Greek Theatre in the 1980s

Greek Theatre in the 1980s

by

Thomas H. Gressler

McFarland & Company, Inc., Publishers
Jefferson, North Carolina, and London

Excerpt pp. 69–72 from "Athens Report" by Thomas Gressler. Reprinted by permission of *Performing Arts* Magazine, a publication of Performing Arts Network, Los Angeles, California. Excerpt pp. 94–96 from "The Magic of Epidavros" by Thomas Gressler. Originally published in *Dramatics* Magazine.

British Library Cataloguing-in-Publication data available

Library of Congress Cataloguing-in-Publication Data

Gressler, Thomas H., 1938–
    Greek theatre in the 1980s / by Thomas H. Gressler.
      p. cm.
    Bibliography: p. 183
    Includes index.
    ISBN 0-89950-411-6 (lib. bdg. : 50# alk. paper) ♾
    1. Theater—Greece—History—20th century.   I. Title.
  PN2664.G74   1989
    792′.09495—dc19   89-45005
                                              CIP

63,348

Printed in the United States of America.

McFarland & Company, Inc., Publishers
  Box 611, Jefferson, North Carolina 28640

To those wonderful theatre people of Greece
whose troubled quest for excellence inspired this book

Table of Contents

Prologue

Like most theatre lovers, I came to Greece expecting to find Sophocles still haunting magical, ancient corners. With vivid images from Kitto and Bieber dangling before my eyes I trekked the holy paths to Epidavros and Dodoni and scoffed at the grandiose ostentation of the second century Herod Atticus theatre. Pericles' hubridic oration about the superiority of that present Athens and the future superiority of the Athenian ideal echoed about me as I greedily purchased theatre ticket after theatre ticket.

I really thought that I could go home to my roots (in the parlance of the TV ads to promote Greek tourism) and rediscover Aristophanes, Thucidides, Phidias and the rest of the gang. Although most of my consciousness about Greece ended with the "tragic" defeat of Athens by Sparta in the late fifth century B.C., I clung to my image of that golden civilization as if it had been captured in some time machine to be revisited at will and revered forever, as if 2500 years of strife had not intervened between me and my idealistic theatrical roots.

Someone should have taken me quietly aside and explained slowly and clearly the obvious: Sophocles and Pericles are rather long dead; there is no extant fifth century B.C. Greek theatre in Greece; Athens is no longer a small city-state at the peak of its power and influence in its Mediterranean world; the Athenian ideal has been badly mauled by millennia of abuse and disuse and now exists primarily in the aspirations of the few idealists left in the world. Someone should have told me that today Greece is "not quite a Third World country," as a Greek producer of films delicately put it. It has the highest per capita foreign deficit and the highest motor vehicle fatality rates in the world, as well as the highest abortion rate in the West. Athens is a dirty, unkempt, crowded, terribly polluted sea of lookalike concrete apartment houses which crowd about the smallest percentage of green space of any major city in the world. Governments change seemingly overnight and the line between democracy and anarchy is fine, indeed. Not only does Athens not identify with its ancient and highly revered predecessor (except for tourist purposes), but it also cannot decide what or whom to identify with at all. Its performing arts, lavishly supported by a government which is in serious fiscal difficulty internally and internationally, cannot seem to produce consistently high quality theatre let alone another playwright or critic of international stature or importance. As every cab driver will tell you, Greece is in trouble.

So, it was not terribly long before I gave up on Phidias, Aristotle and the boys, not long before an honest reappraisal of contemporary Greek theatre forced my idealism aside. Thankfully, this new sense of perspective mollified my feelings of despondency over the state of the Greek theatre. Its accomplishments, given its history over the last 1900 years, are worth noting. While there may not be another Euripides throwing tantrums, there is an avid search for and encouragement of new playwrights. While there may not be a perfect fifth century B.C. amphitheatre, there are several lovely and usable ancient edifices of all kinds in addition to scores of modern playhouses. While there may not be a general societal adherence to the ideals of its forefathers, there is still a recognition and respect for those ideals, especially as exemplified in the constant remountings of ancient tragedies. While there may not be an Aristophanes satirizing the society and the government's postures, there is a modern equivalent, the *epitheorisis* (satiric musical revue) which carries on in the tradition of that great satirist. While the government may not close up all the shops on days of performances, it provides tickets for the elderly and students, is supporting the establishment of new theatres in the neighborhoods and has created theatres in the hinterlands, all of which allows many more people to attend than was possible in that ancient sexist and slave society which we still revere.

The romantic dream of a once-perfect society, however, dies hard. For example, when the theatre lover finds himself in the remarkable ancient theatre of Epidavros and witnesses the opening production of a new season, he may find it difficult *not* to leave a little starry-eyed, muttering to himself, "The pilgrimage has been a success. I have rediscovered *the* Greek theatre."

However, that same theatre lover must remember that, just as Athens is not Greece, and Greece is not Athens, an *Electra* at Epidavros is not the Greek theatre. In fact it is a very small, even if highly visible, part of the total picture. For one thing ancient tragedies and comedies are produced almost exclusively for the summer tourist trade; rarely are they produced during the winter season. Rather, the vast majority of plays produced are international in origin and the vast majority of the performances each year take place in small proscenium theatres. To illustrate, there are only two ancient theatres used regularly during the summer for performances: the Herod Atticus in Athens, used almost daily from late June until mid–September, and the theatre at Epidavros, near the village of Ligurio, used only on Saturdays and Sundays roughly during those same weeks. Another few are used occasionally during the summer: Dodoni, Phillipi, Thassos and

Delfi. On the other hand the winter season in Athens hosts between 60 and 85 professional theatres each of which offers nine performances weekly, six days a week, for about 32 weeks a year. Another eleven regional-municipal theatres operate 10 months a year in communities scattered across the country. Almost none of these produce ancient Greek plays. The over-whelming majority of productions in Greece today are not ancient and are not played in ancient theatres.

In fact, Greek theatre people are very impatient with scholars who wish to study only the ancient plays and their methodologies. Although the Greeks certainly revere their own heritage and know their myths and legends perhaps better than most nationalities, their wish is to be acknowledged as artists contributing to the twentieth century. My sincere desire to accomplish this endeared me to the Greek theatre people more than any other facet of my person or situation.

Conversely I discovered that I was woefully prepared to understand the present Greek theatre. Like any theatrical tradition, theirs evolved out of a long and complicated history, only a small portion of which I knew — that of the fifth century B.C. There seemed no way I could acknowledge Greek theatre and theatre artists as contributors to the twentieth century until I investigated their cultural evolution. Although this led me down un-familiar paths, the information gathered did corroborate and illuminate my own observations of contemporary Greek theatre.

This foray into cultural anthropology awakened in me a new sensitivity to other cultures. For an unconscionable number of years westerners have believed that there were two Greeces. One was a democracy, balanced and wise, a society of incredible invention and profound thought. The other was a society of "takers" rather than "givers," marked by political violence and eternal unrest. Of course neither set of descriptions captures the essence of classical or contemporary Greece. Societies are more complicated than that. In fact on any particular day either or both or neither set of these phrases could describe contemporary Greece.

Like it or not the Greek nation sits, as it always has, at a crossroads be-tween East and West, at the fulcrum of conflicting trade, military and ideological routes. Its present confused condition is partly the result of the forces which have been operating on it for centuries and, most particularly, for the last several decades. As Greece adjusts in its unique ways to the ten-sions of the twentieth century, so we must alter our ways of perceiving it; as it attempts to find its way among the pressures of contemporary life, so we must avoid approaching it as if it had found "the secret" of life long ago and still operates with that secret in hand.

Therefore, although my primary intention in this study is to offer the reader a view of contemporary theatre and theatre production in Greece (1974–1988), I hope even more fervently that the reader will become interested in the people, problems and hopes of this new Greece. Thus the book is intended for theatre academicians and practitioners as well as for the more general educated reader.

Since one of the intentions of this work is to excite the reader with Greek history, culture and the theatrical manifestations of both of these, the manuscript has been slanted toward a more popular style than otherwise might seem appropriate. For example the present tense has been favored whenever possible and the first person pronoun has been used to help create a sense of immediacy. I also attempted to achieve an interesting, informal syntax to help the reader "feel" that this story is happening right now and that Greece's theatre indeed has a reality in the twentieth century.

The book is divided into four parts. Part I offers the background information which is absolutely necessary to an understanding of the rest of the work. In this section Chapter 1 outlines Greece from 10,000 B.C. to the present. Chapter 2 investigates the nature of the Greek character, especially as it has been formed by diametrically opposed emotional demands since mythological times. Chapter 3 presents the Greek theatre as caught between the worlds of East and West. Chapter 4 explains some of the difficulties one might expect to confront when attempting research in Athens today.

Part II investigates the various types of theatre and theatre activities in present-day Greece. Chapter 5 treats the government-subsidized theatres: national and state theatres, semi-state theatres, independent theatres, municipal theatres and theatre festivals. In Chapter 6 the minor forms of theatre are explored: commercial, children's, puppet and amateur. Chapter 7 examines two significant new projects in the Athenian theatre scene, theatre in the rock quarries and a bilingual theatre company.

Part III concentrates on theatre training and production techniques. Chapter 8 is an overview of non-production elements while Chapter 9 offers a view of the production elements. In Chapter 10 I offer an insider's view to the training theatre people are likely to receive in Greece.

Part IV of the book is divided into two chapters: Chapter 11 is entitled Spotlights and Darkspots, in which I include those subjects not easily categorized with any of the previous chapters; Chapter 12 is a summary.

The research was accomplished in Greece thanks to two grants, one from the Northwest Area Foundation in 1983 and the other from the Fulbright Foundation in 1985–1986. I must thank especially "Chip" Ammerman and his wonderful staff at the Fulbright Foundation in Greece. Their hospitality and assistance in so many ways helped make my year there truly a memorable experience. I must also thank Mike Engel at the Linfield College Library for his tireless work tracking down research materials for me; Bill Lingle of the Communications Department for his encouragement of the project; Cherine Bauer for helping with the maps which were illustrated by Sam Lowry. Especially I must bow deeply toward all those wonderfully warm and open Greek theatre people whose contributions made this book possible.

I
Background

1. A Brief History

Greece was first populated about 10,000 B.C. by immigrant tribes from Asia Minor. By 6500 B.C. these peoples had established colonies near Thessalonika and soon after (5000 B.C.) had settled Crete. Around 3000 B.C., other populations from Asia Minor moved into the Cyclades islands and the mainland. About 2600 B.C. the Libyan culture co-mingled with the Cretan one, adding Libyan and Asian skills to the artistic Cretan civilization. The result was a flowering of urbanization on Crete, based on trade with Egypt, Syria, Spain and the Greek mainland.[1] From the very earliest years, then, the Greek culture had profound roots in the "East" and its cities acted as focal points for trade and exchange throughout the Mediterranean.

The idea of *polis*, the city, evolved sometime after 700 B.C. This word encompassed the idea of the city-state, its surrounding territories, its institutions and its way of life. Commitment to and pride in one's own *polis* became very important to one's sense of community and understanding of common values.

Two of these city-states emerged to dominate Greece, the Ionian city of Athens and the Dorian city of Sparta. They bickered almost constantly, but a fifth century B.C. invasion from Persia—now predominantly Turkey—united them briefly. Their victories at Thermopylai and Salamis ushered in what has become known as the Golden Age of Greece—the Age of Pericles—the age of unprecedented accomplishments in the literary arts, philosophy, science, architecture, history and theatre. In short, by the fifth century B.C. this civilization which had arisen out of Oriental roots—Egypt, Mesopotamia and Anatolia—had become "western." That is, it had developed capacities for clear observation, description and precise classification that we still accept as the foundations of western science and rationalism.

In 146 B.C. Rome overran Greece and eventually the entire Hellenistic world. Christianity was established early in this new era and grew in importance and power just as the Roman Empire grew in lasciviousness and crudity. When Emperor Constantine converted to Christianity and moved his capital from Rome to Constantinople, thus establishing a Greek-speaking capital in the East, he split the Empire just as its weakened western half began to be attacked by migrating tribes from the north.

By the fifth century A.D. the Western Empire with Rome as its capital began its demise and the Eastern Empire flourished. The latter was Greek in language and culture and Roman in law and administration — a combination we identify as Byzantine. Thus we can see that as early as the fifth century one of the central conflicts of the Greek people emerged: the conflict between "Eastern" cultural characteristics and "western" institutional characteristics. The Greek people in Constantinople now repudiated the ancient Greek culture because it was pagan and espoused the new "Greek Orthodox" religion.[2]

The Latin Church centered in Rome and the Greek church centered in Constantinople finally split in the eleventh century, creating the schism between Catholicism and Orthodox Catholicism which continues to this day. (The Orthodox naturally considers itself the purer of the two.)

The Greek people lived under the Byzantine Empire — that is, Eastern Orthodoxy — from 330 to 1453 A.D. During those centuries they compromised, if not actually repudiated, much of what was essentially Greek in order to become Eastern Christian. They then had to live under the even stronger Eastern influences of the Turks for the next 400 years. From the Fall of Constantinople in 1453 to the Greek War of Independence which began in 1821 and reached success in 1827, Greece was controlled by Muslim Turkey. During this time, while the rest of the western world was giddy with their Renaissance (based, ironically, on those artifacts and manuscripts that once were secreted away in Byzantine Constantinople), the Greeks were dominated by a society that routinely defaced or demolished irreplaceable ancient statues, monuments and buildings. During this time all those ancient Greek colonies which had been established along the coastlines and on the islands during the heydays of Greek supremacy in the Mediterranean were being conquered and occupied by a continuous assortment of attackers — Venetians, Italians, Turks, Franks, Slavs. It is this fracturing of the ancient fabric of "Greekness" in its race, language, religion and culture that modern day Hellenes tend to forget but must not if they are to understand modern Greece.[3]

After their successful War of Independence the newly freed Greeks were guaranteed their freedom by the Great Powers — England, France and Russia. However, three-quarters of all Greeks living in lands which once had been part of the Byzantine Empire were not included in the new "Greece" created by the Great Powers. Therefore, the Great Idea (*Megali Idea* — Μεγάλι Ιδέα) was spawned. It had as its goal the reuniting of those millions of disinherited Greeks in a great new homeland, a modern equivalent of the old Byzantine Empire with Constantinople as its capital.

The idea simmered while the new country attended to the harsh realities of trying to become a stable entity. Even though nothing much happened to the *Megali Idea* in the nineteenth century, Greece did extend its borders via other means. The Great Powers ceded to Greece the Ionian Islands in 1864 and Thessaly in 1881. After the Balkan Wars in 1912–1913 Greece annexed Crete, Southern Epirus, much of Macedonia and part of Thessalonki. These various accessions increased Greece's territory by 68 percent and its population by 67 percent.[4]

Then, in 1917 Greece entered World War I on the side of the Allies and took part in the occupation of Turkey from Constantinople to the region between Smyrna and the Dardanelles. The Allied wartime promise that Greece would be awarded all of western Anatolia (Turkey) and, thus, achieve for the Greeks the long-dreamed approximation of the Byzantine Empire, seemed at hand. But the rising nationalistic movement in the newly organized state of Turkey as well as political manueverings throughout the area changed the imminent realization of the dream into a nightmare. Instead of withdrawing his troops from Turkish territory after the armistice, Greek leader Eleftherios Venizelos ordered them to attack Anatolia. Turkish troops routed the Greeks in 30 days, and Smyrna was given over to an orgy of massacre and destruction. Thirty thousand Greeks died. To make matters worse, independent Greece was still cut off from millions of Greeks scattered throughout the remaining lands of the Turkish Empire, as well as from those thousands in the islands which were in the hands of other nations.

The Treaty of Lausanne (1923) attempted to address this continuing desire on the parts of both combatants to again unite their peoples. In it the Great Powers decreed that there was to be a mandatory exchange of Greek and Turkish populations on each side of the new border in northern Greece. In just days 400,000 Turks left northern Greece to return to Turkey and almost 1.25 million Greeks living in Turkey returned to Greece. This exchange effectively ended 3000 years of Greek life in Asia Minor. In addition it increased the Greek population by 20 percent seemingly overnight.[5] When added to the population increase of 67 percent in the preceding two decades, these hordes of new people created a situation which was almost impossible to govern. It is not surprising that between 1923 and 1936, nineteen changes of government took place, as well as three military revolutions or *coup d'etats* and innumerable minor acts of sedition.[6]

The Great Powers continued to support a monarchical form of government, a form with which the Greeks never were comfortable. Consequently, there was a constant struggle between Greek monarchists and republicans (as well as anarchists and dictators) almost from the time the first King Otto of Bavaria took over until the beginning of World War II. But when the Axis threat reached into Greece, the struggle over the form of the Greek government suddenly seemed of much less importance than the struggle for survival.

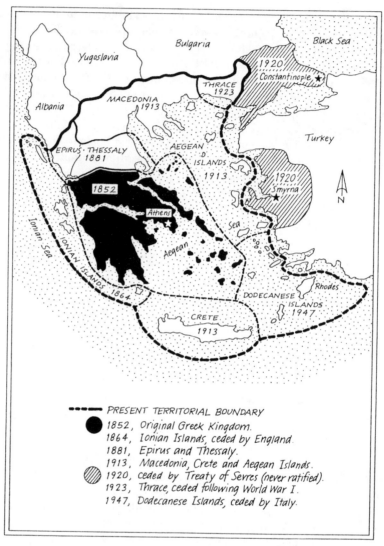

Expansion of Territorial Greece since the War of Independence.

Amost immediately following Greece's fall to Hitler's Panzer Divisions in 1941, the famous Greek Resistance movement began on the rugged island of Crete and spread throughout the country. It is the memories which have become attached to this Resistance movement that continue to divide Greek people of good faith.

One arm of the Resistance movement was Communist, the other was right wing Royalist. The Communist arm grew to tremendous numbers and effectiveness. The Royalist arm also was effective, but became increasingly concerned about the power of the Communist movement. Both sides jockeyed for power, fighting each other as often and with as much ferocity as they fought the Germans. There was truth in Nikos Kazantzakis' statement, "Wolves don't eat each other; Greeks do."[7]

In 1945 after the victory over Germany the well-organized and financed Communist Resistance forces tried to take over Athens by force. A civil war broke out along the same lines as the inter-necine hostilities which had characterized the Resistance throughout the war. Twice the Communists were on the verge of winning; twice they failed to take advantage of their gains. England and America sent extensive aid to the Royalist forces which finally won the day. Hostilities ceased in the fall of 1949. Eighty thousand Greeks had been killed or had died of starvation; 25,000 children from the northern villages had been forcibly evacuated to Eastern Bloc Countries by the Communist insurgents and 700,000 refugees had been created.

As if the German scorched-earth policy as they retreated northward through the peninsula were not enough, these brotherly slaughters created an atmosphere of divisiveness, hate and revenge among the people that still has not fully abated. There is almost no Athenian over 40 who has not had a relative, close friend or acquaintance killed, tortured, lost, resettled or starved to death in that internal feuding. In 1949 Athenians going to work had to step over the bodies of those who had starved to death during the night. It is no surprise that discussions about the pros and cons of various political parties often end with shouting matches that make a westerner twinge.

(One indication of this continued divisiveness was the appearance on the Greek cinema scene of the film *Eleni* in the spring of 1986. Based on numerous interviews with Greeks who had lived through the War and the Resistance, the film had been widely praised in western countries as a truthful, if brutal, account of the atrocities committed by the Communists during the Resistance. However, as Athenian spectators exited the cinemas after the film, they often were accosted by Communists or other sympathizers who felt that the film did not present the truth as *they* knew it. Some spectators were beaten. Sometimes the police had to be summoned. A few movie houses, consequently, stopped screening the film. After a week or so of constant streetside altercations, after a week or more of political pressure from the Communist members of Parliament, the film was withdrawn from the cinemas of Athens by government decree.)

After peace supposedly settled on their country after the Civil War, another three-quarters of a million people were resettled by government forces in addition to the 1.25 million already immigrated from Turkey in 1923. Once again governance became almost impossible. Between 1945 and

1952 there were more than twenty different governments with an average life span of 150 days.[8]

Thus, by the end of World War II and the Civil War that followed, the Greek nation was devastated, bankrupt and exhausted. It was then that the Truman Doctrine was enacted, infusing millions of dollars into the economy, providing hundreds of managers, leaders and advisors to nearly every Greek government committee. Propped up by American hegemony there was only one government in Greece from 1952 to 1963, compared to twenty in the previous seven years. This stability, combined with the American influence over every decision made by the stricken state, firmly pushed the Greek nation into the western sphere. The desperate nation had little choice but to accept the well-meaning directions of its American advisors and the American vision of "freedom." Greece emerged from its wars a democracy, safeguarded against Soviet domination by America and its Sixth Fleet. It even joined the North Atlantic Treaty Organization. Greece was finally "western" again.

Greece was now "free" and able to rebuild its economy. Most of the Greek citizenry were extremely thankful for American aid and advice. Still, to many it seemed that Greece-with-American-aid was just another way of saying Greece-under-American-domination, or just another way of saying Greece-under-American-Occupation. Afraid to bite the hand that fed them, and yet still determined to be totally free as were those ancient democrats of the fifth century B.C., the Greek people felt and continue to feel too dependent on a foreign power.[9]

In 1964 the old scourge of Greece, the estranged and hated Communists, felt strong enough to publicly demand official recognition as a political party. As their power grew the fear of another civil war–like blood bath grew. Army officer Colonel Papadopoulos traded on that fear. On April 21, 1967, just before scheduled elections, he led a group of minor military officers in a military coup. Civil liberties were suppressed, special court-martials were established and political parties dissolved. Thousands of Greeks were exiled to remote islands; many of the intelligentsia fled; hundreds or perhaps even thousands were tortured.

When Papadopoulos' associate, Gen. Dimitrios Ioannides, assumed the dictatorship in 1973, he inherited a sad list of economic indicators. Even though Greeks were long-lived and well-lettered compared to the Spanish and Portuguese, their standard of housing (two persons per room average) was Europe's poorest; their average productivity and average personal incomes were not more than one-third of the Common Market countries'; the problems of unemployment and under-employment were among Europe's worst; even though one-third of the Greek population lived on the land, they produced less than one-fifth of the country's wealth; 100,000 people, nearly always the youngest and most capable, were migrating each year, one-half again as many as the population increase; 95 percent of the country's "factories" were really workshops, employing fewer than 10 people, and fewer than one in 100 employed more than 50 people; poverty-stricken villages were losing their men to better paying jobs elsewhere, for example, in Germany, where slave wages could be accepted with no social stigma of unmanliness which would reflect negatively on the village.[10]

It was at this juncture that the long-standing feud between Archbishop Makarios, president of the new Republic of Cyprus, and the dictators in Athens erupted. Years of incipient warfare between the Turkish Cypriots, hoping for continued British rule or at least connection with Ankara, and the Greek Cypriots who hoped for reunification (*enosis*—ένωσις) with the Greek mainland had resulted in the creation of a Turkish expeditionary force within immediate striking distance of Cyprus. It was placed on constant alert to "protect" its countrymen on that island should the Greek Cypriots attempt any action against the Turkish Cypriots (18 percent of that island's population). Probably unwittingly, Makarios exacerbated the situation by courting Moscow as a possible ally against any overt Turkish action in support of the Turkish Cypriots.

To the violently anti–Communist dictators this courtship of Moscow was seen as a direct affront to their power. The resulting *coup* against Makarios—probably instigated by the colonels, although this has never been proved—was successful in deposing his government even though Makarios himself escaped. To the reunification zealots on Cyprus as well as to the dictators, it no doubt seemed that "democracy" had been preserved, Soviet expansionism thwarted and *total reunification* with the mainland was at hand.

Suddenly, on July 20, 1974, the Turkish expeditionary force attacked. The Greeks were not prepared for the onslaught and the Turkish forces easily occupied the northern third of the island. This occupation of land variously claimed as Greek or Turkish remains a festering political sore to this day. Even though Cyprus had achieved neutral status and independent statehood in 1959, Greeks still consider it a natural part of Greece. The presence of Turkish troops on what they see as sacred Greek land is a bitter pill for the Greeks to swallow. Again, they see American refusal to automatically side with them against the Turks—the American fleet prevented a counter-attack by the Greek naval forces in order to avoid war between the two NATO allies—as a certain sign of American duplicity and short-sightedness.

On January 1, 1981, Greece became the 10th member of the European Community. In October of the same year Greece elected its first Socialist government, the Panhellenic Socialist Party (PASOK) of Andreas Papandreou, a former UCLA professor of economics. In 1985 the new election confirmed this government and it remains in power as of this writing.[11]

Even this cursory review of the history of Greece suggests several facts which must be kept in mind when attempting to understand the artistic accomplishments of the country. First, the Greece which western eyes romanticize disappeared 2500 years ago. Second, the present-day state of Greece is an amalgam of 2500 years of mostly non-western influences within a context of historical classicism. Third, the Greek state has become "western"-oriented again only because of the massive infusion of American military and economic aid in the 1950s. Fourth, Greece is presently a Socialistic Democracy, or a Democratically Socialistic state, depending on which political view each Greek favors.

2. The Greek Character

The Greek is both oriental and native. These two sides sometimes flow "side by side, never joining, sometimes meeting and struggling furiously, and even, rarely, joined in organic union. The modern Greek loves life and fears death, loves his homeland and is simultaneously a pathological individualist; he fawns upon his superiors like a Byzantine . . . yet he will die for his *philotimo* and his personal honor. He is clever and shallow, with no metaphysical anxieties, and yet, when he begins to sing, a universal grieving leaps up from his Oriental bowels and breaks the crust of Greek logic; all at once the East, all darkness and mystery, rises up from the deep within him."[1]

In the winter of 1986 Emilios Vouratinos, Greek Cultural Liaison to the U.S. Embassy in Athens, tried to explain to new Embassy employees the seeming dichotomy in the Greek character. Greeks, he said, are constantly pulled in equal and opposite directions, toward Dionysius on one hand, and toward Apollo on the other; that is, toward intuition, emotionalism and wild abandon on one hand and toward clear logic, reason, balance and proportion on the other. The important thing to remember, he charged, was that these dual and seemingly exclusive biases do not take turns in some neat and tidy way; rather they exist simultaneously.

In the summer of 1983 the dramaturg for the Stavros Doufexis production of *Lysistrata* tried to explain the same dilemma to me while we watched the show being set up in Ioannina. The temple at Delfi, he said, existed first for Dionysius, not Apollo as commonly believed. This explains why Greeks' first predispositions are toward the emotional and passionate. However, because of their excesses in these directions, another god was called upon to moderate their behavior—Apollo. A balance was finally achieved. For untold years the same temple was used for both gods, each for six months. The front door had an inscription to Dionysius over the lintel, the back door one to Apollo.

Although this story may smack a little of legend and folk tale, nevertheless, it does describe a condition of which the Greeks themselves are very aware—the condition of being caught in a temple with equal and opposite gods at each end demanding equal and opposite attention simultaneously.

Both of these vignettes and the Kazantzakis quote above are attempts to discover the exact nature of a people and country that has been and continues to be very fascinating. Although the magic of the ancient Greek ideal continues, history has compromised much of that ideal and has left twentieth century intellectuals either caught in the vise of the romanticized past, or hopelessly cynical about the character of the contemporary Greek and his country. If we are to understand the contemporary Greek theatre at all, we must also understand something about the unique people who make it.

What exactly is a Greek? What are his values? How does he behave and why? David Holden, in his book *Greece Without Columns*, attempts to trace these social, religious and behavioral patterns in some detail. He admits, however, that any attempt to pin down Greece in order to study it is like trying to pin down a butterfly, an action which, of course, destroys "the movement that is the creature's essence." Greece, he says, is an exercise in motion that creates its own significance.[2]

Any attempt to define Greece or Greekness is difficult because there is almost no continuity among the various elements of the Greek experience. Territorially Greece has hardly ever been stable from century to century and recently from decade to decade. Territorially speaking, there is not and has never been a continuous Greek state to which we can refer when trying to answer the question, "What is a Greek?"

Perhaps, then, it would be possible to identify Greece in terms of a long-standing and stable race. With all those years of occupation by succeeding waves of Serbs, Bulgars, Romans, Franks, Venetians, Turks, Albanians, Germans and Italians, though, the Greeks have become "a decidedly mongrel race."[3] Even today the villages along both sides of Greece's borders with Albania, Yugoslavia, Bulgaria and Turkey contain people whose roots are on the other side, whose forefathers may have lived in each others' countries for generations. Contemporary weavings from Greek Macedonia and neighboring Albania, for example, are obviously from the same root culture. Today the people of Veria, again in northern Greece, find it very natural to invite Bulgarian artists to people their new summer theatre festival. It is not only cultural exchange; very likely it is partly the same culture.

Is there a continuity in Greek politics to which we might refer when trying to define Greece or Greekness? Probably not. Even though democratic Athens has become a world-accepted legend, despotism and anarchy have played equally important roles in its history. The despot, Solon, preceded Pericles by not many years; during the Peloponnesian War the vaunted "democracy" was riddled with factionalism, greed, circumventions and the like; Greek city-states of those days often urged moderation on each other because they so often acted like fanatical extremists. Centuries of foreign occupations made Greece politically nondescript, even while it clung vaguely to its desire to somehow recapture the golden, hardly democratic days of Alexander, or the days of its Greek-speaking Byzantine Empire. When it finally attained independence from Ottoman rule in 1827, however, it reacted with an incredible string of governments that ranged from semi-democratic to autocratic to monarchic to despotic, the last of this long line ending as recently as 1974. Even today the catchword in Athens is "democracy," spoken most vociferously by the Socialist-Democratic government as well as by its Communist and other radical leftist opponents. If there is any continuity in Greek politics, it seems to be the absolute necessity of changing the form of government as soon as it ceases to be of personal value.

Is there a religious vein in the Greek people that has remained constant throughout the ages? The too-obvious answer here is "yes." Nearly all Greeks claim Greek Orthodoxy as their religion. Even though few attend church regularly, every Greek is baptized, married and buried in the Church, and most participate in the services leading up to Easter. It was not always so, of course. The first Greek religion was pagan; next came a brief fling with "regular" Christianity. Yet even after their espousal of Constantinople-brand Orthodoxy, they could not and cannot completely relinquish their emotional holds on the old gods. Half of the saints they venerate are from the Pantheon — St. Dionysius is Dionysius; St. Elias is Helios, the sun god who had hilltop shrines everywhere in Greece; the Virgin of Tinos, to whom 30,000 pilgrims crawl annually in hopes of miraculous cures, is really Poseidon, who presided at that very same shrine before her, and Asklepios (Aesculapius), who was there even earlier. When thunder causes the farmer to declare that God must be rolling his wine barrels around the heavens, he certainly could not be referring to the austere Christian God, but rather Zeus.

It may be true that this particular brand of evolved Orthodoxy may be thought of as a kind of continuity between the present and the past. In fact, William McNeill, in his book *The Metamorphosis of Greece since World War II*, claims that the Greek religion is one of only two factors which can define the Greek tradition; but since many other nationalities also are Orthodox, even that is a shaky claim.[4]

The closest one can come, it seems, to a connection between the Greek tradition of 2500 years ago and now is their language, the second of McNeill's suggestions. The Greek victory in their War of Independence captured the hearts of idealistic-minded Europeans. Somehow this victory turned from a celebration of a current victory to an opportunity to recapture ancient glories. The romantics, with Lord Byron ("We are all Greeks!") in the forefront, presented to an overeager world images of an over-romanticized Greece that never existed and could not possibly exist. To recapture the "glory that was Greece" became the battle cry of the enamored. The new European Philhellenes even convinced the Greeks that this recapturing of former days of glory was their unique destiny. One of the methods by which that ancient glory was to be recaptured was the re-evolution of the classical language. However, since the spoken Greek language had progressed far from those classical roots over the centuries, a new language had to be created somewhere between the classical and the Demotic, the language of the people. This new language was *katharevousa*, created by a nineteenth century English schoolmaster from Smyrna who had spent most of his life in Paris—Adamiotis Korais. *Katharevousa* henceforth became the official language of Greece. This new language was supposed to help the Greeks recover their ancient glories, but it was a vision of those glories superimposed upon the society by the romantic pseudo–Hellenes of Europe with almost no regard for the realities of Greece at that time. Consequently, since most Greeks went their merry way speaking their native language, *katharevousa* became the language only of legal matters, governmental pronouncements and instruction in the schools. It was considered "cultured" while the language of the people was considered "common," or "inferior," or "oriental."[5]

Between 1964 and 1967 another language, *kathomiloumeni*, resting somewhere between these two former languages, evolved. It was to be the language of the newspapers. Fortunately it has all but disappeared. In 1964 Prime Minister Georges Papandreou increased compulsory education from six years to nine and also swept *katharevousa* out of all schools in favor of Demotic. Three years later the rightist dictator Colonel Papadopoulos usurped power and reversed Papandreou's decisions regarding compulsory education and the legal language. In 1974, with the ouster of the Colonel and a re-affirmation of the Republic, compulsory education again was set at nine years and the Demotiki language was finally reinstated as the official language of Greece.

There is no way to ascertain what the effect of this constant juggling of the nation's language has had on the development of a literature and an informed public. Athens, for example, still sports various commercial and directional signs which display the peculiarities of that first bastard language, *katharevousa*. As recently as the fall of 1986 minor but official changes in Greek were still taking place in order to make it easier to learn and, one must assume, more "available" to those non–Greeks from the European Community who would be working with or in Greece. So, although it is obvious that the Greek language has been the single strongest tie among all the peoples of this country since the start of its history, even that touchstone has not been without its share of troubles.

If all of these standard measures of a society's homogeneity fail significantly, one must ask if there ever was a time in history when the term "Greek" referred to a unique and definable tradition. The answer would be "yes," and that one time was probably Periclean Greece, when the idea of

Greek-ness was well-known, when the Golden Age was widely respected and when a homogeneity of culture did exist. (Even then, we might remind ourselves, "Greece" consisted of a collection of quarreling city-states.)

Even though the Greek language and Greek Orthodoxy have most often been touted as the two dimensions of the Greek experience which define it, we have seen that they and the others presented above are fraught with historical holes. Are there any grounds, then, upon which we might base our study? Our favorite author, David Holden, suggests that the real constancies of the Greek experience are behavioral:

> Internal factionalism and personal jealousy combined with a proud Greek unity against all outsiders; a recurrent swing between efficient and detested despots and popular but incompetent democracies; a conspiratorial cunning along with much naive gullibility; an intense curiosity and political awareness grappling with a love of talk and rhetorical gesture for their own sakes that often outruns all reason . . . [6]

If we accept this approach that the secrets to understanding present-day Greece reside more in a study of behavior patterns of contemporary Greeks rather than in historical-economic-linguistic studies, then many more ideas of particular relevance to an understanding of the theatre come to the foreground. Within this context several patterns emerge which may be worth considering: patron-client relationships; the primacy of the family; the importance of *philotimo*—a mixture of Greek pride and slight arrogance; the absence of any real sense of responsibility connected to that trait; the tendency to cheat all officialdom if possible, along with a tendency toward cunning and shiftiness; the dislike of social distinctions and hierarchies of any kind; the volatility and unquenchable argumentativeness of the race; the use of personal influence—*rousfetti*. Several of these have a direct bearing on the creation and operation of the theatre in Greece and deserve further elucidation here.

Philotimo. A villager had a large and strong donkey. His neighbor was plowing his fields and needed the loan of the animal. Although the owner knew that his neighbor would work the donkey too hard, and that he himself would not get any work done while the animal was away, he did loan the donkey to the neighbor. Of course the animal came back exhausted, unable to work for its owner. The next day the man returned. He needed help in moving some household goods and wanted to borrow the donkey again. The farmer hemmed and hawed but finally relented and gave the neighbor the animal. The poor creature came back even more exhausted. The farmer was angry but simply could not refuse when the neighbor returned the third day for help in clearing some fields. Close to exploding the kind-hearted farmer said nothing and loaned the animal again. Determined that his neighbor had abused his kind-heartedness enough for one year, the owner decided to make up a ruse to avoid giving up the animal one more day. When the neighbor came back the fourth day and asked for the loan of the animal, the farmer, feigning sadness, told him that the poor thing had been worked so hard that he died in the middle of the night. The neighbor couldn't believe him and, in progressively belligerent tones, demanded the use of the animal. The farmer maintained in his own vociferous tones that the creature had perished. Just then the donkey, which had been hidden behind the house, brayed. "There!" shouted the neighbor, "I thought you said he was dead! He sounds very much alive!" In a magnificent gesture of *philotimo* the angry farmer shot back, "Hey, who are you going to believe, the donkey or me?"

Philotimo demands that one never lose face or honor, either for one's self or for one's village. It is a combination of pride and arrogance. At its most extreme, often celebrated by the ancient Greeks as *hubris,* it may result in a father or brother actually killing a daughter and/or her lover if their activities caused dishonor to fall upon the family. On its more common level it affects every interpersonal and communal relationship and situation. Everyone's village is the "best in the world"; one must not lose an argument and so may bend (and is expected to bend) the facts to his own point of view; one's personal ideas are the best of all available alternatives. The thousands of cars waiting to race through the green light will just have to wait because an ambling man wants to cross the street and will not be cowered into running. A Greek will often give you directions even if he knows absolutely nothing about your destination. He simply cannot let you know that he does *not* know. *Philotimo* can be sensed in the very way the Greek carries himself, in his male dances, in his dress and in his treatment of women.

Lack of a Sense of Collective Responsibility. If *philotimo* requires that a man cannot and should not accept blame for his failures, then it follows that some other explanation for the failure must exist. It is not unusual, then, for these other explanations to reach fantastical proportions. Fact becomes irrelevant; rumor and speculation are encouraged. Since nothing can be believed — because someone is saving face somewhere — any nonsense can win an audience. When, for example, a London paper printed a story about the Parthenon being ravaged by Athenian pollution, Athens papers attacked in force the next day, denying any truth in that report. They fairly shouted that "The atmosphere in Greece is amongst the healthiest and cleanest in the world and the atmosphere of Athens is far cleaner than any other large city."[7] Anyone who has been to Athens can judge for himself or herself the accuracy of that claim.

Blame-placing seems to be an eternal and constant Greek pastime, as is their passionate addiction to a conspiratorial interpretation of events. They still blame the failure of their war to recapture all of the land from Epirus to Constantinople (the war of the Great Idea) on the Great Powers who did not support what was obviously a just and holy cause. They still blame America for the failure of their attempt to win back Cyprus from the Turkish expeditionary force. Even though the entire fiasco probably erupted because of aggressive Greek behavior, nevertheless they felt that America should have immediately sided with the just and noble Greeks rather than worry about the fact that two American Allies were about to go at it — again. Regional theatre directors blame their audiences for the low quality of their shows, or they blame the inexperience of the actors. In fact there may be some truth to all the claims above; the Greeks, however, seem unable to accept even the smallest percentage of the blame. After one understands that this is the system in operation, however, it does not take very long to accept all claims and pronouncements, even those of vaulting irrationality, as reasonable and rational, even noble (at least within the context of this avoidance mechanism).

A truly unhealthy facet of this predisposition to blame others exists at the international level. American hegemony and the Truman Doctrine after World War II saved the exhausted Greek nation. Although of obvious advantage to the Americans who were establishing bulwarks against any further Communist expansionism, the policy reinforced eternal Greek suspicions that they needed do nothing, that their destiny was so important that someone else would do the protecting. Besides, the reasoning went, their history of occupation has convinced them that all decisions were made for them anyhow, that someone else would always determine their fate. And since this was true, there was not much any Greek could do about it but sit back and complain.[8] The infuriating Greek predisposition to take no action in the international arena (e.g. their refusal to condemn Kadafy for terrorism), or to sit on fences until some greater power forces or entreats them to action may eventually have a deleterious effect on their international relationships and may actually become dangerous in times of crisis.

Patron-Client Relationships. Patron-client relationships flourish in environments perceived as hostile or threatening. Because of the insecurity created by such real or perceived conditions, people's natural tendencies are to focus their concern on their immediate families. Since these families rarely can reduce this sense of insecurity, patron-client relationships with a few trusted and/or influential people become a natural mechanism to insure security.[9]

It is a universally accepted principle in Greece that the only way to advancement is through the intercession of knowledgeable and powerful friends. In fact, everyone realizes that the real sources of power are the complex, personal, family and clan relationships, not the government. Dropping the right name or recalling some mutual interest will instantly open all the necessary doors.[10] Therefore, Greeks do not spend much time learning the correct way to accomplish something; rather they spend their time cultivating relationships with the "right" people. It is called *rousfetti*.

This patron-client system reaches every facet of community and political life. It is common knowledge that normal legal and administrative channels are not terribly responsive to citizen needs. One of the reasons is that the line between civil and family offices is not recognized. Civil servants are expected to take care of their families and family friends first, whether that be through their work in the home or in their particular job. It follows, then, that they cannot treat everyone equally or according to the same rules, since to do that would jeopardize the primacy of their immediate circle of relationships. As an outsider to the civil servant's sphere of concern, then, one must use one's own friends to circumvent, supplement or contravene the established channels and/or the servant's unresponsiveness. With the aid of these "expeditors" who exist between the suppliant and the power (thus creating a government-within-the-government), somehow most people accomplish what needs to be accomplished. It is clear, however, that the more friends one has cultivated, and the higher placed they are, the smoother one's entire life is likely to be.

A noted professor in the Polytechnic University tried to build a house in a comfortable suburb of Athens. It took him three years to acquire the necessary documents, permissions, releases, etc. His frustrated response to his ordeal was captured in a few words. "There is the law of the government and there is the law of the people, and you need the law of the people to make the law of the government work."[11] An executive for an international foundation built a house on the coast. He discovered that his legal agreements were not half as important to the contractor as were the contractor's obligations to his own circle of friends and acquaintances. These latter all had a culturally equal and rightful claim to his time and energy. The executive decided that, if he should ever build a house in Greece again, he would find a contractor who either A) was related to a member of his—the executive's—family and/or B) had political clout in the village in order to keep at bay the various officials who require stamped, verified, authenticated papers from the forestry department, the Ministry of the Interior, the local town council, *ad infinitum*. To be more blunt, he said, the new owner must know if the contractor can build the house with the help of the contractor's relatives and political acquaintances.[12]

If you want a telephone installed in Athens today, you must know someone in the telephone company or you are likely to wait months, even years. This same executive above had waited six years as of this writing and still had little hope of an installation. Likewise, renting an apartment with no phone already installed is the same as renting an apartment which will never have a phone installed. It is not that phones are scarce or that there are insufficient workmen, only that all of the above are being used to satisfy the string-pulls of a phalanx of "expeditors" working for their friends.

Waiting one's turn means waiting forever. To let officialdom do its work seems to most Greeks a mark of stupidity or laziness.[13] Admission to private schools, one mark of success, requires making the right contacts, not necessarily the right grades. The Cultural Attache of the American Embassy is annually deluged with calls from parents or uncles in attempts to get their sons or god-daughters into exclusive Athens College. Students who spend countless hours avoiding studying the entire term then spend countless hours arguing with the professors over their surprisingly low grades, or engage their web of influential friends in an attempt to have them argue in their stead.

It is not difficult to see this system at work. At any government office (for example, the passport office) one may witness, among the crush of suppliants, certain individuals who seem to sail through with little difficulty. No one complains; they know that that person had the right connection. "Impossible" cases are suddenly and inexplicably solved after a short, whispered conference with the appropriate official, often in full view of the deluge of people, or sometimes in hurried conferences in nearby offices. Greeks are expected to engage their circle of influential friends toward the accomplishment of anything that needs doing. This, of course, means that family, and the network of friends related to that family, become the most important tools for success in this world.

Over the months I was in Greece I tried intermittently to arrange an interview with the Minister of Culture, Melina Mercouri. All the Greeks from whom I requested help in arranging such a meeting responded by asking, "Who do you know?" I knew no one of import, but I tried calling anyway. The Minister was always too busy, but "please try next week." After several such attempts, I was asked to submit a list of questions which would be the subject for the interview. After an appropriate hiatus for that office to study the questions, I called again. Again I was refused on the grounds that the Minister was too busy. When at last I had the Fulbright Office reach the correct appointments secretary, she said that Mrs. Mercouri was in Paris for the next two weeks. That night Mrs. Mercouri appeared at a gala opening in Athens. I knew then, as all Greeks would have known long before, that I simply did not have the right friends to smooth the way and to make the government really responsive. I do not blame at all the Minister nor her secretaries; they were simply operating on a different set of expectations than I was. It is certain in hindsight that, indeed, the Minister of Culture was too busy; it is also certain that the right relationships with the right people would have resulted in an interview very early in the year.

Mutual back-scratching is not unknown in other countries; in Greece, however, it has evolved into an alternate system of governance which runs parallel to and barely beneath the surface of the formal one.

The patronage system also operates in reverse. Since each Greek is tied to a particular circle of friends and family in order to accomplish anything, those in power are foolish if they do not fill governmental positions with people whose connection with and loyalty to the "family" of that particular party has not already been proven. Therefore, with each change in government, the entire Civil Service is ripe for dismissal and replacement by a whole raft of "trusted" friends. Even the most insignificant posts are filled as political rewards, a practice that is disastrous to sound public administration.[14] Although the practice is certainly not unknown worldwide, the thoroughness of its application in Greece seems unique in modern countries with "western" leanings.

Cheating, Cunning, Shiftiness. From the beginning the centrality of exchange and its requisite skills have been critical for the survival of the villages. Skills in bargaining have always been respected, especially if they resulted in receiving a better price. If this was accomplished by outsmarting everyone else, the victory was even sweeter. It is not difficult to imagine, then, that cunning and deceptiveness must infuse the negotiations on both sides of the table; universal suspicion is therefore inevitable. The concept of mutual benefit is difficult for a Greek to accept because every deal results in one side achieving just a little more than the other. Justice is, therefore, unattainable; each side feels that the agreed-on price somehow did not give them their due.[15]

It is not far from this incipient cheating as a concomitant of the negotiations procedures to outright cheating in the payment of taxes. All the way back to the Roman Emperor Justinian, the Greeks were noted for their ability to avoid taxes. Referring to his Greek subjects, the Emperor said, "The government was cheated by all of its agents. Two-thirds of the revenue extorted from the taxpayers failed to find its way into the Treasury. The evil was apparently incurable."[16] Curiously, in 1964 it was estimated that income taxes were evaded by two-thirds of all Greeks. In 1986 the fact of income tax evasion was so widely accepted that nearly everyone with whom I spoke openly admitted it.

During the non-tourist season hotels often will not give the traveler a receipt, since to do so they must also make out a tax form and, thus, report their income. It is of course much more beneficial if they simply take your money and report nothing. The second jobs so many Athenians take are more often than not unreported. Even the wealthiest of Athenians cheat on little things like bus and trolley fares. One playwright and his wife showed me how they cheat the system simply by throwing loudly into the toll box a handful of small drachma coins adding up to perhaps half the correct fare. Since the transportation system no longer has a separate conductor to watch these things, and since the drivers have refused to pay much attention to duties for which they are not paid extra, like counting each fare, a significant number of people take advantage of the impasse and cheat in this same way.

A Dislike for Hierarchies. Greece has been known as a country of rugged individualists — we recall the stories of Kazantzakis and the uprising of the fiercely independent Cretan people to start the Resistance during World War II. (They *still* wear their Resistance uniforms in many villages!) For most of its history over the past 2500 years Greece has been dominated or occupied by a foreign power; for much of that time the Greek people have had to behave in subservient ways in order to survive. Some have even prospered by so behaving. To voluntarily become subservient to anyone now that total freedom has been achieved must seem like the most outrageous kind of insanity. Therefore, Greeks find it difficult to engage in activities of mutual benefit. The larger the organization, the more secondary levels there must be; the further down the ladder one is, the further one is from free expression of his or her will and personhood.

It is not surprising that almost all commercial establishments in Greece are small, family-run enterprises employing fewer than 10 people. Thousands are tiny, one-room shops easily operated by one person. Taxis in Athens are mobile one-person businesses. Only in 1986 was there any attempt to tie several of them together by radio in order to provide a better service. The vast majority of cab drivers, however, remain adamantly independent. Even those Greeks who do work for large businesses most often also hold outside jobs, partly as a way of maintaining that feeling of freedom so important to all Greeks. One can more easily understand a Dr. Miller who stated 70 years ago that it was impossible for Greeks to form clubs, companies or "anything that requires cooperation and the subordination of the individual to the whole. Two Greeks will do badly what one will do well. Even when they dance they prefer to do it alone."[17] He went on to say that Greeks operate as individuals or not at all. Two Greeks make three political parties, a fact which makes more understandable Greece's long-lived political instability. One Fulbright professor, after experiencing Athens for just a few short weeks in 1985, dubbed the Greek system "genial anarchy," perhaps the form of social intercourse that can approach closest the kind of democracy that most Greeks envision.

On the island of Santorini leaders of the local Society of Architects decided that something had to be done to keep the unique and gorgeous island from falling into the snares of over-building, lack of planning, pressures to commercialize, etc. They called a meeting of the Society to discuss these problems and possible solutions. The meetings quickly became six-hour debates. They held four meetings to decide to meet; six to decide on an agenda and a name for the group; four more to agree on a meeting time, etc.[18] A well-known and respected international scholar of Greek literature who was elected to the faculty at a major Greek university found that every faculty meeting became such a violent and useless argument that he simply had to leave.

There is another old adage — "Greeks make great followers and terrible leaders." Unless there is a clear and unquestioned and powerful leadership, Greeks will argue in order to prove that they are right, to prove that they are not subordinate to anyone, to preserve their *philotimo,* to argue for the sake of arguing. In the process of writing a new Constitution, an endeavor in which the Greeks are endlessly imaginative, the argument to agree on even the *form* of the document is likely to destroy it. However, if a strong leader emerges, they seem infinitely able and willing to follow. One recalls their adoration of the despotism of Alexander, or of head-strong Venizelos who convinced them to foolishly attack the newly strengthened might of the Turkish forces with Greece's woefully unprepared army. As one actress said, "Greeks . . . need to have someone very strong in front of them . . . to control them because every . . . [Greek considers himself] the first and last person in the world!"[19] In 1986 there was still among many a secret respect and sadness that the despotic regime of the Colonels from 1967 to 1974 did not succeed. At least, these supporters claimed, things got done. They quickly added, however, that they could not admit those feelings in Greek society today.

Volatility and Argumentativeness. My son, Mark, and I walked down Eginitou Street on the way to the bus. Two Greek males in front of us slammed out of their cars, shouting and screaming at each other. Their voices reverberated among the concrete apartment buildings walling the small street. I paid no attention but noticed Mark staring at them with some concern. As we passed them he looked away and said, "What are they arguing about?" I realized that I had become accustomed to normal Greek passion. "Arguing?" I replied, "It's just a friendly conversation."

Ever since the fifth century B.C. the danger "of Athenian democracy was that the power of the spoken word sometimes drove out reason. . . ."[20] Greeks will talk indefinitely about anything, whether or not they know anything about the subject. The card halls are always full with a high decibel level of talk; mealtimes are always social events in which loud and friendly conversation is paramount; older men spend interminable hours sipping their coffee and chatting with friends. A haircut is likely to consume an hour, one minute of cutting to every ten minutes of talking. Those waiting their turn do not seem to mind; they even join in. It is not terribly unusual to wait patiently in a ticket line while the seller and a friend buying tickets catch up on all the gossip.

Summary. It should be clear from this narrative that the old images of Greece are no longer of much value in learning how to deal with the present-day reality. It should also be clear that the Greek Tourist Organization brochures, appropriately, present a view of Greece that, while wonderful and truthful as far as it goes, does not touch everyday realities either. Neither our visions of the glory of Greece nor the glory of nude beaches on Mykonos can capture the souls of the people: the former is the manufactured phantom of nineteenth century romantics who refused to allow the newly independent state of Greece to become anything less than their visions of it; the latter is almost an aberration born of the need for income, but antithetical to the life views of the conservative Orthodox Christian Church. The former presents a vision no people on earth can equal; the latter presents a dream unfathomable to most Greeks. In neither case is there presented a reality that will help us understand the vast majority of the Greek people.

All of this is not to say that Greece does not have its immense charms. Its beauty, although tainted here and there, is unquestionable; its much-praised hospitality, if one avoids the tawdry tourist traps, remains untarnished; its passion for and enjoyment of life infuses every moment; its determination to be totally free from all foreign influences, while unrealistic in the twentieth century, is still worthy of praise; its constant and praiseworthy struggle to discover its true soul somewhere between its Dionysian, Oriental, emotionally-based one and its Apollonian, western, logic-based one is endlessly fascinating.

In 1972 David Holden summarized his conclusions of the contemporary Greek state. "The reality of Greece today indeed is that she is an immature, insecure, and poor nation with an unmanageable and bitterly divided legacy of historical glory. Socially and economically she remains largely underdeveloped but historically she is ... overdeveloped and unable, therefore, to treat herself, or be treated by others, on her present merits."[21]

3. Theatre Between Worlds

> Dualism . . . is the Greek inheritance. . . . They are likely to remain both in-
> dividually and collectively authoritarian as well as anarchic, cynical as well
> as romantic, skeptical and credulous, oriental and occidental . . . forever in
> flight between the myriad poles of their existence. . . .[1]

To further grasp the various opposing forces which have been beset-
ting Greece almost since its beginnings, it might be beneficial at this time
to peruse a short history of Greece's theatre. Most people are aware of the
heights reached by the Golden Age and the depths reached by the Roman
adaptations of their theatrical activities; it seems logical, therefore, to begin
this survey at about the fourth century A.D.

Most theatre activities continued to be attacked in the Eastern Empire
as they had been in the western. Church council after council inveighed
against the coarse performances at Constantinople's own Circus Maximus.
As in Rome, though, mimes, jugglers and other popular performers con-
tinued to exist and perform, perhaps even in the laps of the clergy and the
Byzantine Church. (See Benjamin Hunningher, *The Origin of the Theatre*.)
Moreover, connections between the ancient theatre and the upstart
Church were maintained, even if only in minor ways. For example, St. John
Chrysostom (347–407 A.D.) wrote a Mass following ancient Greek thematic
patterns. The religious rebel Arius (3rd–4th c.) wrote a liturgical play,
Thalia, based on the muse of comedy, with explicit references to Greek
drama.

Sometime between the fourth and the twelfth centuries the only complete extant play from Byzantium was written, *Christos Paschon.* Interestingly the play was written in ancient Greek and started with the
phrase ". . . and now, in Euripides' fashion, I will tell the passion that
redeemed the world."[2] In addition the play includes Hecuba's simile of a
ship in danger, her lament, as well as Andromache's dirge for young
Astyanax.

By about 1050 a Byzantine patriarch, Michael Keroularoios, issued a
decree allowing women to participate in clerical performances. Not only
was the Empire unable to quell the rough-and-tumble performances of the

mimes, it was supporting a liturgical drama not unlike that of Europe. Such performances, some of which included female participants, became immensely popular, and were performed in many regions of Byzantium, even to continental Greece, i.e. Salonika.[3] By the thirteenth century the Palatine Codex, compiled on Cyprus, included a play called *The Passion*. The preface contained substantial notes on the practical aspects of performing the play, e.g. hints about scenery, props, casting, etc. This detailing seems to indicate the existence of a rather widespread and particularized form of liturgical drama seen throughout the Empire.

The theatrical impulse also was preserved in various religious and pagan (e.g. spring) festivals, such as the ones to welcome spring, in *panegyri* (religious celebrations which still survive in various locations throughout Greece), as well as in the long-lived Carnival. All of these forms of communal celebration included theatrical-like activities and were so deeply ingrained in the Greek spirit that, when the Turks conquered Constantinople in 1453, they allowed the continuation of most of them.[4] Because of this dispensation, they became the only forms of theatre which could be experienced by mainland Greeks for centuries.

On the other hand the caustic satire and religio-political indoctrination which accompanied the rowdy Circus performances and the religious plays came to a standstill during *Tourkokratia*, the era of Turkish occupation. No public gatherings were allowed. There was great pressure to convert to the Moslem faith. This pressure sometimes took the form of attacks by ferocious janizaries who often abducted young Greek children. Struggling simply to exist, the Greek people had no time for an active intellectual life. Not surprisingly, thousands of intellectuals, artists and educated ecclesiasts fled to the West, Italy in particular. Many took refuge in Crete (an immigration that was to prove most beneficial to the Greek arts a few years hence), and the period sometimes referred to as the "Greek Middle Ages" commenced. Ironically, this flight of the intellectuals from Constantinople provided the fertile soil from which would flower one of the greatest renewals of history, the Italian Renaissance. On the Greek mainland, however, the people's natural talent for poetry went into hiding for centuries.[5] Modern Greek theatre history did not restart until about 1600 on Crete.

Crete at that time was occupied by the Venetians, a people deeply involved with the European Renaissance. Unlike the Turks, the Venetians and other western-based conquerors of Greek territories often allowed full intellectual and artistic freedom to the natives. Therefore, under the influence of that foreign Renaissance, many plays in the Cretan dialect and based on Italian models were written and performed on that island between 1600 and 1669.[6] Eight plays from that period are extant and represent the then-developed forms: lyrical tragedy, historical tragedy, comedy, pastoral drama, religious tragedy or mystery and, perhaps, epic poem, one of which,

Erotokritos, was performed as a play.[7] Although these plays were highly derivative of Italian models, still they may have been seen to signal a rebirth of Greek playwriting and theatre performance. This hope was suspended when the Turks took the island from the original conquerors in 1669, causing the Cretans to gather their precious manuscripts and flee to the neighboring Ionian Islands.

In the longer view the accomplishments of these Cretan writers may have contributed far more to the history of modern Greek theatre than they might have imagined. As Alexis Solomos claimed, "Cretan tragedy is the only bridge—the essential bridge—which takes us from *Iphiginia in Aulis* to *Trisevgeni,* from the last poetic drama, that is, of ancient Greece to the first of the modern."[8]

During the Turkish Occupation of the old Byzantine Empire (1453–1827), many Greeks left their native land along with the scholars and intellectuals and made homes on foreign soil. While abroad they tried to maintain some kind of contact with their roots, partly by establishing Greek schools in their new communities, and partly by keeping alive the dream of total Greek independence from any foreign power. Some Greek writers in places like Vienna, Odessa and Trieste began publishing books which were then secretly disseminated among the Greek communities in their occupied countries. Among these books were plays, of which Metastasio's were probably the first and most important, c. 1794.[9] Their aim was to provide moral support for their relatives still in occupied territory. Although at first just read, from 1814 on these increasingly available plays by diasporadic Greeks became performed more and more. John Zambelios' *Timoleon,* for example, was published in Vienna in 1818 and performed in Bucharest the same year. In the flourishing Greek communities on the Black Sea and the Danube, students presented performances of original plays, translations of French and Italian works, and of ancient tragedies. Again, however, hostilities blunted the newly emerging theatre when the War for Greek Independence broke out in 1821.

By 1834 Greek independence had been guaranteed by the Great Powers and Athens took over from Naplion as the new country's capital. Determined to adjust Athens and Athenian cultural and intellectual life to European models, King Otto and his court encouraged adaptations of Victor Hugo's work—about 60 plays in his style were created—the translation of Shakespeare, and the hosting of operas from France and Italy. Although Athens had no regular theatre life of its own until 1862, its newly forming theatre companies toured throughout the new country, as well as visiting cities still held by Turkey (Smyrna and Constantinople) and other nations like Romania. In Constantinople their reception was extremely warm because of the audience for Greek plays that had been nurtured by several amateur theatre groups which had been operating there for years.[10] About

1865 Athenian consciousness of and desire for its own theatre to emulate European prototypes resulted in a permanent company being formed. Shortly afterward the first modern playwright of merit, Demetrios Vernadakis, appeared.

It was not unusual for this newly freed people to turn away from the realities of the day and imagine a return to days of former glory. The ancient world, therefore, became a prime focus. For awhile re-creations of ancient tragedies appeared constantly, the presenters believing that ancient Greek tragedies were best for the people. However, these tragedies were presented in the ancient language and so were not readily available to the masses of Greeks who spoke Demotic, the language of the people. Other plays, therefore, were more popular—e.g. French melodramas and especially pantomimes.[11]

It was obvious nearly from the start that theatre would be important to the new Greek nation. Fifty years after independence Greece hosted 15 theatrical companies and 16 theatres. From 1880 on better theatres were constructed.[12] In 1894 the first *epitheorisis* (satirical musical revue) appeared, creating a form which remains today the single most popular form of theatrical entertainment in all of Greece.[13]

From the turn of the century to this day the Greek theatre has created its own theatrical forms and has adopted and/or adapted nearly every eastern and western theatre tradition to its own ends. In modern Athens one can enjoy Arthur Miller's *All My Sons* or Feydeau's *A Flea in Her Ear,* Chekov's *Three Sisters* or Shaffer's *Equus,* a Turkish mime or *The Merry Widow,* an original *epitheorisis* or *Hello Dolly,* a Bulgarian basso or a Yugoslavian puppet show. During the tourist season one can even see ancient Greek tragedy.

Present-day Greece's theatrical history, then, began with the fifth century B.C., waned during the next 200 to 300 years, took a rest of 1500 years, showed a brief flurry in Crete during the seventeenth century, then started seriously on the long road back to respectability in the nineteenth century. It is still on that road, but the number and significance of an increasing number of people and productions may be an indicator that it is again approaching true international respectability. Certainly it has achieved that in its productions of ancient Greek tragedy and in some films.

The many rivers of time which have flowed through this nation, changing its landscape and its people, depositing foreign influences and sweeping away some native ones have affected the theatre as much as the people. Cultural, political and economic dichotomies have created natural tensions in the Greek theatre of today. It may be beneficial to present some of these rather specifically. They may be perceived as themes which recur constantly in their modern history and which will recur throughout this present work. They are

1) Eastern emotionalism and mysticism versus western logic, control and discipline;

2) traditional acting styles versus modern ones;

3) traditional training methods versus contemporary ones;

4) Greek-style Socialism which pits Socialism against Democracy and both against traditional village organizational systems;

5) Socialism versus the autocratic necessities of theatrical art;

6) the Socialist need to provide work for everyone versus the artistic need to use only the best people;

7) individual freedoms versus the ability to subordinate one's self to the artwork;

8) the realities of civil servantism versus the requirement for excellence;

9) the need to preserve the past yet live in the present, or, put another way, the need to emulate the impossible ideal of the ancient world versus the need to "make it" in the commercial 1980s;

10) the need to create world-class theatre events in the face of the world-respected accomplishments of the West, e.g. British television;

11) the need to create a theatre suitable for a small but increasingly upward-bound, sophisticated and international population in Athens versus the need to create a theatre suitable for the still poor, conservative, Orthodox people of the villages, which still comprise over 60% of the population;

12) the morally conservative traditions of the country versus the increasing encroachment of western standards of morality.

Some of these topics will be treated as discrete entities in the course of this book. Many of them will surface again and again in various guises. It might be beneficial at this time, however, to offer some general contextual comments against which they all may be more easily seen.

Theatre Versus Its Audiences

I became aware very early in my research that there was hardly unanimity among theatre workers and their audiences concerning the Greek theatre of today. When I started an interview with one of the leading playwrights in the country, she looked startled when hearing that my subject was contemporary Greek theatre. "Contemporary Greek Theatre?" she fairly cried aloud, "There *is* no contemporary Greek theatre."[14] The overall reaction among all foreign-educated Greek theatre people was much the same. In fact I was told by many to go home and study something worthwhile. At the same time, however, there were sufficient spectators to attend as many as 80 different and simultaneous productions in Athens alone (not counting the 30 children's theatre shows), an activity ratio unequalled by any major city in the world. Overflow crowds filled the Orpheas Theatre for the entire season, paying a mind-boggling 1000 drachmas (about $7.50) to see the hit revue *Prasina Damaskina Psiles Elies* (Πράσινα Δαμάσκινα και Ψιλές Ελιές). The government had recently begun subsidizing eleven regional theatres throughout the country to the tune of 20 million drachmas each a year. Even in the face of some abysmal production standards audiences flocked to see their favorite performers. As noted director Minos Volonakis said with a shrug, "Greeks must have their theatre just as Americans must have their music."[15]

Still, no Greek director or actor with whom I spoke supported his country's theatre. It was the single most disheartening situation I encountered. As a group they were the theatre's harshest critics, convinced that, except for the ancient tragedies, they had little to offer the world. Even the noted international director Jules Dussin, husband of the Minister of Culture, Melina Mercouri, summed up his view of the current theatre scene with, "Well, there's nothing to say."[16]

Yet the Minister of Culture proclaimed in interview after interview that the ancient Greek culture is the country's most saleable commodity. Since tourism accounts for a perhaps disproportionate percentage of the nation's income, her claim has met with generally positive support within the present government. Theatre, Greece's most obvious contribution to the world's performing arts, therefore, has been supported incredibly well. Hundreds of millions of drachmas support the State Theatre, the National Theatre and the Lyric Theatre; several hundreds of millions more support the regional-municipal theatres, semi-state theatres and independent theatres. The *per capita* expenditure for the regional theatres alone in Greece was 244 drachmas in 1985, or the equivalent of $1.86 at an exchange rate of 131/dollar. This does not include government support for all the other national, state or independent theatres. Compare this to a *per capita* federal government expenditure for all theatre in America of 43 cents; if the states' contributions are included the total is 88 cents.[17] Irony aside, one might explain these figures simply by stating that Greece after all proclaimed itself to be a Socialist-Democratic country and the government, therefore, is expected to support these kinds of activities. On the other hand Greece is a poor Socialist-Democratic country and expenditures like these may indicate that, if the country does not have a contemporary theatre, it certainly seems to want one.

Unfortunately, the majority of these contemporary theatre efforts in and out of Athens simply would not be able to compete in any major western city in any way. Indeed, far too many are at the level of mediocre community theatre. Therefore, it may be true that the contemporary Greek theatre is in no danger of challenging the rest of the industrialized world in the imagination and profundity of its drama or in its production methods.

There is no brilliant new theorist or director to whom the world will make obeisance. There is no innovative new theatre company which will provide grist for the now-evolving drama of the late twentieth century.

There is, however, an incredibly avid audience; a truly remarkable devotion to the form; support from the government perhaps out of proportion to its ability to pay; several international-calibre directors, e.g. Michael Kakoyiannis, Minos Volonakis, Karolos Koun (recently deceased dean of the Greek theatre), Yiannis Houvardas, Lefteris Voyiatzis, Giorgos Michailidis, etc.; a fervid desire on the part of a score of writers to place their poetic talents in the service of the drama; an inevitable but inexorably slow sharpening of aesthetic tastes nationwide due to the omnipresence of television.[18]

An audience devoted to the theatre is a necessary and important step toward the realization of a fine theatre environment. It is also true that to have great art this devoted audience must be informed, experienced in theatre-going, and developed in its taste. Even in Athens, the center of theatrical activity, there is not a great audience. The overwhelming majority of new Athenians are immigrants or children of immigrants from the villages and small towns of the countryside and the islands.[19] When this fact is combined with the minimum mandatory education level of only nine years (only recently changed from six), it is not surprising that the majority of the present Athenian audience will accept nearly any level of quality from their theatre.

This rather unsophisticated audience naturally gravitates toward shows which play at its own level. This may explain the incredible popularity of the *epitheorisis* (επιθεόρισις), the satirical musical revue. Although a few of these shows employ the finest available writers and their comedy is based on wit and observation, most of them use humor which appeals to a rather low level of taste. In 1983, for example, the recently passed Equal Rights Law was the "hot" subject. One comic at the outdoor Menandrios Theatre shouted—they always shout—"You women out there, you think you are equal? All right, stand up and pee!" The audience rolled over in laughter.[20] One producer, Dimitri Kollatou, has made a remunerative career of producing sex and nudity shows. Disguised as tracts for freedom of expression, these shows appeal to the puerile interests of a population only recently emigrated from the strictures of village life. By masquerading as a leader in the fight for sophistication, modernization and urbanity Kollatou is able to take advantage of the villagers' curiosity about the enticements of the modern world and to make, therefore, a living (one is tempted to say a "killing"). His production of *Sodom and Gomorrah*, for example, was an artistic abomination with no socially redeeming value in my eyes. Generally Greek audiences truly enjoy themselves at these abominations as well as at the numerous star-headed sitcom vehicles and other grossly overplayed entertainments that seem to deluge Athens. They support their beloved theatre even as they demand little from it.

Audiences in the villages are even more unsophisticated. Theatre activity is very important to them, not as an event in which knowledge and insight are offered to a quiet, absorbing crowd, but rather as a social occasion. Attendance at these shows reminds one of attendance at medieval farces. Everyone is involved, often loudly, often actively partaking in the performance, whether or not the actors wish it. Sometimes talking to one's neighbors is more important than the performance. What westerners would call respect for the actors often seems minimal, even absent. In the village of Anoia in the mountains above Iraklion, Crete, actor-producer Yiannis Voglis had just started the second act of *Captain Michalis*, based on Kazantzakis' story. An old woman, a large shopping bag hanging heavily from each hand, ambled out of the entryway of the amphitheatre there and onto the orchestra circle. She crossed directly to the center of that space, looking out over the audience, presumably looking for her family, completely unaware of the smouldering, rolling-on-the-stage-floor love scene which was taking place behind her. Of course no one asked her to move, and finally members of her family shouted for her to join them. She smiled and climbed up into the *theatron*. After the show the same audience charged down the aisles and across the stage area at the same time as the actors were trying to take their bows. For a long minute the stage was a confusion of actors bowing while being jostled by audience members who were threading their ways through the actors' lines. Some spectators even patted the performers on the backs as they went by on their way to the exit.[21]

By way of contrast the audience for the State Theatre of Northern Greece's production of Genet's *The Balcony* showed extreme interest, western-style attentiveness and critical acumen. Although I thought the production very well done (with the exception of some acting style conflicts which we shall deal with later), this audience was decidely cool toward it. Part of that may have been the long tradition in Saloniki of cultural elitism. Ever since Alexander established his numerous cities in Macedonia in the fourth century B.C., attracting scholars and masters of all sorts from his conquered lands, Salonikians have considered Athens culturally backward. However, another part of this reaction may have been the influence of the university (45,000 students strong) which might have raised the average level of the audiences' artistic sensibilities much higher than usual.

A more perceptive audience, then, may be developing under the influence of more widely available university educations and, more importantly, under the influence of universal television. Even the smallest villages bristle with aluminum antennae over their various style roof tops. The presence of these antennae is so universal and unsightly—nearly one for every TV set in the land—that in April of 1986 the government began placing TV cables underground in the Plaka, an attempt to improve the look of that heavily touristed area. The fact that 80 percent of the fare on Greek television is produced outside of the country, mostly by Great Britain and America, may be of far-reaching importance in terms of raising the country's taste and production standards.[22]

Another fact that may eventually improve production standards as well as the audience's expectations from their theatre is the incredible emigration of Greeks to many other countries, mostly for education and for employment. When they return—and most Greeks maintain at least visiting ties with their native land—they inevitably bring with them a different set of expectations. Just as inevitably these expectations clash with the values of a culture still rooted in village traditions. The sitcoms which may have been superb entertainment before a young person left for England, America or Germany to study may on return seem tawdry or silly.

In the summer of 1984 Yiannis Houvardas directed an experimental version of *Alcestis* at the famed Theatre Festival at Epidavros. For years this festival has been producing traditional versions of the great classics and the place is seen as holy by most Greeks. It seemed to some unconscionable that a revered work like *Alcestis* could be interpreted by anyone. Toward the end of that production an estimated 1000 spectators tried to storm the stage and stop the show. Cordons of police had to be placed around the orchestra to prevent a melee. Old and new Greece had nearly come to blows.[23] This constant confrontation between past and present is one of the sources of tension in Greece as well as one of its most promising hopes.

Yet not everything is discouraging. There are sometimes rare and beautiful productions which appear often enough to keep the avid theatre-lover excited. For every half-dozen stupid sitcoms this last year, there was a wonderfully original and moving Εν Βρασμό Ψήχης ; for every sad attempt at a Broadway musical there was a Πρόσοπο με Πρόσοπο, directed with infinite Stanislavskian care; for every group of off-color revues there was an excitingly produced Σημφορά απο το Πολύ Μυαλό or a finely acted Καλυνήχτα Μητέρα. These shows each found an audience sufficiently knowledgeable and supportive to keep the productions open all season.

Politics

"Politics are the morning and evening pablum of Athens and the debates are followed in the papers . . ." with such overwhelming attention to the minutiae that it may be "fatal to the real progress of the country."[24]

It is difficult to over-emphasize the importance of politics on the Greek consciousness. It is understandable, given their history and cultural make-up, that they should be inordinately interested in the gentlest whiff of political movement. After eons of being told what to do by foreign occupiers, they are paranoid about the possibility of some other power reimposing its will on them. Because the quality of their lives depends so much on their network of politically placed friends and what these friends can do for them, they of course are immensely concerned with the eternal squabbles and maneuverings of each political party. Since nepotism and political patronage are the prime paths to government employment, intimate familiarity with the latest wisps of gossip concerning hirings, firings, new projects to be funded, personnel about to be changed, *et al.* is almost *de rigueur* for the successful Greek. And since there is a substantial belief in secrecy and conspiracy—traceable to the earliest behavioral patterns in village bargaining sessions—any opinion or trace of hearsay is apt to be accorded as much veracity as anything appearing in the papers. All of the above result in a political climate that is constantly alive and charged, permeating all social activity. It has been this way for a long time.

Theatres are not outside these political traditions and turmoils. All of the state-run and supported theatres have substantial political ties, proclamations to the contrary notwithstanding. In many cases belonging to the right political party (that is, the party in power) is an aid to employment and retention. In these theatres everyone is a civil servant, a fact of obvious political ramifications. In 1983 up to 30 members of the State Theatre of Northern Greece were being terminated. Why? A former Executive Director for that theatre pointed out, leaving the intimations clear, that it was curious that none of those people belonged to the present Party.[25] Many independent theatres who either support non–Party platforms or support unpopular causes may find it difficult to win support for their projects. A most poetic production of an original show by Yiannis Voglis never received government funds. Voglis told me the reason was the content of the show, the poetry of Communist writer Yiannis Ritsos. On opening night Voglis' lovely wife, Miranda, leaned over to me and whispered, "It's not going to work. They won't let it work."[26] Miranda also told me that, when Yiannis was preparing this show, he knew that the PASOK (Panhellenic Socialist Movement of Prime Minister Andreas Papandreou) government, adamantly opposed to any strengthening of the Communist Party ever since the brutal Civil War, would probably not award him financial support. A government simply does not reward a theatrical endeavor for criticizing it. Nevertheless Yiannis argued for a grant on the democratic grounds that the government should allow all political voices to be heard. The fear of Communism, however, runs deep; his argument fell on deaf ears. On the other hand the Communist Party did promise him support in all areas, from funding to promotions, production help, etc. Those promises were not honored in any way;

Voglis created, produced and directed the entire show with his own funds and friends. It was a foregone conclusion, though, that without support from either avenue, the production would close. It did and was supplanted with a rather farcical and successful *Good Soldier Schweik.*

Spectators often become embroiled in old political emotions. Many will not support productions in which the leading personalities hold or even held in the past strongly antithetical political views. Sometimes Socialists will not attend a play produced by a Communist; a rightist will refuse to see an avid Socialist in a leading role; Communists certainly will not support imported American hits (except on the sly). Although this practice is not terribly widespread, it does occur often enough to remind us of the passionate political nature of the Greeks.

One of the most recent boondoggles which enmeshed party politics and theatre occurred in the spring and summer of 1986. The Minister of Culture needed to name a new Artistic Director for the State Theatre of Northern Greece. A young and vibrant theatre artist, Yiannis Houvardas, was her choice, that is, the government's choice. After all, Houvardas was internationally respected, worked well with the staff up in that northern theatre, and was willing to take on the onus if he was allowed to maintain his international directing assignments. A vote by the often politically opposed Board of Directors, however, did not win him the majority needed. Suddenly another top-notch director, Minos Volonakis, was named as another contender. Volonakis first found out about it when it appeared in a newspaper. Hounded by reporters he refused to take part in a discussion that had not included him in the first place. The Actor's Syndicate came out in favor of Volonakis. Weeks of interviews, stories and gossip burned up the press. Still he had not been approached by the government. Houvardas withdrew from the hassle, saddened that the former friendship between the two men had been soured by this sensationalist coverage and had placed two apolitical men at the mercy of antagonistic political ideologies. Suddenly Volonakis read in the papers that the government had appointed him the new Director of the State Theatre of Northern Greece, still without discussing it with him personally. He, therefore, refused to entertain the notion until he had met with government officials. After a summer of indecision, he accepted the position in September, 1986.[27] He was still at the helm in spring 1988.

Obviously politics permeates all levels of Greek life. Its interface with theatre creates untold opportunities and untold grief. Its effect will continue to be a very mixed bag as long as there are socialist-run theatres, fully capitalistic-style theatres, and those that fall between these two extremes.

Socialism and Democracy in the Theatre

For a country so dedicated to the ideal of democracy to have elected such a strongly pro-socialistic government seems illogical. Yet it is the "ideal" of democracy to which they are dedicated, not the reality. The ideal was championed by those nineteenth century romantics determined to re-create the glisten of ancient Greece with little regard for the realities of modern Greece. But the story of Greek democracies simply does not support this kind of idealism.

The history of the modern Greek state has rarely included a viable democracy; a parliamentary monarchy has predominated for most of the last 150 years. Especially after the despotic years of the last *junta*, just over a decade ago, Greeks seem to have embraced the idea of unfettered freedom with a passion that is sometimes frightening. A phrase which more accurately describes their vision of democracy may be the one used by that American professor — "genial anarchy." A democracy which depends on mutually cooperative freedoms has never been in the lexicon of modern Greek political terminology. It is the *idea* of democracy for which the Greeks passionately shout. It seems to coincide very well with the Greeks' own sense of personal worth and individualism, with their deeply held determination that in the modern world, finally! they *will* decide their own destinies.

On the other hand their image of this pure democracy is hardly un-tainted. After all, they elected a heavily Socialistic government. Perhaps their need for the *feeling* of democracy as well as their need to have some-one else provide for their well-being (after all, they are Greek and deserve this care) may make this particular brand of democratically-elected Socialism perfect for their needs.

Socialism is dedicated to finding work for everyone, qualified or not. It is a form of government which offers ample opportunities for "padding," or nepotism or "make work" positions. In turn the people in these positions soon realize that they may do almost nothing in order to get a paycheck. That, in turn, allows them ample time and energy to get out into the capitalistic sub-culture of Athens and get another job. Since nearly every-one has a second job, dedication to the primary management system or enterprise is rare. Since everyone is working on that special deal, that second-job project which will be of stupendous financial or prestigious im-portance, absenteeism is a major factor in corporate and governmental in-efficiency.[28] As F. Eleftheriou said, "The Monstrous [sic] public sector created by both conservatives and socialists during the years 1974–1985 — with its blatant bureaucratic inefficiency, its civil servant mentality of mediocrity, its tendency to corruption and its sole usefulness as a tool for political patronage and favoritism — has become a mirror image of society as a whole. . . . Nothing that has to be filtered through the state apparatus (and most things have to) functions any more, even in an elementary level."[29]

In the theatre the fallout from these kinds of behavior results, at least in state-run theatres, in the same kinds of nepotism, favoritism and overlapping as is common elsewhere in the economy. One actor at the National Theatre was hired to deliver two lines in one play of the ten produced during the 1983 season. He had to report daily and spend his time in the theatre, doing nothing, even though he was used not at all 90 percent of the time. Even during the rehearsals for his show he was used for only a few minutes each day. Of course he slipped out to do other jobs whenever possible.[30] At the State Theatre of Northern Greece about 20 actors complained to the Executive Director that they had nothing to do all year and were tired of coming into the theatre and sitting. Could he please add some plays so that they would have something to do? they pleaded. No doubt some of these people also slipped out for some healthy commercial activity on the side, perhaps appearing in TV shows or announcing commercials.[31] Ironically, Socialism gave these employees the freedom to become capitalists.

Since hierarchical structures are inimical to the Greek sense of personal worth (someone has to be above everyone else), Greeks take most unkindly to anyone who sets himself up — or is set up by someone else — as their superior. Subordinating one's self, therefore, to the dictates of a director or producer or technical director is difficult for a Greek, even though they manage to do it. Moreover, since Greece is now a democratic state (the term is used whenever it suits the purpose of the speaker), everyone has a right and duty to voice his opinion concerning any element of any project. That is, in a true democracy everyone has an equal right to approach anyone else in the chain of command (even that phrase would raise Greek hackles) and offer one's opinion with as much passion as is necessary to prove that he is right. That means that the bus driver can command equal time of an Executive Director as can the imported stage director or the President of the Trustees. (This egalitarianism is practiced all the way to the Prime Minister's office.) This characteristic of Greek political behavior would seem to be a great benefit to a nation, whether it be democratically socialistic or socialistically democratic. Greeks really *do* participate in the fullest possible way in all decisions. Yet their love for unending debate and rhetorical gesture has always proven an obstacle to a full realization of any organization's goals.

Of course these kinds of scenes do not always take place, certainly not in those well-established and high quality professional theatres such as have been mentioned. In most of the rehearsals I witnessed the respect for the director was admirable, even if at times sycophantish (one wonders if this was a respect for his art or for his political power). The rigorous rehearsals of Karolos Koun, the Father of all modern Greek theatre, or the 6–12 month rehearsals of Lefteris Voyiatzis certainly belie any tendency toward laxness or laziness. The highly disciplined back-to-back productions of Beaumarchaise' *The Barber of Seville* and *The Marriage of Figaro*, by the Anoikto Theatre Company reflected an attention to detail, control and organization that would have been applauded in any theatre circle anywhere.

In the worst cases Socialistic attitudes toward providing work for everyone and supporting a low level of performance work directly against the requirements of the theatre as art. If everyone is an equal worker in the eyes of this system, then how is a leading role cast? Indeed, why are most of the leads given to a very small number of leading players? One answer to this obvious political-artistic dilemma may be found in the curtain call method used in state theatres. The more senior members of the cast are given the final, "star" calls. In a production of *The Taming of the Shrew* Katherine and Petruchio, young members of the National Theatre, were relegated to a back row in the curtain calls while several secondary and even minor role players were awarded the final, down-front bow.

At the same time the propensity to use "democracy" as an excuse to avoid chains of command or to excuse endless debate also works against the theatre art. Great theatre has rarely been democratic; indeed, much great theatre has been the result of autocratic forms of leadership. Given the various Greek responses to the concepts of socialism, democracy and autocracy, it is amazing that so much theatre is even produced and that a fair percentage of it is produced very well.

4. Difficulties in Research

Contemporary research in any field is a tricky endeavor, like trying to analyze and contextualize a constantly changing organism. Very little is "set" yet. The slithering thing is still searching for its form.

Contemporary Greek society and its theatre are both those kinds of organisms. In a very real way their latest transformations were as recent as 1974, the year of the Colonel's ousting. And even though since that time there has been relative calm and stability in that country, even though the government was elected by a whopping 48 percent of the people, and even though they finally have decided to speak the Demotic Greek language in all situations, nevertheless, Greek society is undergoing incredibly rapid changes daily.

Even a casual observer may ascertain the rapidity and extent of some of these changes. Between the summer of 1983 and the fall of 1985 I was struck by several: incredibly, pornography had appeared on open display in many Athenian kiosks; bra-less females rode their own motorcycles; anti–Americanism was much more rampant and open; development of nearly any island with a beach seemed out of control, e.g. the heretofore quiet island of Agistri; educated Greek females were unafraid to call males for social purposes; the pursuit of material wealth had become almost palpable—Greeks had suddenly become ". . .like kids in a new candy store!"[1]

Caught up in the same leaps as its society was the drama. Professor Varos Paselidis of the University of Thessaloniki said that "The Greek theatre is really a very new thing." Until the ousting of the Colonel all "theatre" teachers in the universities were really classicists who knew nothing about the theatre. Modern literature of any kind was kept out of the classrooms in deference to the classics taught in a classical way—rhythm, grammar, etc. When freedom was re-established in 1974 these same classicists undermined any attempts to include new playwrights or theories in the educational system. It was only very recently and with a great deal of effort that writers such as Williams, Brecht, Ionesco, Pinter, etc. have been included in the curricula.[2] (Interestingly, much of contemporary Greek playwrighting echoes the same kind of metaphysical anguish and existential cynicism of the playwrights of the Absurd.)

In theatre practice the contemporary Greek theatre also may be said to have restarted with the fall of the Colonels. At that time there was a fresh flow of exiled Greeks back into the country (although many stayed away when they realized that opportunities abroad were infinitely more available than those in their native land) and the government increasingly has supported a country-wide effort to bring theatre to all the people. Freed from the fear of censorship, new voices spoke out in an attempt to define the new Greek experience. Total nudity, male and female, now appeared on stage with few repercussions. Experimentalism was more accepted. For example, in the summer of 1986 experimental productions of classical plays in the ancient theatres were actively encouraged by the government, just three years after the audience at Epidavros nearly attacked Houvardas' experimental *Alcestis*. In 1988 the National Theatre of Great Britain under the leadership of Peter Hall was invited to perform three plays at Epidavros, a theatre usually reserved for Greek companies. Between 1984 and 1986 there have been established a fully subsidized regional theatre program and a major new summer festival in Athens (Festival of the Rocks) as well as a bilingual (Greek-English) theatre group, two new theatre spaces in the totally renovated Plaka area beneath the Acropolis, the beginning of a restoration of the ancient theatre of Dionysius in the same area, a plan to construct a new amphitheatre on Santorini, the beginning of the restoration of an ancient theatre near Agrinio, the construction of a major new amphitheatre eventually seating 17,000 in the neighborhood of Nikia, Athens, etc. The activity is simply staggering, a situation which presents enormous challenges to those trying to study it.

In addition to the constantly changing nature of the subject, there are several other difficulties in researching the contemporary Greek theatre which might be worth mentioning. Some of them grow naturally and understandably out of the Greek consciousness, and others grow out of the practical realities of day-to-day life in Athens. I offer them for their own sakes but also as *caveats* for those researchers who might follow.

First is the attitude on the part of the Greek theatre people themselves, the "there is no contemporary Greek theatre" syndrome. It may be clear that there is no *great* contemporary Greek theatre, no great movements or geniuses. There are, however, an incredible amount of activity and significant attempts to improve, to be acceptable in the international marketplace. Greek directors like Kakoyiannis, Dussin, Houvardas, Doufexis and others are already widely sought by theatres in many foreign countries. Actors like Telly Savalas and singers like Dafne Evangelatos have made respectable careers in America and France respectively. Greek productions of Greek tragedies are still respected world-wide.

It seems that the "no contemporary Greek theatre" syndrome refers more often than not to the lack of outstanding playwrights, insightful experimentalism, consistently high production standards, training programs and almost no perceptive and consistent criticism. Of course there are exceptions to all of the above, but in general the Greek observations of their own theatre seem accurate.

Second, the amount of material written in Greece about their theatre, rather than the drama, is minuscule. It was only within the last few years (1985) that a book on stage design written in Greek appeared. This is partly because most practical theatre artists leave the country to learn their trades, or learn it on the job. The education and/or training of non-acting production personnel is almost nonexistent in the country. The need, therefore, for written materials which investigate these areas is absent.

A similar situation applies to the areas of theory and criticism. Until 1983 there was no advanced degree in theatre offered anywhere in the country, a situation that director Minos Volonakis called "a national disgrace."[3] Since then, however, at least one university, the University of Crete, has established a degree in "Theatrology," which seems to include dramaturgy, history and criticism. Since it is a very recent development, it is unclear what effect its recipients will have on the quality of criticism in Greece. Two leading Greek theatre personages, Aliki-Bacopoulou-Halls and Spyros Evangelatos, have received doctorates from the University of Athens. Mrs. Hall's daughter also was accepted as a doctoral candidate in 1985. She faced three years of independent research and the presentation of a dissertation. Certainly the continued awarding of such degrees should improve the overall level of critical commentary eventually. In 1986, however, most newspaper criticisms which I read or had read to me seemed to be uniformed puff pieces or scathing, baseless attacks. When I asked a Professor of Literature how these "critics" could dare call themselves by that title, he scoffed, "In Greece you are what you state you are."[4]

Again it is those theatre workers who have been educated outside Greece, or who have worked in the theatre in other western countries, often during self-imposed exiles during the military *junta,* who find the greatest fault with the Greek system of criticism. It is also this group from which informed commentary is slowly starting to be heard. People like Thassos Lignati or Anee Kortzedopoulou are gaining respect, at least among the theatre intelligentsia, for their perceptive and informed criticism.

Third, it is difficult to know whom to believe. Greeks for centuries have placed more weight on *philotimo,* on being in the right, on winning, on protecting friends and family than on any sort of objective truth. This tradition causes facts and ideas to change shape in Greece, to blur; everything is of potentially equal importance or potentially irrelevant.[5]

In the summer of 1986 there were 17 newspapers in Athens, all interpreting the events of the world through their particular political biases. Since Athenians normally bought only the paper which presented their party's view, one wondered if there existed anywhere in that city a clear, objective view of the facts of anything. If a critic came out with a particularly scurrilous attack on an actor or director, the first response by the attackee was to find out which newspaper printed the piece. Depending on the political persuasion of that paper, the attack would either be accepted or sloughed off as irrelevant. Since these reviewers rarely had any formal training for these jobs, anyway, their criticism was often devalued to nothing. Of course, if it was a rave review, regardless of the paper which printed it, it became a wonderful promotions artifact, blown up and pasted on a sandwich board outside the theatre in which the praised play was appearing. This warmly human trait touches on a Greek tradition; a judgment that goes against a Greek is obviously the result of someone else's evil machinations; a judgment that applauds a Greek's accomplishments obviously recognizes true value.

In Greece today it is, therefore, difficult to believe the response of anyone who says that a particular play is "wonderful." That response is more likely to be a function of *philotimo* than of accurate judgment. This is especially likely when the judgment is spoken in front of a *xenos* (ξένος), a foreigner. A Greek is behaving traitorously to his culture if he openly admits to a ξένος that something Greek is not wonderful. In village terms this means that there can never be a village where the water is purer, the fruits sweeter, or the women more chaste than in one's own village.[6] In theatre terms it means that the designer of one's play is "the best in Greece," the composer is "wonderful, a very important man," the leading actor is "very good, very good," and the director is "a genius."

On the other hand if one disagrees with such a hyperbolic judgment, i.e. finds the play mediocre, the setting tawdry or the acting unconscionably overdone, he is likely to run into a kind of reverse *philotimo*. Since the original adjudicator cannot admit a mistake, he may offer many reasons to explain why the production did not attain high enough artistic goals — Greece is a poor country; the audience is tired from fighting its way through the demonstrations tonight; we do not have the money to get enough lighting instruments; the best actors were hired elsewhere before we started into rehearsals, *ad infinitum.*

This response may grow out of the nation's basic insecurity about itself and its place in the world. Unable to articulate comfortably a statement concerning its own identity, unable to feel totally secure and free to determine its own destiny it might choose to operate on the levels of intense national pride and insecurity at the same time. In the theatre this may take the form of judging a show "wonderful," because everything Greek is wonderful, even while the critic knows that the production does not come up to world standards. Aesthetic judgment is only partly a function of aesthetics; more often it is the result of politics and/or national psychological mind sets.

This shell-game-with-facts is played constantly and by everyone. I have already mentioned how my attempts to get an interview with the Minister of Culture failed when I was told she was in Paris when she really was in Athens, or the Volonakis story in which the papers had him accepting the appointment to head the theatre in Saloniki when he had not even talked with the government to that time. On January 17, 1985, Kostas Laliotis, the former Minister of the New Generation and Athletics, was interviewed for the Athens News Agency by Haris Livas. The Minister waxed eloquently about 15 of the 300 planned new recreation centers that the government had set up throughtout the country, all of which included amateur theatre groups. He claimed that "we now have 3000 teachers to teach the theatre seminars."[7] Three years later, in February, 1988, there was no trace of such centers, nor had anyone heard of their being established anywhere.

To obfuscate the facts even more there seems to be an "oh, well . . ." attitude on the part both of most Greeks and of non–Greeks who have lived in that country for awhile. When a "fact" is presented today and contradicted tomorrow the general reaction is likely to be, "oh, well." Even I began to accept the fact that "Greeks live in a state of total and permanent contradiction to each other . . . if you don't like what they do or say today, just wait until tomorrow to find them doing the opposite."[8] Like the impossible traffic jams, the constant strikes, the gross inefficiency in government offices, this contradictoriness became just another fact of life and certainly nothing to become concerned about. No one was surprised that these recreation centers and their amateur theatre groups had never been established and even wondered why I was so aghast that they had not.

It was difficult, then, to ascertain the trustworthiness—in western terms—of anything. Logic, control and reason seemed lost somewhere. Eastern mysticism and mythology seemed in the ascendant. One came to suspect all information and at the same time came to accept contradictory claims as part of the whole truth in some culturally mysterious way.

The same dichotomy applied to the press. Journalism in Greece may best be described as a creative art. One recalls White House Chief of Staff Donald Regan's television statement regarding a Greek newspaper's report regarding the Iran-Contra scandal: "Anyone who knows anything about Greek newspapers would not lend much credence to their claims."[9] A highly placed officer of the American Embassy, in a fit of frustration over her dealings with the Greek press, intensely declared, "I can't respect anyone who has so little regard for the truth."[10] Again, taken in the perspective of Greek culture and tradition, this *modus operandi* is eminently understandable. If the "truth" resides primarily in the effects the "facts" have on one's family, village, political party or country, then "facts" do not become objectively truthful entities; rather they become malleable tactics toward more important ends.

Fourth, planning an efficient day of research, interviewing and theatre-going was never possible. Although this may seem a trivial point, it did have an effect on the amount and quality of research accomplished.

It took quite a while, for example, to get used to the unique work schedule of so many businesses and offices. Like most Mediterranean countries, Greece takes a siesta break in the middle of each day. Each group of stores and offices, however, establishes its own break schedule. Some break between 3 P.M. and 5 P.M., others between 4 P.M. and 6 P.M., others go until 5 P.M. and do not re-open, except on certain days of the week, others work until 5 P.M. and still report during their second work period, variously placed at 5–7 P.M., 6–8 P.M., 7–9 P.M., 7–midnight, etc. The tiny mom-and-pop stores sometimes closed while the single proprietor visited a friend down the street. With no one but the occasional customer to complain (and only people whose expectations were much more western than those of the Greeks would complain), these tiny stores were more flexible in their schedules than the larger businesses having international dealings with the Economic Community.

In late January 1988, the government announced an entirely new schedule of shop hours, primarily to limit the suffocating pollution caused by vehicular traffic in the city's center, secondarily to suggest a more western approach to business activities. Naturally thousands of small shops and supermarkets went on strike. For weeks no one seemed to know which shops would be open or closed which hours or days. Even after all these schedules were sorted out, individual shop owners adhered to the older, more traditional hours. This individualism, of course, created some difficulties with those of us who liked to adhere to firm schedules. For example, the Curator of the Theatre Museum on Akadimias Street worked only four hours on two mornings each week, unless he was out or unless he decided to work late or early, or unless he changed his work days.

Even planning attendance at performances was not as smooth as one might expect. For a fair percentage of the time particular performances did not take place, or were moved to another date. Sometimes strikes, holidays, demonstrations or a lack of transportation caused performances to be canceled. Sometimes the tickets were not on sale where they were advertised to be, or they had not arrived at the box office yet, *ad infinitum*. When taken as a whole these glitches in the public performance system caused countless hours to be lost. Some entries from my diary may illustrate the point.

On October 21 a general strike was called to protest government devaluation. . . . Not everyone went on strike at the same time. My phone has been out for five days and the workers will not fix it. . . . I try to remember to call people from a kiosk but forget their numbers or my phone book or there's a line there waiting for the phone or the line is busy. So this morning

I was determined to get to the downtown box office of the National Theatre to get tickets for the touring production of *John Gabriel Borkman* as soon as the box office opened.

I did. It was not open. While I stood inside the vestibule a workman said he had to pull down the steel grates across the lobby. (Because of the strike no offices would be opened, he said.) So I left to buy stamps. Ended up at a parcel-post-only post office which, of course, did not sell stamps. They sent me to the correct post office where I did manage to purchase stamps. It turned out to be my only accomplishment for the day.

Passed the box office on my way back to the office. It was opened! Delighted, I asked for the tickets. They said they did not have the *Borkman* tickets (even though it was advertised thus) and that I had to go out to the National Theatre box office itself.

. . . Since the public transportation system was not operating I had to walk the couple of miles past incredible traffic jams and thousands of people out to Omonia which was blocked off by a rally—posters, loudspeakers at hundreds of decibels, thousands shouting *et al.* Tired, hot, nervous, feet hurt. Reached the National Theatre. Closed for the strike. DAMN! (Of course, they are government employees. Why do I always assume that theatre workers are above this sort of thing?)

Walked all the way back to the office to catch a few minutes' rest before my 11:45 appointment for lunch with a theatre and movie editor. Walked up to Kolonaki. SHE never showed up! Starving now. Decided to go home.

City is using military buses and 2½ ton trucks as bus system replacements. I was lucky and caught an Army bus. Realized that I had no food in the apartment and so tried to go shopping. Forgot. All the groceries were closed because of the strike. Made a huge, non-nutritious meal with what I had and fell asleep.

. . . decided to leave 1½ hours early [instead of 45 minutes] for my 6 P.M. appointment because of the strike and the fact that the appointment was across town. A few streetcars were suddenly running—why? While waiting for the trolley that would take me within a few blocks of Nikos' apartment, I realized that another Navy bus was going in the same direction. Caught it. Got off exactly where I had hoped it would stop. Proud of myself. Even a little early. Great. Waited until 6 P.M., walked up his stairs—lift was not operating. HE wasn't there! Angry, frustrated, I stopped at every candy shop on the street.

Stinking with sweat by now. A light rain starts falling. I was determined not to walk the several miles back home. The only transportation was a crowded, jostling Army 2½ ton truck. Everyone is bent over because the tarp is so low. So crowded that I could not shove or plead my way out at my stop. By the time I elbowed my way to the lip of the tailgate on the next stop, the truck started up again, unaware that I was perched there precariously. Thrown off balance, I leaped for my life into the traffic.

Seven hours of hard work today for absolutely nothing. Need an *ouzo.*[11]

Scheduling interviews likewise was frustrating. Most often, once I actually contacted a Greek theatre worker for an interview, he or she would want to conduct it that day, even within the hour. If my schedule was booked up for that day and the next, they would ask that I call back when

I was again free. Consequently, I was able to schedule interviews mostly one at a time and almost always had to save large blocks of time the day of the call just in case the interviewee suggested an immediate meeting. It was grossly inefficient and plodding. I began to understand the advice of most westerners living in Athens: "Be happy if you accomplish one thing each day." When I once asked why Greeks shied away from scheduling appointments days in advance, an actor-director told me, "Who knows? Something better might come up in the meantime?"[12] When once I vented my frustration on Nikos Skiadas, a National Theatre actor, he smiled kindly, closed my heavily blackened appointments calendar and said, "Tomas, you must learn to be a Greek. We Greeks love to eat well, drink good wine, make love and talk. . ."—not one word about the importance of appointments.

Fifth and perhaps most importantly, the highly political and conspiratorial nature of Greek society caused many of those I met and talked with to be a little hesitant about offering information. The reader no doubt will have already noticed that several references in this work have been labelled, "Name withheld." The reason is clear to anyone who has spent time in Greece.

For centuries this poor and almost consistently dominated small country has evolved a particular behavioral pattern that ensured at least the survival of its basic social units, its families. Basically this survival has been accomplished by trusting no one outside the immediate sphere of the family. The world becomes divided between friends and enemies (δίκοι μας και ξένοι) and these are mutually exclusive. There can be no middle ground; therefore, there can be no room for an understanding of one's opponents' views.[13]

Hence, criticism of the ruling party, its officers and, by extension, any of its familial or official "relatives" immediately places the critic outside the embrace of those entities. Once outside, the critic faces the distinct possibility that the airing of his criticism will directly affect his personal and/or professional aspirations. This does not mean that people are thrown in jail for being outspoken; heavens, if that were so the entire country would be behind bars. Rather it means that there exists a paranoic fear of reprisal, objectively true or not, that recalls centuries of history in general and the bitter civil war brutality of just a few decades ago in particular. (For years after that conflict, for example, Athenians rolled up their newspapers on the buses and trolleys so that no one could see which paper it was, and, therefore, report them.)[14] Whether or not there are covert observers on every block, most Greeks stride through daily life with a suspicion that there just might be.

Thus it was not surprising that some of my interviewees at least mentioned that I should not mention the source of the particular information which had been offered; others simply wondered how I was going to use the information. A few said outright, "Do not write this down." Others were more circuitous — "Don't tell anyone *I* said so, eh?" Some strong or financially secure or well-placed individuals seemed freer from this tension than most and expressed no fear at all with the ultimate disposition of the information they were providing; these, however, were in the minority.

The fact that nearly every Greek with whom I spoke was open and hospitable and warm to me, a foreigner, the fact that they were willing to express their judgments and concerns about the theatre to me, and the fact that by so doing they could be charged with breaking trust with their "Greekness" exhorts me to tread very gently when identifying my sources. I cannot determine what information other Greeks would consider damaging or culturally traitorous or false, nor can I determine what information is absolutely neutral when seen through the Greek consciousness. I can only try to be as careful as possible in finding the balance between intellectually defensible statements, culturally sensitive references, and Greek *philotimo.* I trust that the reader will understand my sometimes purposeful circumlocution.

II
Types of Contemporary
Greek Theatre

5. Government-Supported Theatres

Perhaps reflecting the many types of political preferences in Greece, the theatre has evolved several types of financing and organization, several purposes and several audiences. Greek theatre today may be propagandistic, educational or escapist in its purpose, capitalistic or socialistic in its method of financing, communistic or dictatorial in its organizational structure, or any of the above within any of the above. The permutations seem endless, a quality which may give the present-day Greek theatre its vitality.

In general the vast percentage of financial assistance to the Greek theatre stems from direct government subsidy. Even the independent or "free" theatre movement depends too often on at least modest government support. The commercial theatres do not request nor do they generally need such assistance. Children's theatre normally operates through a parent independent theatre company but the children's theatre productions are most often supported in some way by the government.

Even though the divisions among the various types of theatres are sometimes muddled, they generally may be categorized as government-supported theatres (national, state, semi-state, free and municipal), commercial theatres, theatres for children, *karagheozis* theatres and amateur theatres. In this chapter we shall examine those theatres with official government-supported status.

State Theatres

Three institutions exist which are totally funded by the national government of Greece: the National Theatre in Athens, the *Lyriki Skini* (Lyric Stage or Opera) also in Athens, and the State Theatre of Northern Greece located in Saloniki. The buildings are government buildings; the furnishings, including touring buses *et al.* belong to the government; the workers are nearly all civil servants. The budgets and staffs are enormous compared to all other Greek theatres'. Their productions range from stunning to tawdry, although the northern theatre group seems to produce

49

shows of a higher quality more consistently than either of the other two.

Governing a huge, tradition-bound, civil service–oriented government bureaucracy while still producing worthwhile art must be enormously difficult. Perhaps that is one of the reasons these institutions have had difficulty finding and retaining suitable leadership. For the first time since 1983, as a matter of fact, both the *Lyriki Skini* and the State Theatre of Northern Greece now have strong and capable artistic leadership, Spyros Evangelatos at the opera and Minos Volonakis in Saloniki. As of this writing the National Theatre still was being headed by the President of the Board, Kyrios Varkopoulous, a lawyer. To my knowledge it has been without strong artistic leadership since the spring of 1983.

As with any civil service–bound organization in Greece, these state-run theatres no doubt face the same kind of traditional practices that infuse all other governmental offices. Inefficiency, a slack attitude (and the usual concomitant, mediocrity), holding second jobs, protecting family and familial interests (including political ones) before those of the theatre, featherbedding, etc. all pervade these structures. Since employment, advancement and retention are more functions of *rousfetti* (personal influence) rather than talent or dedication, and since it is the goal of the socialistic state to keep people working, it is not difficult to understand how normal human beings could become less than committed to their work in these theatres. Since this traditional system of sub-official operation constantly has been a source of concern in all the government services (in fact, each new government promises to attack these problems energetically), then the quality of work, the sense of artistic mission, of dedication to excellence is almost impossible to maintain. At least two directors who worked at the National in 1983 ranted at me almost daily about the gross inefficiency, the laziness, the absenteeism running throughout their companies. Both said that they would never work there again.[1] Theatre people outside the government-supported theatres, themselves more often than not past members of those establishments, generally denigrate them and their work. These "outsiders," many of whom now operate their own theatres, dismiss the civil servants in those state-run theatres as "workers," not "artists." National Theatre members, especially, are disparaged for "putting in their time" rather than dedicating themselves to the art.

There may be some truth in this. In my observations inside the National Theatre it seemed that a great deal of time, energy and money were spent at least very inefficiently, and often at cross-purposes — although this should not surprise anyone who has spent any time with the Greek people. On the other hand I also observed a great deal of true dedication and striving for excellence among individual artists, many of whom were totally committed to a national system of theatre production. (Their productions of *Orestes* in 1983 and *The Ghost Sonata* in 1986, for example, were wonderful.) It was difficult to determine how much of this animosity, therefore, was warranted or how much arose out of some real or imagined emotional slight. It might have arisen also from the normal Greek belief that, if person A achieved something person B did not, then person B must have been cheated and/or person A had better "fixers."

The National Theatre of Greece. The National Theatre, established in 1932, is a fully subsidized branch of the Greek government and is its most visible contribution to the nation's performing arts. It operates directly under the aegis of the Minister of Culture. Its payroll includes approximately 100 actors, 100 technicians and 30 administrative personnel. It is governed by an Artistic Director and a General Director, although sometimes both positions are combined under one man. These directors are selected by the State, but they report directly to a volunteer Board of Directors who normally are outstanding citizens in some realm of endeavor. Some members of this Board have direct and practical experience in theatre production, others are simply influential citizens. One is a government representative.

Normally the Artistic Committee, composed of the highest echelons within the permanent establishment, recommends to the full Board a season of plays as well as proposed directors and designers. (There are no staff directors or designers in the National Theatre; only the Technical Director carries full-time, permanent responsibilities.) Although technically the Board can veto these suggestions, usually the influence of the Artistic Director holds sway.

The directors which are hired usually have casting privileges, but sometimes certain casting decisions have already been made or are strongly urged upon the incoming director. The leading roles are not always cast from the resident company, or, conversely, they are cast from a very small group of talented (and privileged?) actors from within the company. Not unlike elsewhere in the world, these procedures sometimes ruffle feathers or create interesting tensions in the company.

The National Theatre resides in a large, Renaissance-like building at 50 Constantinou Street in Athens, just off Omonia Square. It contains two theatres, a once-lovely 700-seat, gold and beige proscenium originally built under King George I, and a 100–150-seat experimental house which is also used heavily for student work. This large building contains a few storage and production areas, but many of these necessary spaces are scattered throughout the city.

In the winter of 1985–1986 the National opened a second major facility in the port city of Piraeus. It is a large and imposing, if badly deteriorated, classical-style building which covers an entire block. When current renovations are completed, this 1000 seat theatre should be truly lovely both inside and out.

During the winter season the National produces about a play a month in each of its theatres. These productions most often are taken from the dramatic literature of the post–Renaissance western world and from new Greek playwrights. Almost never does the season include the ancient classics. "That," I was told by a cynical actor, "is for the tourists."

It is true that almost all classical plays appear in summer productions in those ancient theatres naturally suited to them. During the winter season classical tragedies and comedies appear, if at all, in the independent theatres. This is one example of the Greek theatre's attempt to serve both tradition and the modern world. Greek theatre people, while deeply respecting their ancient heritage, decry western attempts to define their work only in those terms. In 1983 while I waxed hotly about my profound theatrical experiences at Delfi and Epidavros, the actors in the cast of the National Theatre's production of *Trojan Women* said simply that I *had* to return during the regular winter season because "that's when we do our real work."[2] In my first meeting with TV soap star Tasso Kavidia, I mentioned that attending a performance of a modern play that afternoon was impossible because I had made previous plans to go to the Parthenon. She fairly yelled at me in that small cafeneion. "The Parthenon! The Parthenon will be there tomorrow! Everyone wants to go to the Parthenon! If you want to learn about the real Greece, you must go to this performance!"[3]

This was my first indication that the vast majority of Greeks wish to be treated as inhabitants of the twentieth century, not the fifth century B.C. Neither they nor anyone else on this globe can live up to the accomplishments of that ancient society and it is unfair to expect them to. In fact, the widespread undercurrent of expectation among the Greeks as well as among other nationalities that Greece today should somehow be a direct copy of its ancient predecessor may be one of the greatest obstacles to progress in that country. A noted director vented his frustration in this regard: "The best thing that could happen to Greece is for the entire Acropolis to disappear."[4]

On the other hand tourism comprises an enormous percentage of Greece's foreign income. With the largest balance of payments deficit in Europe the country must encourage and support those activities which will assist with the problem. Ancient plays produced in ancient theatres are, of course, a tremendous drawing card and a great deal of state money and effort is expended in order to maximize their attractiveness. It is natural that these plays are presented on those perfect summer nights in the Peloponnese when most of the tourists are in the country.

From 1954 until 1970 the National Theatre was the sole producer of the ancient playwrights in the Festival of Epidavros. Over the years, however, as other theatre groups became established and competent, they also were invited to perform there. By 1983 the National was expected to produce in addition to its winter season two new shows for the summer Festival at the Theatre of Epidavros as well as to remount two shows from the previous summer's repertory for the same festival. Since 1986, however, the government has invited many more groups to perform at that festival and the National Theatre may no longer have to provide the majority of the shows there.

In its home space on Constantinou Street the National Theatre also hosted touring companies primarily from western nations. This probably added another 6–10 productions to its main stage season. Athenians flocked to these touring shows and standing-room-only was almost a foregone conclusion. The National also maintained a Drama School and some "moving" or touring companies. These latter were normally short, small-cast, minimally produced shows which traveled to schools and factories throughout the winter season.

A word should be said about touring in Greece. A disproportionate percentage of the Greek population, almost a third of the country, resides in Athens. Naturally, a disproportionate percentage of the country's theatrical activities has gravitated there to serve these immigrants. Because Athens is the center of theatrical activities, most actors and directors far prefer to serve Dionysius in the city than in the regions. After all, there is more professional theatre activity there than in any other place in the country; the best talents in the business are there; prestige and star-making arise from that metropolis; international opportunities await almost wholly in Athens; nearly all broadcast commercials, radio, TV and cinema are centered there. Asking an actor to leave that potential to spend time on the road is asking a great deal. Nevertheless, the government and the Actor's Syndicate fortuitously have enacted guidelines which, when taken together, do encourage and support touring.

The government requires that all recipients of a subsidy of any sort must take shows to nearby villages and towns. (Actually, the interpretation of the rule by some theatre producers goes something like this: If you tour to nearby towns and villages, your chances of winning a subsidy the next time you apply is greatly enhanced.) The Communist-led Actor's Syndicate, meanwhile, has stipulated that if you hire an actor for any purpose, you must pay that actor for three months, whether or not the show goes on. This of course protects the actors from unethical producers who might "cast" someone and then pull out before the first rehearsal, but it also places a sometimes undue burden on the producer. The upshot of these rules, consequently, is that a producer like Christos Tzangas, who feels personally obligated to take shows to the smallest villages, tries to rehearse for one month and tour for two, jamming into the schedule as many shows as union rules allow in order to insure sufficient income to cover the mandated salaries and still make some profit.[5] It is exhausting work, but the combined rules of the government and the actor's union do encourage theatre groups to take their wares to the villages.

Even though the National Theatre does not face these salary stipulations (most of the company is on season contracts), it still is required to tour because it receives a subsidy. These small "moving" companies, therefore, as well as the summer productions at Epidavros and at other festivals satisfy both the government's conditions for subsidization as well as its ideological goal of taking theatre to as many people as possible.

Depending on your source of information the National Theatre has saved or is killing serious theatre art in Greece. I met no one outside that organization who had kind or encouraging words to say about it. Even the gentle Dean of Greek Theatre, Karolos Koun, sadly reflected that "It was healthy at that time [when it was formed]. And there was great enthusiasm, excellent actors. Now I think it's declined."[6]

Lyriki Skini (Opera) Theatre. Organized in 1940, the national opera employed in July, 1983 some 300 people of which 70 were musicians, 35 were dancers, 100 were singers, 20 were administrative personnel, and the remainder are divided between the front-of-house, technical and box office staffs. There was one staff conductor and one permanent designer. With the installation of a new Artistic Director in 1984, the total number of employees rose to 500. Like the National Theatre the opera presently is led by an Artistic Director who is selected by the government, and who is overseen by a Board of Directors. Selections of the operas, singers, designers, etc. are all handled operationally pretty much like the National.

The Lyric Theatre produces 12 to 15 operas each winter season for a total of about 100 performances. Three of these each year are new productions or remountings of old ones. If at all possible a new Greek opera is presented each season. One of the last spring productions sometimes is remounted to open the summer Athens Festival at the 161 A.D. Herod Atticus Theatre.[7]

The successful presentation of what must be considered a truly western art form marks still another attempt by the Greeks to adapt to a western tradition. The furs, the curving marble staircases in the foyer, the intermission imbibing and snacks, the "social elitism" all remind one strongly of opera attendance in any major center in the States. Yet it all is a curious adaptation.

Opera certainly is not indigenous to Greece, nor widely supported by the masses of the people. In fact, even if there were widespread yearnings for this form of theatre, there are only two other theatre facilities in the entire country extensive enough to house even a small touring opera production—one in Corfu and one in Saloniki. While the subsidy keeps the ticket prices low enough to permit the usual theatre-goer to attend, the location of the only opera theatre in Athens, the 1500-seat Olympic Theatre on Akadimias Street, is simply too far from the majority of Greeks who might wish to. Under these circumstances it seems difficult to claim that this institution is for "the people" (even though attendance in 1983 hovered around 85 percent and attendance in the 1985–1986 season approached capacity).[8] One might deduce, then, that its existence stems from Greece's desire to present a strong "western" cultural attachment as well as to preserve for those high officials and rich businessmen a lavish form of exclusive entertainment in the best traditions of practical Socialism. The 1983 budget for the opera, reputed to be 400 million drachmas, certainly could have been spent more effectively if the prime goal of the program was to take musical theatre to as many of "the people" as possible. Yet, if one accepts the fact that Greece is trying to become at least nominally "western" in its orientation, then encouraging and supporting a national opera company is a laudable attempt to introduce and encourage an incredibly rich and important musical tradition.

Greece claims that it creates singers by the dozens, but they all leave the country for more lucrative and challenging opportunities. Andreas Evangelatos, Head Conductor of the opera for 30 years and father to the present Artistic Director, told his son that "Greece has three things to export, wine, oil and voices."[9] Designers and directors are more difficult to find, as are musicians and conductors capable of handling western music with the required facility. Many of these major artists, therefore, are imported. The opera house itself is not totally adequate, but it certainly is one of the nicest major houses in the country and all of its other production spaces seem adequate—even if they are scattered about the city. While productions like the 1986 *Rigoletto* were mounted in truly terrible fashion, other productions like the 1985 *Boris Godunov* with Bulgarian basso Paata Bourtsoulatze were surprisingly enjoyable. By most accounts Greece is successfully supporting—for at least a few of its people—a western opera tradition.

If there is a reason for the general insufficiency of the musicians working on these shows it may be that, as a string player for the Athens Orchestra told me, "The musicians simply refuse to cooperate. Everyone has to do it his own way."[10] If there was one overriding musical comment possible after witnessing several of these operas and concerts, it was exactly that; no one seemed to be working together. If that observation is accurate, then it would underline the all-pervasiveness of several Greek behavioral patterns already mentioned: rampant individualism; refusal to be subordinate to anyone; refusal to be seen as wrong; refusal to lose face in public. The fact that Greek musicians, steeped for centuries in Oriental modes of expression, *are* performing western music in spite of these centuries-old *modi operandi* may be an index of the seriousness with which they are grasping for the western way of life.

In May of 1986 the Artistic Director, Spyros Evangelatos, was nearing the end of his 18-month contract to head the opera. Always a man of incredibly high energy, he had already directed in the 1985–1986 season two shows for the opera and two shows for his own theatre company, Amphitheatro, and had provided leadership and administrative control over both organizations. He admitted that he accepted the opera job partly because the opera had fallen on difficult times since there had been no strong Director there for several years, the job usually being pawned off on a dedicated and willing member of the Board. He accepted primarily because the Minister of Culture "begged" him "to undertake this very difficult obligation" and partly because of his father's 30-year commitment to the same organization. Evangelatos recognized that there were few people in Greece capable of handling the unique requirements of opera production, so he took the job—for 18 months only, a period "too long for me." It had not been an easy 18 months, but he was satisfied that the company was now looked upon as successful. Part of his success, he suggested, was that he was able to keep everyone from "talking too much," a smiling reference to that vaunted Greek love of passionate but often aimless conversation. Nevertheless, he was looking forward to having only one major job again. "I am tired," he whispered after our interview was interrupted for about the sixth time by yet another matter of the most urgent importance.[11]

The State Theatre of Northern Greece. Established in 1961 the State Theatre at Saloniki is the leading theatre outside of Athens. (At one time the State Theatre of Cyprus was considered of equal importance, but since Cyprus became an independent state in 1959, its theatre is outside the realm of discussion here.)[12] The natural jealousy between the State Theatre and the National Theatre is long-standing, although not very rancorous; in fact, artists from both theatres regularly work in the other for short periods. There is a distinction, however, one put rather vociferously by Stella Zografou of the National: "There is only *one* National Theatre. The others are only State theatres."[13] The northern tier theatre receives a subsidy only slightly below that of the National, but its personnel and facilities seem slightly better than the Athenian institution.

This northern province theatre is housed in a huge building only a short walk from the sea. (See photo, page 57.) It operates with 100 actors, 30 administrators, 100 technicians (which includes several chauffeurs, ten ushers and ten maintenance persons), three buses, four trucks, ten cars and a budget in the hundreds of millions of drachmas. Until 1985 it operated two outreach branches in Macedonia and Thrace; at that time, however, these

The main building of the State Theatre of Northern Greece, Saloniki.

minimally operational facilities were transmuted into fully independent municipal theatres in the government's regional theatre program.

Not unlike the other government-run production companies, this theatre has had its share of administrative and artistic troubles. In 1983 the sense of impending doom seemed to cling to every doorway—a new government had been installed and the ramifications of its new policies were still unknown, thus creating a pall of fear among the theatre's personnel. Thirty people were being terminated and no one knew who would be next. Rehearsals held at the International Trade Center were theatrically emotionless, an understandable reaction to the fear of firing or of strike. There seemed to be no disposition to work toward excellence since hirings or firings were perceived to have no connection with talent or the ability to work hard. At the outdoor Theatro Thassos on a hilltop above the city a rehearsal for an upcoming summer production was conducted in an incredibly anarchic and slovenly manner. The Actor's Syndicate had mandated a minimum of 100 actors for the theatre; 80 had been hired and even that number was too many for the work available. Many waited around all day. The policy was to send them home if they definitely were not going to be used, but to have them wait around if there was a *chance* that they would be. One young, waiting actor, who had been quietly biding his time for the last six hours, leaned over to me and whispered disgustedly, "This is the hardest work I have ever done."[14]

Former General Director Nikos Bakolas, whose primary employment, incidentally, was that of a journalist, explained that the problems were almost totally political. Members of the theatre who are on the "right" side, that is, the side in power, he said, feel they have jobs forever and do not have to work. But if the next election installs a new government of the opposite stripe, then there is likely to be wholesale housecleaning again, with all the changes in policy and personnel going in the opposite directions. Division along political lines, then, is inevitable. "How can any sense of ensemble be created? Any sense of continuity?" he exclaimed. After the demise of the despotic *junta*, he went on, the country and its theatres decided that the quest for total freedom was primary. But everyone went overboard in that quest.[15] Now nothing is under control. The theatres are not governable. There is only one thing to do, he said. "The state theatres must close." After a time they should start over with an unassailably non-political plan which utilizes the best people regardless of their political views.[16]

Yet in that same year of this statement the State Theatre of Northern Greece produced the hit of the Athens Festival, a neanderthal version of Euripides' *Helen*, complete with Babylonian fountains, 1940s Hollywood-style sound track and skyrockets. (See Appendix A for a review of this production.) It was so popular, in fact, that it was revived for the 1986 Festival at Epidavros. Their production of *The Balcony* in the winter of 1986, while not perfect, certainly was rigorously produced and directed, revealing not at all any sense of anarchy or organizational malaise. In the fall of 1986 internationally respected director-producer Minos Volonakis, a strong leader and fiercely independent person — "genius" is sometimes used — took over the reins of the State. Considering his education and experience in both the English and Greek theatres, it would be difficult to imagine a more perfect person to test whether or not that organization was governable.

It seems clear that inconsistency in national politics and, consequently, administrations of nationally supported theatres create a sense of malaise that seems difficult to avoid. In a way the entire system echoes accurately the Greek way of doing anything. New governments install their own people — not unlike governments anywhere — who are then beholden to that government. Wholesale change-overs in the civil servants involved with those systems are likely. Scurrying for "position" or rank or even employment, therefore, becomes a function of politics, of *rousfetti* (personal influence) rather than of talent or experience or longevity. "Expeditors" arrange assignments based on personal relationships or obligations. For example a *koumbaros* (godfather) is often expected to find employment for his godchildren. If the older man is in a position to find them employment in the theatre in which he happens to be working, he is expected to do so.

The client-patron system of operation may not permeate every level of the Greek theatre, as it probably does not totally permeate any other national institution. However, since it seems all-pervasive in the Greek social system, and since newly elected national leaders for scores of years have inveighed against the practice, we can assume that a large percentage of all assignments in the state theatres of Greece are the result of this traditional procedure.[17]

The seeming inability to achieve consistency and high quality in the administrative and artistic facets of state-run theatres has no doubt contributed to the plethora of independent or semi-independent theatres in Athens. For the most part the men who established these other theatres had spent some time within the state theatre system. They had become angry and frustrated and moved out to create their own theatres, determined to prove that high quality theatrical endeavors could be fashioned without the politics, frustration and inefficiency of the national system. Of course not all of them have achieved their goals; two of them, however, have provided such a high level of accomplishment over so many years that they have been awarded the status of "semi-state" theatres, a rank between the fully subsidized national system and the occasionally subsidized independent theatres. These two theatres are the Art Theatre of Karolos Koun and the Amphi-Theatre of Spyros Evangelatos.

Semi-State Theatres

Semi-state theatres are those independent theatres which have proven themselves artistically over a rather long period of existence. They are awarded annual government subsidies with only minimal bureaucratic maneuvering. These subsidies are not intended to cover all expenses as they are with the state theatres; rather they are meant to insure a basic minimal operational base so that the continued existence of the recipient theatre is not wholly dependent on box office receipts. Of the two theatres accorded this unique status, the first of these, headed by the old master, Karolos Koun, has been and may still be the most important theatre in all of Greece.

The Art Theatre of Karolos Koun. For many years the statement "Karolos Koun *is* Greek theatre," would have been unchallenged. Until relatively recently Koun established the standards of production against which all other shows were judged. During his last few years (he died on February 14, 1987) his fire may have been diminishing, his vision may not have been as startling as it once was, his influence on the fabric of Greek theatre may not have been as direct and immediate. However, it is one mark of his stature that no other director dared name himself heir-apparent.

Koun started in 1933 working with children between 12 and 16. He discovered then that plays were to be produced, not revered on some shelf in some library. He realized then the importance of unearthing the right environment for the play, an environment which grew out of native soil, light and sound.

In 1936 with a group of amateurs and laborers, he attempted to produce Aristophanes, trying to find the connection between the ancients and a twentieth century Greek culture formed by the Byzantines, Turks, Venetians, Franks and Europeans. Because of World War II this work was interrupted. In 1942, however, in the midst of the Nazi Occupation, he founded the Art Theatre. From then until 1957 the Art Theatre explored the works of Williams, Miller, Lorca, Brecht, Albee, Weiss, Beckett, Genet, etc., and was awarded a long-term Ford Foundation grant for its work in exploring the bases of Greek theatre in the twentieth century.

In 1959 the Art Theatre decided to focus on the ancient drama. By 1962 it had won first prize at the Theatre de Nations with *The Birds,* a production many Greeks still recall with pride and amazement. From that year until 1982 Karolos Koun's theatre had participated in and won prizes at nearly every important international theatre festival—Zurich, Israel, Stuttgart, Stockholm, Oslo, Bonn, Berlin, Moscow and many more.

In 1983 the weakened and sickly master had been written off by nearly every jealous theatre worker in Athens; his revival of the Art Theatre's famous production of the *Oresteia,* however, revealed that Koun was still able to command the theatre's materials impeccably. The trilogy, all three hours of it, "formed a continuous, sinuous, graceful path of such detail and control it seemed that no actor—or audience—could maintain the intensity."[18]

His 1986 production of *Agrotes Pethainoun* (Αγρότες Πεθαίνουν) by Franz Kraitz revealed the same kind of care, detailing and intensity as the former show. Because of his continued illness he had to relinquish control of some of the theatre's productions to former students of his. Unfortunately, none seem to exhibit the talents of their master.

The Art Theatre's facade is on busy Stadiou Street; in fact the theatre shares its facade as well as its foyer with a wildly popular *epitheorisis* theatre, the Orpheas. Spectators for the revue ascend from this common foyer up a grand set of stairs tó a large lobby; spectators for the Art Theatre descend a plain set of stairs to a mini-lobby whose walls are plastered with photos of past Art Theatre productions.

The Art Theatre is one of the very few non-proscenium theatres in Athens. It is a three-quarter arena seating about 250, with thick supporting pillars at the front two corners of the stage. There is the usual problem of inadequate storage space—the lobby doubles as storage, costume construction, administrative and box office areas. Koun's office is dark green, about six by eight feet, barely large enough for a small desk, two chairs and a tiny napping couch. It reflects the director's artistic philosophy, that of a "poor theatre," that is, "a theatre that presents everything as it should be but with a means that are not too costly, too inefficient."[19]

In 1986 the Art Theatre opened a second theatre in the Plaka, an area long run-down, but recently renovated. The Plaka, Athens' oldest district and long-time tourist haunt, is situated directly below the Acropolis. It is an area which contains some of the finest examples of early city architecture as well as some significant ruins. For years it had acquired a reputation of also housing sleazy discos, bums, rip-off joints, houses of prostitution and similar activities. Between 1983 and 1986 the government cracked down. With the expulsion of these undesirables and the granting of massive loans to encourage local citizens to refurbish their properties, the Plaka came back to life. People started living there once again, instead of simply renting out their properties to shady interests. The result is now a delightful pedestrian mall lined with colorful and increasingly well-appointed shops and tavernas. It is a perfect environment for the second Art Theatre facility.

This new Art Theatre–Plaka was carved out of a small warehouse and retains the charm of old wood and unique construction. The stage sits exactly in the center of the gutted space, so the lobby area and hallways are defined by temporarily pulling up large blinds which surround the stage. It is obvious that the hallways and lobby thus defined can also become playing spaces or audience spaces for some future productions, productions which illuminate once again the "poetic realism" style often associated with Koun.

Although the master director rejected this often-quoted summary of his style, there did exist a Koun touch which was eminently discernible to the practiced eye. It was characterized by grace and control, imaginative use of space and, especially, ensemble. This last was accomplished in large part by hiring almost entirely his own students (dubbed "monks" by the rest of the Athenian theatre establishment because their lives of total dedication to the theatre recalled the extreme demands of a monastery). He explained that very early in the training program they all developed unique ways of working together as well as a common set of values that made later projects much more efficient. He also intimated that during rehearsals he did not pay much attention to the constricting rules of the actor's union regarding breaks, number of hours allowed in rehearsal, etc. "When you begin to work," he said with a great fire rising in his voice, "you don't want to be interrupted by these petty things!"[20]

With the gradual diminishing of Koun's personal influence on the stage, the continuation of his work, his particular kind of total commitment and his poetic style will be relegated to his subordinates. Even if none of them can equal the master, however, Koun's influence on the evolution of the modern Greek theatre is incalculable. As one admirer stated,

> The contribution of Karolos Koun constitutes a chain of explosions which started long ago and which, by now, are so numerous and indirect that we have difficulties determining their origin.
>
> This contribution and its continuation does not limit itself to the uninterrupted, priceless work of the Art Theatre. It can be measured with the progress of the modern Greek theatre as a whole. And if you want to see this progress in its real dimension, just compare it to the Fifties. The difference is that of night and day. For me who experienced this change from within the theatre, that "day" in the modern Greek theatre is, to a very large extent, the day brought by Karolos Koun.[21]

The Amphi-Theatre of Spyros Evangelatos. One of the hardest working theatre directors in Athens is Spyros Evangelatos. In 1986 he was chief executive for both the state-run opera company as well as for his own Amphi-Theatre. Between 1977 and 1980 he undertook a similar onus, heading the State Theatre of Northern Greece at the same time as running his own theatre in Athens. The almost-daily flights back and forth nearly killed him. But now, at 46 years of age he shows no signs of slowing down.

Evangelatos graduated from the National Theatre School of Drama and within a year produced the first in what was to become a long series of previously undiscovered plays from seventeenth century Greece. As a result he received several scholarships to study theatre in London, Paris, East Europe and Vienna. In the latter city he was first introduced to the pleasures and horrors of directing opera. He returned to Athens and founded in 1975 his Amphi-Theatre, dedicated to reviving the ancient tragedies from a modern viewpoint and, even more importantly, to uncovering and producing sixteenth to nineteenth century heretofore unproduced plays from Crete and other Greek-speaking islands.

The Amphi-Theatre's reputation for producing these rare texts has been rewarded by a continuous stream of invitations to present these plays in England, Italy, Brussels, Moscow, Bulgaria, Australia, Switzerland, etc. Each season finds still another previously unproduced play bouncing about the Amphi-Theatre stage. Even though few of these can be considered treasures, still the Amphi-Theatre must be applauded for bringing to full production little-known works of drama which connect the Greek islands with the Italian Renaissance.

Until 1985 this theatre was located in a small space at the end of a narrow alley off Stadiou Street just a block or two from Koun's Art Theatre. With the revamping and purifying of the Plaka, however, Evangelatos moved into a delightful theatre there, again just blocks from Koun's second theatre in the same area. It holds about 300 on plush blue velvet seats which surround in a wide 150 degree arc the open stage. It is one of the most comfortable of all new theatres in Athens.[22]

Evangelatos' company numbers only about 30. His wife, Leda Tasopoulou, like Koun's administrative assistant, Olga Pavlatou handles many of the day-to-day administrative details in his absence. This husband and wife team are proud of their theatre's accomplishments working with only a fraction of the people and money accorded the huge state-run theatre organizations. When asked if he liked being a state theatre his reply was immediate, "We are *not* a state theatre—thank god!"[23]

State-Supported Independent Theatres. There were between 60 and 85 professional theatres operating in Athens during the height of the 1985–1986 winter season. The vast majority of them were independent or "free" theatres. That means that their offerings were not totally commercial, but that their prime method of support was the box office.

For several years governmental support to these theatres was relatively rare, more often than not awarded for exceptional stability and/or touring. At that time the designation "free" theatre reflected a financial reality—free from government support. Recently, however, under social pressure to shift the cornucopia of subsidy toward more theatres, and under cultural pressure to give person B what person A was given, the government seems more disposed to helping nearly every theatre which requests it. The limited funds for this kind of support, therefore, have been diluted to the point that nearly no theatre really benefits from the pittance it is given.[24] "Free theatres" now are more often than not "government assisted" theatres, although they may again become "free" if they do not receive any subsidy during a particular year. The theatres which will be mentioned here may or may not be "free" or "government assisted" at any one time; they do, however, fall generally into this third category of relatively independent theatres.

The majority of these operations were formed by strong Greek personalities probably convinced that they could administer and create theatre better than anyone else. Very commonly this single individual then became the leading actor for his own theatre. Dimitris Potametis runs his own Theatro Erevnas; Thanassos Papajorjiou appears in his own productions at the Stoa Theatre. The pattern is standard: Rena Vlachopoulou at the Bretania, Alekos Alexandrakis at the Poreia, Xania Karlojerlopoulou at the Porta, Giorgos Panza at the Chatzokou, etc. Sometimes husband and wife teams (or teams of lovers, I am told) run theatres for the display of their own talents such as Jenny Karezi and Kostas Kazakos at their Theatro Athenaion or Yiannis Fertis and Mimi Denisi at the Theatro Athena.

Although no doubt there is some Greek pride, refusal to be

subordinate, and fierce individualism working here, such arrangements should not be dismissed out of hand. In Athens producers are almost unheard of—at the time of this writing there was one only man, Giorgos Lembesis, who controlled more than one show: *Extremities, All My Sons* and a satirical revue. Yet, maintaining some sort of quality control requires producer-like financial control. Actors who are wealthy enough—usually from their work in what they consider "illegitimate forms" (TV, radio and the like)—find it artistically comfortable as well as financially necessary to produce their own shows. No one else is available.

One might hypothesize that, without the inflated salaries paid TV and cinema actors, or without the inflated salaries paid Greek actors who work in other countries, a large portion of the "free" theatre movement would disappear. For example, director Stamatis Chondrojiannis shifts all his income from his international-level TV directing into his Theatre Alpha; Rena Vlachopoulou supports her Bretania Theatre with her earnings from film roles; Xania Karlojerlopoulou supports her children's theatre operation from her TV and film work. Of course there are stars whose theatre appearances alone would finance a theatre; normally, however, some other source of income is necessary for these "free" theatres to continue existing. If they ceased to exist, then hundreds of actors, directors, musicians, etc. would be out of work. This argument may be one reason the government has decided to offer at least some help to as many as possible.

In addition to those theatres which are relatively stable, that is, those which have produced plays in the same place over several years, there are scores of other theatre spaces which are rented by their owners to whoever can pay the fees. These other "producers" most often are actors or directors with a theatrical property and a fierce desire to present it. So, they form their own production companies, made up for the most part of friends and relationships, rent the place and start rehearsals. In fact, surrounding a goodly part of Athenian theatre is a kind of Judy Garland–Mickey Rooney "Let's get a barn and do a play" amateurism that seems as violently out of place in the birthplace of tragedy as it seems fetching and noble.

The latest rules from the Actor's Syndicate stipulate that no more than 20 percent of any cast may be non-union members. Generally that means that 80 percent of each cast has graduated from a licensed drama school. Since many of the licensed drama schools can hardly be called training academies—a subject I shall treat later—the talent and training level of many Athenian actors is low. When added to the producer's natural inclination to fill 20 percent of the roles with non-union friends and family in order to save money, and when added to the fact that there simply are not enough highly competent actors in Athens to populate the scores of shows presented each season, one can imagine that some of the productions offered by these "free" theatres can be truly dreadful.

On the other hand some of these independent producers gather wonderful talent around them by virtue of their particular projects or the talent level of their friends. One notable example may be the experience of playwright Giorgos Dialegmenos, whose first play, *We Lost the Aunt (Stop)*, made him one of Greece's more important playwrights almost overnight.

Dialegmenos received his actor training at Karolos Koun's School of Drama, then taught there for five years before entering the three-year ordeal that resulted in the completion of his first play. Supported by his lovely wife, Sofia, he then devoted all of his time to producing it.

Searching for an appropriate theatre space proved complicated. He found only four theatres whose work he respected. Some who found the play acceptable also preferred that changes be made in the manuscript so that it would better coincide with their audiences' interests. One theatre owner, for example, would have accepted the play if the heroine would appear bra-less, an obviously commercial attraction in the predominantly conservative Orthodox society. The playwright refused. In another case Dialegmenos suddenly discontinued negotiations because the theatre owner plied him with increasingly probing questions about the play's content. The playwright felt that, if the owner was privy to every detail, he would also find a way to re-work the story to suit his own sense of the commercial. In fact it was about this time that Dialegmenos decided that he had to play the leading role himself if only to protect the integrity of his work. (This latter reaction may also be an example of typical Greek paranoia, their predilection toward a sense of secrecy and conspiracy as well as a determination to remain in complete control of everything.)

After a theatre had been engaged, Dialegmenos hired a director whom he trusted, then other actors, designers, etc. and began rehearsals. Then he, his wife and a close friend, Dora Litinaki (who also turned to playwriting a few years later) became the production's promotion team, designing, producing and putting up posters, producing their own commercials and eventually selling their own tickets. In true Hollywood fashion the show was a hit and provided a foundation upon which the attractive and twinkle-eyed writer has built a playwriting career.[25]

This method of production is not uncommon in the professional theatre of Greece. State theatres, of course, have regular staffs to accomplish these tasks; all the other types of theatres and theatre producers, however, must find ways to do the work themselves. Although normally some friends or family can be pressed into this service, it is not unimaginable for a well-known director or actor to be seen putting up his own posters or selling his own tickets.

The production of new plays, however, is not always this exhausting. Sometimes plays like Dialegmenos' appear on the regular schedules of established theatres, even the National. Three new one-act plays, one each by Georgos Almenis, Spyros Papadogeorgos, and Narkos Xaritakis were forcibly combined by the director, then produced by the National Theatre under the title *Akalyptos Xoros* (Ακαλήπτος Χορός) in the fall of 1985; a new play by Dora Litinaki was given a loving production by the Art Theatre of Karolos Koun in the spring of that same year. By and large, however, play production by most independent producers was and is an all-consuming task, requiring that a few dedicated people accomplish an incredible range of tasks outside of their primary ones as actor, writer or director.

Generally each theatre production in Athens tries to remain open the entire season; that is, in each theatre there will be only one show each winter, even if that show is constantly on the edge of breaking even. The difficulty of finding a new show, of re-casting, re-designing, re-rehearsing, re-promoting, etc., is almost too overwhelming a task to face. Remember also that the actor's union requires that all actors be paid for at least three months, regardless of whether or not the show plays. Even failing shows are kept open, therefore, sometimes playing to 12 or 15 people, in an attempt to recoup some of this cost. An audience of less than 40 people at any particular performance was not that uncommon during the 1985–1986 season.

If the show is a true flop and the theatre still rented and the actors still being paid, a producer may try to rush into production another, more commercial show to recover his investment. When Yiannis Voglis' lovely *Makria Poreia* (Μάκρια Πορεία) failed probably on political grounds, the producer closed that show and within weeks mounted a lively if somewhat rushed version of Brecht's *The Good Soldier Schweik*, which allowed him to break even.

There are several theatres and theatre directors in Athens which have developed reputations for consistency and excellence in production. Very few have long histories and some may prove to be unable to maintain such high standards over the next few years. Nevertheless, at this time, they do boast enviable reputations. It is with trepidation that I note some of these, knowing that others not mentioned will be irate. However, I believe that this inventory is fair, with the selections garnered both from the recommendations of Greek theatre people as well as from my own experience viewing their productions.

Karolos Koun's Art Theatre must top the list, although there are a few wrinkles in this recommendation that did not pertain a few years ago. When Koun himself directed, the productions there were top-notch, once the auditor accepted the director's predilection for the "poor theatre" approach. When his underlings directed, though, the product could be anything from wonderful to tawdry. With his death it is unclear how the Art Theatre will fare.

Minos Volonakis is an independent producer and, as of this writing, also the Director of the State Theatre of Northern Greece. His work is always of a high standard and sometimes brilliant. His visions for theatre in Greece seem at the cutting edge of contemporary thinking, for example his idea for neighborhood theatres in the rock quarries surrounding Athens or his idea for a bilingual, international centre for the study of ancient Greek theatre.[26] A highly educated and well-read man, Volonakis has produced ancient tragedies in several other countries, most recently at the International Cultural Festival which accompanied the Los Angeles Olympics in 1984.

The Amphi-Theatre of Spyros Evangelatos must also be considered a solid producing establishment. The work is always detailed and conceptually complete, even though some complain about the lack of variety in its production style. If nothing else it is the only theatre which produces on a regular basis Greek theatrical works from the sixteenth to nineteenth centuries.

The most well-founded experimentalist in the Greek theatre seems to be Yiannis Houvardas, an independent director who probably works outside of Greece more than inside. Highly educated, intelligent and perceptive, Houvardas' productions are significantly richer and better produced than most of the shows in Athens. Even at the National Theatre with its reputation for wearing down the most imaginative director with civil service-type sluggishness and mediocrity, Houvardas manages to mold his shows there into wholly rewarding, even impressive, evenings. He is part of a minority who believes that the Greek theatrical world was cut off from the rest of world theatre from ancient times until the beginning of the twentieth century and, consequently, it must run far and fast to catch up just to the mainstream, not to mention the *avant garde*. As for this experimental theatre, it is non-existent in Athens, he says. "Some can do it and don't; others *call* it experimental and it isn't; others should not be doing it and do. Few really *do* it."[27]

The Stoa Theatre of Thanassos Papajorjiou has a solid if not inspirational reputation. It consistently produces a kind of middle-of-the-road show which will not antagonize anyone but which also will not excite anyone. These shows are produced well and almost all of them include Papajorjiou in major roles.

Director Lefteris Voyiatzis seems to have found his particular niche in recent years. In his *Skini* (Stage) Theatre he produces consistent, meticulously mounted and rehearsed semi-realistic plays in the nineteenth century Russian manner. That is, he rehearses each show for several months and opens only when he is ready. Normally his productions are among the last to open in a new season and most of the theatre community awaits these openings with some excitement. His 1986 production, *Symphora Apo to*

Poly Myalo, (Σημφορά απο το Πολύ Μυαλό), included some of the most detailed acting and directing I saw the entire year. It was the show nearly all Greek theatre people recommended for my viewing.

Giorgos Michailidis' Anoixto Theatre has been presenting conceptually strong and imaginative productions for several years. His 1985–1986 hit was a double bill, *The Marriage of Figaro* and *The Barber of Seville*, back to back, done in two different styles (*commedia* and eighteenth century), connected right before intermission by a clever visual melding of both styles.

The Athenaion Theatre, which always stars the husband and wife team of Karezi and Kazakos, has produced some of the best shows in Athens over recent years. Once a popular, commercial theatre team, these actors decided about six years ago that they would do only the best quality shows possible from then on. Their *Virginia Woolf* is still considered one of the best productions ever in Athens. In 1985–1986 they produced a Russian play, *Prosopo Me Prosopo* (Πρόσοπο με Πρόσοπο) by Alexander Gelman, which played to full houses the entire season. They first saw the play in Russia and immediately hired the Russian director to come to Greece and direct them in it. The production was stunning (with the exception of a little over-acting on her part), full of Stanislavskian detailing rarely seen on any western stage.

Of course one should not miss the work of that internationally respected theatre and film director, Michael Kakoyiannis. His work occasionally may be seen in the more established Athenian theatres.

Although very few Greek theatre people would argue with these choices above, no doubt other names and theatres would be recommended. Of course there are stunning shows produced occasionally by other theatre groups and directors. These offered above, however, have been proven over a number of years and offer promise of continuing in the future.

Throughout this narrative the subject of touring has been mentioned repeatedly. In a country geographically divided into innumerable islands and covered by mountains over 80 percent of its land mass, reaching the hundreds of isolated coves of habitation has always been difficult. Touring is the only way to provide live theatre to these people.

Few westerners, though, understand the physical exhaustion and the emotional trauma which often attend such tours in Greece. Since both the free theatres and the municipal theatres which I am about to discuss spend a large percentage of their time performing such chores, I would like to offer here my own eye-witness account of just one day of a typical Greek theatre company tour. The theatre group was called Palkoseniko (The Stage), the time 1983 and the leader was Kristos Tsangas.

He looked and acted like Alan Bates, thick, rough, shy, guarded, yet with a noticeable twinkle in his eyes. But he was really a Greek actor, director and leader of an Athenian splinter group at odds with the National Theatre Establishment and determined to create his own theatre in his own way. And his own way in this case was to tour high quality theatre to all those scores of villages which saw no theatre at all. That day it was a trip to tiny Irakia, a village near Lamia about two hours northwest of Athens. Its people had never seen a live theatrical presentation.

Tzangas, then 44, started Palkoseniko about six years before. A respected actor on the Athenian scene in live theatre, cinema and TV — his economic life was still dependent on those "illegitimate" forms — Tzangas realized that the inhabitants of those villages needed him. So, working out of a space which combined a workshop, office, rehearsal, construction and storage in the basement of a Trias Street house near Victoria Station in Athens, he created a company which became dedicated to touring. This was necessary partly because he had not been able to secure a permanent theatre and partly because he could enlist the financial support of the government, at that time supporting touring groups lavishly. For one year at a time groups such as his received enough funding to tour. But few lasted as long as his; with discouraging regularity most appeared, took their turns on the stages of scores of villages, then disappeared.

The flatbed truck and battered bus, bought during the one "lush" year five years previously, bounced off the main highway, a relatively smooth, two lane road, and onto a back country road leading to Irakia. No signs marked the majority of these roads and, so, great confusion and discussion attended the approach of each intersection. With each slowing the oppressive heat and dust caught up with us, permeating everything before we regained speed and the air again rolled in the open windows. Although we could see delightful country scenes roll by, we rarely could hear reassuring country sounds because of the sound of gravel crunching under the tires.

An actor's wife and her two small girls were entertained by some of the best story tellers they could have hoped for, and touched and loved by them too. One tiny girl crawled up to sleep across a seat and anxious hands pulled down the window blind to shield her from the blazing sun.

Two actors had throat infections and could barely talk. One of them was Lambros, Kristos' brother. Lambros also acted as bus driver, technical director, business manager and all-around handyman. Kristos concentrated on the artistic side of the venture — planning, dreaming, performing; the rest fell into the hands of his brother. They had been performing outdoors in the night air for noisy village crowds six days a week for three weeks then, and the travel, dust and vocal strain had taken their toll. They all felt, Kristos more than the others, that the schedule was too rigorous. Next summer, he said with a determined punch at the seat in front of him, he would do fewer performances but charge the villages more. But as of that moment, since the Actor's Syndicate required that each actor be hired for a minimum of three months whether or not he was used, Kristos felt that he must keep them all working constantly, often just to make expenses.

The hills showed more rock than trees and the scrubby pines that managed to survive must have struggled through cracks in the rocky soil. A few heat-loving junipers surprised us here and there, and the tiny villages flashed a few flowers as we tumbled by.

In what seemed just another village we slowed to a stop, then carefully maneuvered the bus between two rock walls, and bounced down an alley next to a schoolyard. Several kids ran after the bus, past posters pasted on the schoolyard walls by Kristos' advance man. We all gratefully performed a quick *exodos* from the metal torture chamber and immediately gravitated to the shade of the one decently tall tree as Lambros and the company leaders discussed where to place the flatbed truck-stage in the tiny schoolyard.

An old volleyball post stuck up in the center of that yard, blocking easy positioning of the truck as well as eventual sight lines. Picks and shovels suddenly appeared and the base of that poor, old grey post—really just a chunk of tree—was attacked. Eventually it succumbed to the team's efforts and was laid gently aside. The hole was covered gingerly with large rocks and then filled with loose dirt so that the post could easily be resurrected later.

The tech staff took over, lowering each side of the flatbed trailer to create a playing area of surprising dimensions. All the flats for the scenery had lain without any protective covering in the truck and now magically became three "houses" for the play, *The Peasants*, adapted from three sixteenth century *commedia scenarii*. A sound system and rudimentary lighting appeared. The crowd of kids swelled to 20 as the excitement mounted. But none of it rubbed off on the half dozen goats chomping grass in the yard not 20 feet away—they ignored us totally.

At 6:15 P.M. the cast when to a village taverna for lunch. Everything there, including the wine, was home-made or pulled from the garden that day. The cheese was the best I ever tasted. At 7:30 we started walking back to the school.

About that time the kids started bringing wooden, straight backed chairs from somewhere into the "seating" area, that is, the gravel school yard facing the stage. By 8:00 P.M. the village officials started draping old parachutes over the wire fences along the side of the playground so people couldn't peek in. After all, these village officials had helped pay for this performance out of the village's meager coffers and had to sell as many tickets as possible to recoup some of the expected loss. Both their contributions as well as the government's subsidy were necessary to pay all the salaries involved.

At 8:30 P.M. the procession started. People from all over the village, each carrying his own chair from kitchen or living area, each dressed according to his or her interpretation of the importance of the occasion, each loudly greeting friends and relatives paraded in and set up his chair in what looked like a good spot. One couple, dressed as if they were going to La Scala, sat next to a grandma in traditional black dress and scarf; teenage girls dressed as if awaiting a dance date passed young men wearing clean shirts, white belts and white shoes—polished. Most brought something to eat or drink. And everyone knew everyone! I hadn't experienced such a feeling of "community" since I was growing up in the Polish ghetto of Pittsburgh and attended one of our picnics or religious holidays.

A feeble grandmother without a chair wandered around looking rather helpless. No one offered her a seat. A healthier-looking grandfather without a chair but with a cane followed almost immediately; one young man about 20 years old literally ran out to get him one and, just as he returned with it, a family man of about 40 also rose and insisted that the older man take his seat. He did. The family man took the newly arrived chair. The youngest man sat on some concrete steps behind them. I never saw the grandmother again.

The announced starting time was 9:00 P.M., but announced starting times make almost no impression on the Greeks. So, at about half-past, the mayor finally monotoned his welcoming speech amidst good-natured catcalls and kibitzing. Huge applause welled as he left the stage. Then, rapt attention, at first.

The play, a typical *commedia* farce, fast-paced, rough-and-tumble, pleased immensely for awhile. Soon, though, the younger children grew tired of this new experience. Some babies cried, which caused all their concerned relatives to try keeping them quiet which, in turn, created more disturbance than the tots did. Then the audience started talking back to the actors and began commenting hysterically among themselves. Occasionally a late-working farmer roared his tractor down the alley immediately behind the stage. I knew that this kind of situation made playing extremely difficult and exhausting for the actors, almost not worth the effort. But by and large the majority of the audience enjoyed the show at some level right to the end.

Of course one could not tell by the applause the level of this enjoyment. There was almost none; everyone started hurrying home immediately at the final dim-out, totally ignoring curtain calls which devolved into some kind of hodge podge.

Kristos, disappointed that the response had not been more enthusiastic for the sake of this American who had traveled with him to see the show, swore that this kind of work was too hard. He could not continue doing it, he shouted, even though he felt strongly attached to these villages, very much like his own. "They tug at my heart," he said with a mixture of sadness and embarrassment.

As the truck and the set started to reverse roles again those not involved went to another taverna for dinner about 11:45 P.M. One actor broke us up with a rendition of Prime Minister Papandreou's hard line on the American bases. "By God, I told those Americans," he shouted. "They just had to get their bases out of Greece and they only had seven years to do it!" The local wine from the barrel wasn't very good but the effect was the same. After a few glasses to build my courage, I offered a woozy toast to the company, thanking them for their wonderful hospitality toward me. An avid Communist member of the company offered his own toast in return, "Get rid of the American bases but let Tom stay." People hugged and kissed me. Lambros, his voice barely audible, brought two glasses of wine, gave me one, kissed me loudly on both cheeks, then wrapped his curled drinking arm around mine. We both gulped the hot wine and he hugged me. "We are now brothers," he whispered.

During the trip back I wondered aloud to Kristos how he could think of giving up a type of theatre that was so desperately needed in Greece. How could he give up the incredible excitement and surprise in the eyes of so many villagers? How could he give up wonderful experiences like the old gentleman who, completely unaware, walked across the front of the audience, blocking many people's view, stopped dead center and looked for his family? How could he give up the garden fresh, special-only-for-you banquets that were given after so many performances? How could he give up his special, glorious-unglorious calling?

"It's easy," he croaked after we arrived back at his Athens workshop at 3:30 in the morning. "I'm tired."[28]

Municipal (Provincial) Theatres

One of the most laudable attempts by the government to take theatre to more of the Greek population—the 67 percent which is flung over 50,000 square miles and 400 islands—has been the municipal-regional theatre movement of 1985. It has entailed the establishment of new theatres in major cities or the legitimization and reorganization of those theatres which had already been in existence in these cities.

Although the gossip mills had already been grinding out horror stories about the ultimate details of the plan in 1983, the final announcement of this huge project appeared (some already established theatre companies would say "descended") in 1985. In all there were ten municipal theatres which thenceforth would be subsidized in large part by the government. They were to be located in Rhodes, Crete, Kalamata, Agrinio, Ioannina, Lamia, Larissa, Veria, Serres and Komotini. (Later, under pressure from the theatre community, the well-established theatre at Volos was added to this list, making eleven officially supported municipal theatres in the regions outside Attika. (See map on page 73).

Twenty million drachmas in state funds would be added each year to each theatre's box office receipts and the contributions of the concerned municipalities. Generally the local city was required to provide usable spaces, even though the government often agreed to renovate them or otherwise make them habitable. The theatres were to maintain minimum ticket prices, and were to produce at least three shows each year, one of which toured, and a show for children.

One can only imagine the political maneuvering which accompanied the cities' requests for recognition or the debates which raged over the selection of the artistic directors for these new theatres. Even in the summer of 1983 some already established theatres—for example, the Organization of Epiratic Theatre in Ioannina—were jockeying for favored positions (in this case in opposition to the Theatrical Studio of Epirus). To complicate this particular situation even more the founder of the latter, Giorgos Nakos, also had established the former; friends on both sides of the debate found it difficult to maintain civil relationships. Volos, too, had a long-established director and it seemed reasonable to simply re-appoint him under government tutelage. Larissa had long been the leader in the northern Greek theatre movement and it seemed silly to appoint anyone other than the person who had taken it to that peak.

Of course, reason and coolness under stress are not strong Greek

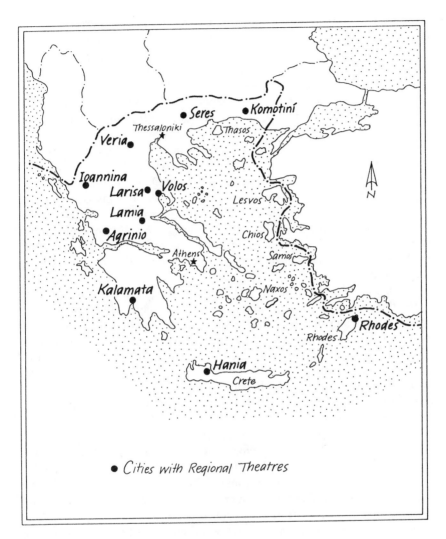

Locations of Regional Theatres in Greece.

characteristics. Yet it seemed that at least some cool heads prevailed, some compromises were made, some political differences were overlooked, because after the dust had settled most agreed that the government had chosen its artistic directors wisely. In nearly all cases the men who had been installed represented substantial professional experience both artistically and administratively.

In general these theatres are led by this government-appointed artistic/managing director who is responsible directly to a voluntary local

Board of Directors. Together they forge the season and determine directorial and design assignments—to be frank the artistic director holds a
significant power advantage in any disagreement. The companies are cast
from available Athenian actors as well as local performers, this latter situation encouraged by both the national and municipal governments.

Hiring local actors may have become an inherent dilemma for these
theatres. Some maintain that, like professional actors in any country, a
goodly percentage of the best Greek actors really prefer to flee the rat-race
and pollution of Athens to work in the provinces where the air is cleaner
and the pace of life more human. Too, many have families and find life in
the smaller cities much healthier for their children. Some fine actors, they
say, are truly altruistic and wish to perform in those regions which are
culturally deprived rather than in the metropolis which is bulging with
native and imported performing arts. Besides, they continue, seeing local
people on the stage helps create a feeling of local identity with the theatre
establishment, a very real necessity in cities which do not have a long
theatre tradition.[29]

Others argue that that all may be true, but if excellence is the goal,
these theatres must hire primarily Athenians actors. It is clear that,
although there may be an occasional fine actor in the provinces, most actors
of any real talent remain in Athens where opportunities abound. The
cultural life is better, audiences more perceptive, the quality of one's acting
partners better, the possibility of a truly remunerative TV or cinema role
near. Under these conditions, they insist, it must seem to a successful actor
the utmost madness to join a struggling theatre group in the country, even
if it is only for three to nine months.

The actuality probably lies somewhere between those two poles.
Although there are some fine actors who join the province players—the
reasons are irrelevant—there also are many moderately and even minimally
talented players who join these troupes. This wide range of achievement
continues into every phase of the operations. The general production standards range from embarrassing to quite good; audience sophistication
seems as low as their excitement, energy and support is high; audience support fluctuates from "barely" to "enthusiastic"; facilities vary from non-
existent to quite lovely, even at times impressive.

The most impressive element of the entire municipal theatre movement is that it has taken place at all. The state government is in the throes
of a national deficit second to none in the European Community; with so
many financial pressures on the internal economy it is unbelievable that the
government has managed—not without great opposition—to provide 220
million drachmas each year to the municipal theatres. These theatres, in
turn, have managed in varying degrees of success to attract some credible
talent to their regions. Living in these conservative and agrarian regions

must be difficult for citified artists, yet many have left the hedonistic pleasures of the city to commit themselves — at least for a time — to a life which is far more strictured in many ways. For those local actors and those who support their continual appearances on local stages the program has worked beautifully. Some of the local boys and girls have become very popular fixtures in the plays, providing a valuable link between the policies of the national government and the emotional attachments of the municipalities.

My visits to these municipal theatres took me over most of the country in 1986. I visited nearly every one of these organizations with the exception of Hania (which I visited in 1983), Volos and Komotini.[30] In most cases I was able to see a current production and speak with the directors.

Kalamata. That curious Greek gesture, fingers together, hand tracing small circles in the air, eyebrows raised, lips pursed, releasing a small stream of air was the response nearly everytime I asked about the theatre in Kalamata. My respondents were saying, "*That* one! That is quite a nice set-up." Compared to most other operations around the country, Kalamata is, indeed, a "class act."

I accompanied a government official and her daughter to this southernmost Peloponnesian city of 150,000. Somehow all the bills were paid, cocktails were served in the director's house on the shore after which we were driven to a remote and historic taverna by the sea for lunch, theatre tickets were waiting, and a small taverna party with the mayor was arranged after the show. It was treatment unique in all my travels outside Athens.

Somehow it came as no surprise that Kalamata's mayor was the first to sign an agreement with the government to run an entire municipal arts project, including a theatre, a theatre for children, ballet school, ceramics studio, cinema school and music school. Kalamata's theatre sparkled with newness, even though it sat next to a railroad track (see photo, page 76), the music school twinkled with new paint and total retro-fitting for sound control, the children's theatre served the 100 or so kids who attended very well. Since it supported the only such center on the entire Peloponnese, the city might have easily accepted its growing reputation as Cultural Center of the South. (I am unsure whether or not the massive 1986 earthquake which struck that city destroyed or damaged any of these edifices.)

The envious might have ascribed the excitement and achievement of this entire project to the mayor's affiliation with the PASOK party. This may have been true in some sense. However, it also was obvious that this man, know to me only as Kyrios Benos was immensely gifted as an organizer. He also believed intensely in the efficacy of the arts, especially in an area such as Kalamata which is about as far from centers of culture in Greece as one can get.

Entry facade for the Provincial Theatre of Kalamata.

The theatre itself was a beautifully renovated warehouse. The glass-enclosed lobby, still smelling of new carpeting, was tastefully decorated with posters of past plays and led easily into the grey-blue auditorium of about 250 plush, velour seats.

The rather open proscenium stage itself seemed well-appointed, even though obviously needing more side stage space. As the production of the show that night, Chekov's *Uncle Vanya,* progressed, it became more and more obvious that lighting had been a priority when the building was designed and equipped. The stage actually included a sufficient number of lighting instruments and there was obviously sufficient control capability so that a sense of artistic lighting design was attained. (Usually one feels that these theatres barely have enough equipment and control to provide basic illumination.)

A theatre had been operating in Kalamata since 1973, but the new theatre building was only three years old and full subsidization only one. The Music Odeon had just been finished, and work was just starting on the ceramics studio.

Interestingly, the artistic director of the theatre was depressed by the lack of progress of the theatre to that date. The audiences simply refused to come to shows he wanted to do, like *Hamlet,* and he refused to produce those kind of silly sitcoms to which they would come. (Even the night I attended there were fewer than 40 people in the house.) Later he suggested that there may have been one further reason Kalamatans did not attend: many of them disagreed with the PASOK-party beliefs of their mayor.[31] In not-so-unusual Greek fashion they simply decided not to support any project with which the mayor was involved.

If the lack of support was as debilitating as some conversations seemed to indicate, then the situation was unfortunate. The facilities as well as the dedication and talents of those in leading positions were among the best in Greece's regions. The mayor for whatever reason seemed to have a direct line to the money in Athens and remained determined to create an exciting cultural environment for the people. It would be a shame to have impatience and/or political disagreement obviate the good work of many people. Then again, it would not be the first time political differences overcame noble human intentions.

Rhodes. (See photo, page 78.) Rhodes has long been a privileged island. Blessed with incredible beauty and a temperate climate, rich in cultural traditions from ancient Greece, Turkey, the Crusades, Byzantium, Italy, etc., it has long been a favorite destination for sun-worshippers and culture-seekers. Its long connection with the British culture as well as its inheritance of a twentieth century Italian infrastructure after the War has allowed it to attain a privileged position among the Greek islands. For example, it is one of only two islands (Kos is the other) which is allowed to retain an income tax for its own purposes. A small percentage of each tourist dollar remains in Rhodian coffers to provide an enviable windfall each year. The mayor and his deputy, both highly educated in English systems, are determined to use these extra funds to find a balance between the cultural and physical destruction being wrought by hordes of tourists and the island's need for the tourist dollar. One solution is to support the island's cultural organizations and, thus, present a more varied menu to the tourists. The result, hopefully, will be the creation of a more respectful attitude toward the Rhodians and their homes than is normally the case. One of the first steps was to legitimize and fully support a "National Theatre of Rhodes."[32]

There had been several theatre groups trying to establish a permanent theatre in Rhodes before Mayor Vangelis Pavlides and Vice-Mayor Litsa Papathanassi-Fraraki took office. When these two leaders decided to provide two-thirds of the operating budget for one of these groups, the competition to be named the city's official theatre became fierce. The two officials decided to combine several of these theatre forces and awarded the new composite organization the use of the city's three major theatres. The two indoor spaces were built by the Italians and remain remarkably modern and usable. In addition there is an outdoor amphitheatre constructed in the moat of the medieval city which had been built by the Crusaders.

In 1984 this new composite group produced its first full scale production, Arthur Miller's *All My Sons*, and toured a children's show. The next year it produced Molière's *The Thoughtless* in the medieval moat theatre, toured it to the villages and then traveled up to Athens' Lykabettos Theatre

The Municipal Theatre of Rhodes.

where it received most favorable reviews. With two major successes behind them, they applied to the Ministry of Culture for a full municipal theatre subsidy and received it. Considering the subsidy this theatre group already was receiving from its host city, the additional state subsidy may have made it the wealthiest municipal theatre in the country. Its facilities certainly were (and are), if not the best, certainly among the best.

As I left the group in November of 1985, they had just started rehearsing a play by a new Greek playwright. Their young director, who had been trained by Nikos Charalambus in Kalamata, and who had only a very few plays to his credit, already was displaying a typical Greek characteristic: he wanted to leave these backward hinterlands and move to Athens where he could set up a theatre the way *he* dreamed one should be set up. (Ironically, one of the actresses in the company had just left the National Theatre in Athens where she had appeared in a Brechtian production of *Trojan Women.* She had moved to Rhodes temporarily because she simply wanted to breathe some good clean air for a change.)

Hania, Crete. Since 1973 this theatre company has been producing plays consistently each winter and summer. Between 1973 and 1983 it presented twenty, concentrating on those from the 1600–1900 period of Greek playwriting. Formerly operating as the Theatre Company of Crete, this group has been housed in the centuries-old Firca prison almost within touching distance of the obelisk which guards the port of Hania. (See photo, page 79.)[33]

Displaying the fierce pride of the Cretans, this theatre company was

Site of Summer Theatre of Hania, Crete. Located in the ancient Firca Castle, this theatre contains space for about 800 spectators whose view of the play is previewed by sights of the setting sun and accompanied by the gentle chug of fishing boats entering the harbor.

committed to its stated goals: to take theatre to *all* of the people of Crete; to raise the spiritual and cultural level of these people; to cultivate their artistic sensibilities; to entertain with high quality work; to encourage the people to read and to become familiar with the authors and the plays that were produced.[34] In addition this was the only municipal theatre which intended eventually to form its own drama school as well to establish a new annual festival of ancient drama to be held in the capital city of Iraklion.

Since reaching the people of this large island has always been one of its most important goals, touring has been its major activity. Each year the group has visited between 50 and 60 villages while performing 150 to 200 days out of the year. Its audience averaged 300 to 500 per performance. Such numbers made procurement of government financial support easy even before the group was legitimized as a municipal theatre.

The Board which governs this municipal theatre is comprised of any Cretan who wishes to run for the office. It meets once a month to consider the recommendations of the subordinate Artistic Council which, with the Artistic Director, selects the season, the artists, etc.

Although the old Theatre Company of Crete hired mostly Athenian actors on a per-show basis, their new designation as an official municipal theatre has allowed them to hire a small, permanent company of actors and, like the other regional institutions, actually hire and pay a small administrative/technical staff. For some reason they seem to have no trouble enticing actors away from Athens.

Headquarters for the Provincial Theatre of Ioannina. This old school building housed the main offices and storage spaces. The political graffiti is a common feature of a large percentage of public buildings throughout Greece.

Ioannina. This northwest city, the fourth largest in the country with a population of 80,000, has been home to one of the most unique theatre organizations since 1976. At that time 20 to 30 people of various backgrounds banded together to form the Organization of Epiratic Theatre. By 1983 it had grown to four staff members and was receiving some government subsidy for its many activities. For example, it booked other performing groups into the city, formed a special cinema club, sponsored amateur musical and theatre groups, etc. Its theatre produced four shows each year, each of which played the high schools or churches in Ioannina before going on a 70-village tour. A schism, however, occurred when government funds pressured the theatre into producing higher quality shows which in turn meant hiring more actors from Athens which in turn prevented local performers from having a platform. The splinter organization and the Epiratic Theatre fought to be named the new Municipal Theatre. The government, however, started with a clean slate.

A new Artistic Director was brought in and a small staff formed. For the 1985–1986 season nine actors from Athens were hired, five from Ioannina, and three amateurs from Ioannina, the latter paid only for actual rehearsal time and performances. The municipality offered the theatre the non-exclusive use of an old theatre and the Church of Ioannina also rented their space to the group for use as a second, small performing space. (See photo, page 80.) The city contributed three million drachmas to the budget to supplement the 20 million sent by the government.

Even with a decent ticket income, however, this theatre, like most of the others in the regions, must operate on an austere budget. This was especially true when the drachma was devalued by 15 percent and the subsidy was not increased by a like amount. When coupled with the 20 percent inflation rate, the actual buying power of the total was reduced by about 35 percent. One rarely saw, therefore, stunning physical production in the regions.

Since most of these regional institutions are similar, it may be interesting to provide here some general information on salaries and other financial matters. Athenian actors were paid between 55,000 and 75,000 drachmas a month. At an exchange rate of 131 drachmas to the dollar that equalled $419.00 to $572 in round figures, a healthy sum if the actor had not had to pay for travel and the expenses of living away from home. The technicians earned 65,000 a month; the designers 100,000 to 150,000 per design. Directors made 170,000 to 250,000 drachmas (about $1300 to $1900) per show—a very substantial salary in Greece. And the General Manager/Artistic Director made exactly the same as his actors, 75,000/month.[35]

Ticket prices were generally 250 drachmas ($1.90) for adults and 150 drachmas ($1.14) for students. The children's show at first was priced at 100 drachmas ($.76), but the people in that vicinity were so poor that General Manager Papadakis asked the Regional Council for a supplementary grant of one million drachmas so that those shows could be free to all.

The tradition of touring to the surrounding villages comprised a strong percentage of Ioannina's theatre activities. All of the season's five shows toured during the entire last month of the winter season. In addition the theatre planned a comprehensive two-month summer tour of *Romeo and Juliet* for 1986.

(This practice of touring during the hot summer months is standard throughout Greece. Very few theatres are air conditioned and the weather is far too hot to remain inside. Conversely, Greek summer nights are almost perfect for outdoor activities. Attending any show under the stars with a sweet-scented breeze wafting over an excited, colorful crowd comes close to theatrical heaven.)

Agrinio. Agrinio sits in an eternal envelope of barren, arid, rolling hills between Ioannina and the Gulf of Corinth. With a population of only 50,000 it did not strike me as a hotbed of culture which would support a professional theatre. I was only partly right.

The Agrinio group, led by its quietly determined, trilingual, cultured

Headquarters for the Provincial Theatre of Agrinio.

mayor and an intense, former director of the National Theatre of Cyprus, were in the second year of creating a new brand of theatre. (A municipal theatre group had been trying to operate there on a semi-professional, on-off basis for at least 10 years.) Long-time friends, these two men were committed to establishing a theatre-going tradition of high quality in an environment with no such leanings. Their 1985–1986 season, for example, consisted of a Goldoni, *The Wrestlers,* a new Greek play, Ibsen's *Ghosts,* Gogol's *Pantrolina,* Shakespeare's *Othello* and Aristophanes' *Acharnians.*

When the government announced its plans to fund municipal theatres in the provinces, the mayor lobbied intensely for his Agrinio group to be named one of them. Agrinio, a town far out of the mainstream, he argued, needed substantial government support for its people. He was successful and in 1983 requested that his old friend from Cyprus be named the Artistic Director. He then turned over to the new group the town's theatre — one of the few regional theatre facilities which had actually been built as a theatre, not a cinema — promised municipal financial support and even convinced the regional Prefecture to contribute financial support on a regular basis. (See photo, page 82.)

The two friends and their staffs then decided that some kind of theatre event must be regularly and consistently available if they were to establish a theatre-going tradition. Therefore, they decided to freeze ticket prices at 100 drachmas (about 70 cents), to produce six shows a year rather than the required three, to perform every day but Monday, and to tour constantly. Their performances were never cancelled even if there were only ten people in the house. Between December 1, 1985 and September 1, 1986 they had given 299 performances in Agrinio and the surrounding villages. They also claimed a higher percentage-of-house attendance than the Athenian theatres.[36]

The Artistic Director, Nikos Siafkalis, believed deeply that a viable and high quality theatre could be established even in Agrinio. But, "Art needs continuity to establish a tradition," he said. "Because the municipality *can* guarantee this continuity, the tradition *can* be created." And in the case of Agrinio the municipality was "obliged" to make theatre happen because "it was the wish of the people."

At the same time he echoed the strong sentiments of the mayor regarding programming. "There can be no compromises to village tastes when it comes to play selection. . . . [We accept the fact that] this selection *is* an intrusion to their tastes because it is the obligation of a non-commercial theatre which is supported by the municipality and its mayor to raise their expectations."[37]

The theatre group at Agrinio had other dreams also. They often tried to book into their small town foreign touring groups which happened to be in Greece. They already succeeded once when they hosted the Abbey Theatre's magnificent production of Beckett's *Endgame,* and even enticed the Artistic Director of that theatre to travel to this tiny town, to design the sets and costumes as well as to direct *Dierdre of the Sorrows* in English. Bolstered by his experience with the International Theatre Institute on Cyprus, director Saifkalis also hosted the International Conference on Regional Theatres and has tried to establish a Commission in order to revive ancient theatre performances in the still-to-be-renovated theatre which is in ruins near Agrinio. When that project is completed the mayor and the Artistic Director hope to establish an International Workshop and Study Centre for the Revival of Ancient Greek Drama.

To actually accomplish all of this it was evident that the two men relied a great deal on their own enthusiasm as well as on the influence of the mayor because the theatre's administrative and production staffs were minimal. As with most regional theatres they included three administrative personnel: an accountant, a promotions/publicity person and a personnel manager; and a production staff of five — electrician, stage manager, stage hand, advertising assistant and driver.[38] In the bleak hills of Agrinio this staff and the enthusiasm of two men seemed scant ammunition for confronting the challenge they had set for themselves.

Veria. Years ago, when the State Theatre of Northern Greece was attempting to serve more of the people flung across the northern tongue of Greece, it created two outreach programs, one in Veria and one in Serres. These programs operated on a part-time and piece-meal basis, but at least they existed. The one in Veria was called Macedoniko Theatro but was formally licensed as the official Municipal Theatre of Veria on November 9, 1983. Without strong leadership until November of 1985, it languished. With the arrival of Nikos Nichailidis in that month, however, it became an extremely active producing unit.

By far the most organized of the municipal theatres I visited, this group had an office next door to the city council building. In it a staff of only two worked with the Director. They produced six shows and a children's show each year, performing 230 times with only 60 of those performances taking place in the group's temporary theatre.

This theatre was a minimally equipped 300 seat facility deep in the bowels of the city's administration building. As the municipality's only meeting space, however, this space was also used for various city functions, for major municipal organizations when they needed meeting space, for amateur theatre groups which needed rehearsal space, and for the cinema which operated every Friday night. It was the only available space for theatre in Veria at that time; there was no indication that other indoor facilities were even being considered.

In a way the absence of a completely equipped theatre structure in this small town did not totally compromise the purpose of this municipal theatre program. Before its formalization local theatre groups had long performed in high schools and gymnasia and, in the summer months, in playgrounds and parks. Of course this kind of adaptation most often minimized the amount and quality of the technical complement, but the shows did go on. In fact while I was in Veria the company was in a local village grammar school playground offering a children's show.

One of the most exciting developments in Veria was the announcement that their new outdoor theatre in a nearby forest was to be opened. This new facility would give the new theatre company an outdoor space in which to perform as well as to offer the people of that region the opportunity to witness performing arts groups from all over the northern tier regions.

Immediately after the war the people of Veria decided to re-forest the mountainsides which had been devastated by the fighting. In one huge area, Papagos, they planted countless thousands of pine trees which now have reached maturity. In the exact center of this beautiful green Forest of Papagou — appearing even more lush because of the aridity of its immediate surroundings — they erected a new amphitheatre. In the summer of 1986, primarily in August, they hosted their first full season of artistic events — plays, ballets and musical events given by groups from northern Greece (including the Veria municipal theatre), Bulgaria and Czechoslavakia.

Serres. The second of the outreach theatres sponsored by the State Theatre of Northern Greece in 1979 was the one in Serres. Called at that time the National Theatre of Thrace, it operated on a haphazard basis until December of 1983 when it was officially included in the list of municipal theatres to be subsidized by the government.

With a typical complement of three administrators, four tech men and 7–15 actors, this group tried to mount its required three shows plus a children's show. It was difficult. The theatre space was a rented cinema and had to be shared with a regular movie schedule. Scenery, therefore, had to be extremely flexible and durable. The quality of the production I saw, *Axecasta Kronia* (Αξέχαστα Χρονιά), was a little above community theatre level, with many moments of "breaking up" by the actors. The audiences were probably the most rude of all I had encountered in my travels. Elpidophoros Gotsis, the artistic director and leading actor, once had to drop character, come downstage and deliver a short but intense chastisement about manners.

To be fair, these audiences in Serres, a town of 70,000 near the Yugoslavian border, probably had little exposure to live theatre and needed time to understand the difference between movies and TV and this live form. They were truly excited about being there — noisy and rowdy but interested. All ages attended, with a predominance of teenagers apparent. Their years of mandatory English instruction in school helped in a confrontation I had with an avid Communist who was seated next to me, paranoically wondering about those notes I was making. These teenagers helped translate our intense and hurried political discussion with each other which, gratefully, was terminated with the rise of the second act curtain. Although we all entered the second act with rapidly pounding hearts, by the end of the show the gentleman and I shook hands and hugged and wished each other a warm Κάλυ Νήχτα (good night) to the smiles and giggles of the girls in the row behind.

The government was renovating a small, lovely old cinema into a theatre for this municipal group. It had been in construction for about four months, though, when suddenly and inexplicably, all money for the project stopped flowing from Athens. As of April of 1986 the project was simply on hold. Assuming that the political and/or bureaucratic foul-up is untangled, however, the completion of this nearly new space will ameliorate some of the group's space problems. It will not, unfortunately, solve the problems of money, inept actors, and lack of production spaces which the artistic director, Gotsis, enumerates as the basic problems confronting the group.[39]

Larissa, Lamia, Volos and Komotini. These municipal theatres are being grouped here because they offer nothing extraordinarily different from the rest of the theatres discussed thus far. Komotini, as has been mentioned, still was in the process of organization and had not produced anything by the time of this research. The Volos theatre group was touring and had closed the theatre for that period. I did visit the other two and offer here those few details which may be of interest.

Reputed to be the longest-living of the several regional compaies, the Municipal Theatre at Larissa claimed an annual audience of 80,000–100,000 people. Most of this claim derived from its extensive touring program: each play was presented nine times in their renovated movie house home to every 50–60 performances in the villages. Under its old organization (Thessalonikon Theatro) it built such a reputation for consistency and dedication to the people of its region that it was offered some government subsidy even before the new Municipal Theatre law took effect.

Its usual small staff remained loyal and proud of the theatre's accomplishments. The old cinema was slowly undergoing expansion, most immediately in the backstage area which was acquiring more space via the rather difficult ordeal of pushing out the rear walls of the building. The lighting equipment was relatively new, even though there was the usual insufficiency of lighting positions and instruments. Interestingly, this theatre continued to be used as the cinema for the town, so scenery again had to be constructed very flexibly.

Lamia's English-trained director, Kostas Tsianos, was fortunate enough to work in a wonderful, pillared and marble facility that seemed almost out of place in the dreary industrial city of Lamia. The lobby was airy, light and clean, the auditorium of about 600 seats comfortable and unostentatious, the stage, remarkably, fully rigged. The mayor himself, dressed in his nattiest suit, took tickets and gave me a quick and proud history of the theatre since 1973, interrupting himself only to hold friendly mini-chats with all his constituents coming through the door.

Volos also had been hosting a theatre group for several years under the direction of Spyros Vrachoritis. This director long had favored experimental plays and approaches reminiscent of Off-Off-Broadway during the 1960s. As obtuse as some of these had been (e.g. his touring production of *I Apokalip-sis Tora* Η Αποκάλυψις Τώρα) they did exhibit a strict discipline and a production concept. For his work he too was rewarded with occasional government grants before the major subsidy program was enacted. In addition he was the only producer in the country who regularly tried to mount ancient Greek tragedies in the ancient Greek language, a tactic which no doubt endeared him deeply to the hearts of many classicists.

Festivals

It is almost mind-boggling when one considers the extent of government support for theatrical activities in Greece. In addition to the state theatres, the semi-state theatres, the increasingly funded independent or "free" theatres and all eleven municipal theatres, the Greek government also spent great sums of money supporting summer festivals and international tours into and out of Greece. (Examples of these latter would be the Volonakis' tour of *Oedipus* to the 1984 Los Angeles Olympics and, through the National Theatre, the booking of touring companies from Germany, Spain, Ireland, etc.) It is unclear how much in additional monies is required to support the major summer festivals or how much the government awards the many regional festivals which sprout up in the tourist months. If one considers the extent of these festivals *in toto,* and the calibre of the artists presented, however, a considerable sum begins to suggest itself.

The major performing arts festivals sponsored by the government are the Athens Festival and the Epidavros Festival. The former is held annually in the 161 A.D. Roman Theatre of Herod Atticus as well as in the modern steel amphitheatre atop Lykabettos Hill, the highest spot in Athens. The latter is held in the magical, fourth century B.C. ancient theatre at Epidavros near the village of Ligurio in the Peloponnese. (See photos, pages 88, 89, 90, 91, 92, and 93.)

(It was unclear exactly how much support the government gave to other, smaller festivals, but it seems likely that without such monies they could not exist. There was a recently developed annual Festival of Ancient Theatre presented at the holy theatre at Delfi in June, which hosted producing groups from all over the Mediterranean. Through the Ministry of Agriculture and the Ministry of Housing, Environment and Public Works monies were being allocated to support The Festival of the Rocks which took place in the abandoned rock and marble quarries which ring Athens. [See photo, page 92.] A much-touted Balkan Theatre Festival to be held in Saloniki failed, but the idea was still very much alive in 1986. It can be assumed that the Annual Puppet Festival on the island of Hydra received

Top: **The Roman Herod Atticus Theatre, Athens.** *Bottom and following page:* **The Lykabettos Theatre. Used mostly during the Athens Festival, this steel theatre was constructed in an ancient marble quarry high above Athens.**

The Ancient Theatre at Epidavros. This view shows some of the stone steps which seat up to 13,000 people during the internationally famous festival. Note the narrow exit aisles, the deteriorated seating stones, the foot space behind each raised seating band.

The Ancient Theatre at Epidavros. A view from a parados.

An overview of the Theatre of the Rocks, Athens. The middle-sized theatre sits in the center of the photo. Directly below the camera and out of sight is the largest theatre, consisting mostly of graded dirt. The smallest theatre can be seen nestled into the cliff at the right of the photo.

some government support, as did the Performing Arts Festival in Veria. Perhaps the government also contributed to the Karezi-Kazakos-sponsored Mime Festival in the spring of 1986.)

The Athens Festival regularly produces over 80 performances by an average of 50 performing groups from all over the world. In the 5000 seat Roman theatre spectators have seen groups like the San Francisco Ballet, the Moscow Symphony, the Nakane Japanese Theatre Company, the State Theatre of Northern Greece, the New Shakespeare Theatre of London, etc. At the steel amphitheatre which sits in the gouge once made by a marble quarry, spectators have attended rock and folk music concerts, an imported *Medea,* a National Theatre rendition of Aristophanes' *Peace,* Dave Brubeck, Joan Baez, the Alvin Ailey Dancers *ad infinitum.*

The Festival at the incredible theatre at Epidavros, however, is always dedicated to the ancient drama. Traditional and experimental versions of ancient texts are presented by Greek theatre companies each Saturday and Sunday. (The Cyprus Theatre Company is still considered Greek and, thus, still performs there.)

This latter festival is probably the most important one in all of Greece, summing up in many ways what is best and most exciting about the Greek theatre. As famous director Jules Dussin offered, "What works [in the Greek theatre] are the ancient plays at Epidavros."[40]

In an attempt to recapture the flavor of attending a performance at

The setting for *Electra* at Epidavros. The all-steel scenery was designed for the opening production of the festival in 1983. It was directed by Michael Kakoyiannis and starred Irini Pappas. (See Appendix B for a first person account of the performance.) In this photo one can easily see the open space between the ruins of the skenae and the tree line. The acoustics are so tuned in this theatre that the steps of the actors crossing that gravel space can easily be heard in the top row.

this world-famous festival, in this case the opening performance of 1983, I would like to offer the following first-person account (see photo, page 93):

If there is one theatre in the world which epitomizes the universality and excitement of the theatre experience, it is probably the ancient theatre at Epidavros. Since 1954 it has reminded us of the ancient Greek drama festivals by hosting ancient tragedies and comedies each weekend from June through September.

For theatre people, attending a performance at this remarkable place is like going on a pilgrimage to their "roots"; it is almost a holy experience. Here in the fourth century B.C. they were still playing Aeschylus, Sophocles, Euripides, Aristophanes and, eventually, probably that upstart, commercially-minded newcomer, Menander. Here in the same spot modern Greek actors play the same plays.

Not only is the theatre's size impressive and its park-like surroundings beautifully preserved, but also the natural acoustics of the place are unbelievable. In the last row, 195 feet away from the center of the orchestra, you can hear clearly a match being struck, or a small piece of paper being crumpled and torn in half. A coin dropped on a piece of metal sounds as if it had been dropped next to you.

Modern directors are just now discovering the variable acoustics built into each section of the orchestra circle. The proximity of the speaker to the orchestra's center as well as the direction the speaker faces determine the strength and the quality of the sound produced. And when you stand in the center of that sacred circle and look up around you, the immediate sensation is that of intimacy. Actors *feel* close to their audiences both visually and orally. It is no wonder Greek actors consider the theatre "magical."

I was fortunate enough to make friends with many directors in Greece and sometimes traveled to Epidavros to attend their "general rehearsals" (dress rehearsals) each Friday night before the Saturday opening. Traditionally, the descendents of the people of the local village, Ligurio, also have been allowed to attend this rehearsal free because they are thought to have first discovered the remains of the theatre and helped in its excavation and repair. Many friends and relatives of the cast and crews join them.

Ligurio has only three small hotels and so finding housing always is a problem. Napflion, the next largest town with hotels, is 30 minutes of tortuous road away. Athens is three hours away. (Nevertheless, most people drive or are bussed in from that city for each performance.) One other alternative is to ferret out rooms in private houses, still an infant industry here. Now that the actors and technical staffs for the productions also stay in these rooms, even private rooms are sometimes exceedingly difficult to find. One Friday a coffee shop owner, seeing the desperation in my eyes, called every friend he had who might have had a room for me. Failing, he finally moved his daughter out of her room so that I might have a bed for the night. Thank God for Greek hospitality toward travelers.

Ligurio is really a quiet, sleepy, laid-back place during the week. The men sit around all day at the outdoor cafes three feet from the road sipping their terribly strong coffee or alcoholic *ouzo*, talking politics and bickering by the hour. It's really too hot, they seem to be saying, to do much work. It is wonderfully quiet then, with only an occasional bus going through.

More sound comes from dogs barking, cocks crowing, mules braying and goats baaing than from any man-made activity.

On Saturday morning, though, the air changes—"The Festival is on today," it seems to be saying. You can actually feel the tension mounting. About 6:00 P.M. ("afternoon" to the Greeks) police seem to appear from cracks and crevices. You can see tradesmen readying their goods for the thousands of people who at least will go through their village and, at best, will spend a few hours shopping. By 7:00 P.M. the traffic starts clogging the only street through the village. Cars from several nations share the street with many minibikes, motorcycles, and buses of every conceivable make and color combination. By 7:45 P.M. the police whistles are stuck on "steady" as are the horns of the more impatient. The shops entertain steady streams of customers. At this time of seeming chaos it is reassuring to watch many natives sitting placidly sipping their apertifs as the hurricane roars by—gives one a sense of proportion.

At the theatre the police direct countless cars into open spaces between the trees and the scores of tourist and local buses into a huge, mostly-paved parking lot. The thousands of pilgrims are walking now, funneling naturally down one main road arched with trees and huge, blooming laurel, past the expensive Xenia Hotel, up two sets of stone steps until they reach what looks like a clearing but is really the open space behind the theatre's *skene* (stage house). And there, in front of the pilgrims rises the 13,000 seat theatre. It simply takes your breath away.

You may have difficulty finding your reserved seating section (there are no reserved seats), or finding a seating stone that is not cracked in the wrong place, or slopping downhill or whose weathered gouges are not filled with water from the last rain; you may have difficulty getting used to the thousands of spectators all around you who are smoking incessantly. You may decry the presence of those thousands of flash cameras which will be used continuously throughout the performance. You may discover that you are one of the few who have not brought something to sit on, a pillow, blanket, piece of styrofoam, a bamboo mat. Within 20 minutes you notice that stone, regardless of how well worn by antiquity and use, can be very hard on the old epilogue. After 40 minutes you consider violent crime a viable option in order to acquire a nice, foam-filled pillow.

These unfortunate conditions, however, suddenly seem trivial when they are placed in the context of the whole experience.

The audience members have found their places on the ancient stones and wait patiently past the 9:00 P.M. curtain time. A limousine purrs up to the open space behind the *skene*. A celebrity gets out and walks to his privileged seat in the first row, the seats once used by the priests of Dionysius, the only seats with back rests. The audience applauds. A politician arrives for his entrance and receives mixed boos and applause. Minister of Culture, Melina Mercouri, evokes a rousing standing ovation. Like a well-directed scene they appear, one by one, to receive their entrance acknowledgement and be seated in the priests' chairs.

The last orange glow has left the rims of the hills behind the trees and the first stars sneak out. A huge cymbal crashes, the first of three to signal the impending start of the show. The trees behind the *skene* are shading into black against the purple hills and iridescent blue sky. Suddenly some shadows start moving across the open space from the tree line to the *skene*—

actors, in black. They move slowly and ceremoniously in a long line. After a brief flurry of applause the audience grows silent. A second cymbal crash. More black figures seem to detach themselves from the shadows and approach the stage area. Torches are lit around the orchestra. A third crash. House lights dim out. Eerie electronic music touches the absolutely silent night air. A torchlight procession winds slowly around the orchestra as the stage lights fade up slowly. The first speaker takes a breath and the entire theatre world pauses.

Then, the first word.
The rebirth.[41]

6. Commercial, Children's, Puppet and Amateur Theatres

Commercial Theatres

All of the theatres which have been investigated thus far have had as their primary goal the creation of serious works of art. Of course each one has had to consider in some degree the economic potential of the production it presented—only the state-subsidized theatres can afford to ignore that reality. The commercial theatre, however, has as its primary goal the financial success of its product. It can afford to ignore art as well as subsidy.

The secret to the success of these theatres is almost entirely their stars. Whether the vehicle be a silly sitcom, Broadway musical or satirical musical revue, the primary draw is the star quality of the major performer(s). This is entertainment with a capital "E" and commercialism with a capital "C." As likely as not the star has become identified with a particular theatre, just as some of the stars on the "legitimate" stage have acquired their own spaces. Thus Aliki Voujiouklaiki has a winter theatre as well as a summer outdoor theatre in Green Park. Rena Vlakopoulou resides at the Bretania Theatre. Some theatres, because of their production capabilities, naturally become associated with large revues since only a few houses in Athens are able to accommodate the tremendous scenic requirements of such shows. Thus the Orpheas Theatre most often houses these kinds of revues and may be termed a commercial house.

Such musical shows often are very expensively—if garishly—produced. Most include at least some bow toward female nudity, especially in the Las Vegas-style costumes of the show girls in the major revues. Almost every one of them utilizes taped music in their lip-synch routines, but the more lavish of them use both live and recorded music synchronously.

Tickets are expensive by Greek standards (1000 drachmas is not uncommon) and the theatres in which these shows are housed most often have large capacities (1500 plus). These seats are needed: the Greek people adore these shows.

Although the sitcoms, Broadway musicals and European operettas are the standard fare of commercial theatres in most parts of the world, the Greek revue is the most popular *form* of theatre in Greece, "much more popular ... than other forms of theatrical art." It is "the Athenian form of theatre par excellence."[1] The revue form, called *I epitheorisis* (Η επιθεόρισις), also is probably the most unique form of theatre to develop in Greece since the fifth century B.C.

Although the Greek revue varies somewhat in its several manifestations, some few elements are normal: political satire, songs and girls. In the most Spartan versions the revue consists of a few stand-up comics who also sing, or try to, and a few girls who wear slinky costumes and provide sexual humor. In the glitziest of these shows there may be a half-dozen such comics of national recognition, a large mixed dancing chorus with lavish and revealing costumes, enormous sets and a large band enhanced by impeccably timed taped music.

The show normally starts with the usual full chorus and showgirl production number and quickly patterns itself into a series of stand-up comic routines, with very short musical sequences included, followed by a duo routine or choral number followed by another stand-up comic. Sometimes the comics perform together in set "scenes" and sometimes with a chorus girl or two. Large production numbers appear occasionally and often rely on gargantuan stage machine devices, like the huge mansion interior which changed into a jungle with a 20 foot gorilla trying to grasp the leading female star who avoided his clutches by riding a swing up into the flies.[2]

For all of its bowing to spectacular effects the revue relies on politically oriented comedy for most of its content. One famous actress described the scene backstage before every performance of a particular revue which played to full houses during the 1985–1986 season. The leading comic for this particular revue was an avid Communist and naturally wished for the demise of the current government. A short time before curtain a group of local Communist bosses entered his dressing room and closed the door. Afterwards, during his "free" stand up routine (that routine which could change nightly) new anti-government humor had been inserted.[3] Based on the latest political events—no doubt gleefully presented by those Party messengers—the material never failed to shock and tickle the audience with its street-fresh commentary. Although this kind of direct political influence may be rare, its existence indicates the importance of political commentary to the core of these shows.

In the best of these shows the writers provide truly witty humor for the comics, without forgoing their traditional scatological leanings. In all cases the effect on the audiences is electric; people doubling over in uncontrollable laughter is not uncommon. Wave after wave of such laughter reverberates through the houses. Handkerchiefs dab at streaming eyes and people hold their sides in pain. At times it seems that human beings simply cannot continue to laugh that much over that long a period of time.

It must seem obvious that the revue form is not particularly indigenous to Greece, even though the particular mixture of the various elements may be so. The satiric revue form probably appeared in Paris in 1894, curiously the year of the first revue in Athens. The Greek revue was called *Ligo ap'ola (A Little of Everything.)*[4] After a few more attempts the form disappeared until 1907; since then, though, it has lived a wondrous and even charmed existence. Like the Parisian, English and American revues a la Ziegfeld of 1907 these revues have included girls, comedy, song and spectacle in varying degrees. Even during the Occupation the Nazis allowed the heavily satiric revue theatres to exist even as they censored the dramatic theatres. Regardless of the political situation the revues continued holding up to ridicule the government currently in power. Even today a change in government causes hardly a ripple in the revue theatres; they simply change the names in their routines and charge straight ahead attacking the new politicians with the same fervor as they attacked the old.[5]

Theatre for Children

In a way nearly all theatre one sees in Greece is for children. That is, children often attend nearly any show. This is especially true outside of Athens where the appearance of any theatre group is an event not to be limited only to certain ages. Although many westerners no doubt would refuse to allow their children to attend certain of these shows, apparently the Greeks have no such hesitancies. For example 500 people from the town of Ioannina attended a traveling, Brechtian-style production of Aristophanes' *Lysistrata*. The ages of the audience spanned nearly 100 years and parents were not at all concerned that their tots or teenagers were watching when the dialogue focused on the withdrawal of sexual favors to stop the war, nor when enormous phalluses appeared. (See photos, page 100.) All ages in the village of Anoia, Crete, attended *Captain Michalis*, as they did in Irakia for Palkoseniko's *The Peasants*. I am certain the same age groups would have been represented in any village regardless of a play's subject matter or treatment. To the degree that these audiences contained healthy percentages of children, all theatre in Greece could be called theatre for children.

By most standards, however, theatre for children refers to a specific group of literatures and methods of presentation which make the offerings more palatable and exciting for younger audiences than for older ones. In Greece this particular kind of theatre exists in Athens as a kind of

Actual performance of *Lysistrata* at Ioannina. A Brechtian-inspired version which included a male Lysistrata, mixed chorus, night club routines, modern music as well as more traditional masks, songs, etc. Directed by Stavros Doufixis.

Actual performance in a school room by the Provincial Theatre of Agrinio.

appendage to a regular theatre's offerings. One gets the feeling that many of them are thrown together haphazardly to insure the theatre against financial losses incurred by the adult production currently running. Of the 30 children's shows running in the winter of 1986, for example, the vast majority were connected with a theatre which played an adult show in the evening. Often the cast of the children's show was drawn primarily from the cast of the adult show.

In the outlying regions this kind of show for younger audiences most often takes the form of traveling troupes which go to area villages. (See photo, page 101.) Although these shows are produced partly to satisfy the stipulations of the municipal theatre contracts with the government, no doubt they also would be produced without such encouragement. They are small, minimally produced, highly flexible shows, it seems to me, and serve an extremely important function: they take live, professional theatre to audiences which otherwise might never travel to the major cities to see one.

In Athens some theatre companies have established reputations for consistently producing above-average shows for children. The National Theatre is one, Stoa Theatre is another. Theatre Erevnas once created a highly acclaimed show which was comprised of portions of several Aristophanic comedies. The one person, however, who is most identified with high quality and dedicated children's theatre is TV actress Xenia Karlojelopoulou.

Karlojelopoulou's first experience with an exciting children's theatre production occurred in London where she saw Brian Way's *Pinocchio*. That experience convinced her that children's theatre in Greece could be an artistic as well as an economic success. She already controlled an adult theatre company. Even though this group had no knowledge of children's theatre at all, they embarked on a children's theatre production as an experiment. Her first such play took place in 1962 at the Children's Stage in collaboration with Yiannis Fertis. Not surprisingly, it was Brian Way's *Pinocchio,* directed by Marsha Taylor.[6] The show was such an enormous success that she decided to drop the production of adult plays to concentrate on plays for children. It was time, she said, because "children's plays fit the cultural mosaic; that is, no one else was regularly producing this form and a contribution in this area was sorely needed in Greece."[7]

Fortunately her name was a household word from her fame in over 40 films and 40 notable plays. That notoriety not only provided sufficient funds to start the project, but also it imprinted it with a respected, positive and stable reputation. Even today she admitted that that fame allowed her to engage in such a lucrative activity as a TV game show hostess, from which she received enough income to support her children's theatre project.

By 1983 her salaried staff included the Artistic Director, two administrators, three tech people and various box office staff as well as the actors. Although she produced only one show each year, it played 6–8 times a week, mostly on tour. It was a schedule which she admitted was terribly exhausting.

Both the Ministry of Culture and the Ministry of Education were involved in funding and coordinating her tours. Sometimes the Ministry of Education told the schools which plays they could see (Karlojelopoulou's was not the only theatre company bidding for these contracts). Sometimes the Ministry of Youth would buy performances outright for small towns and villages. At still other times factories might purchase performances for the children of their employees. Regardless of the specific situation, the producer-director operated under one cardinal rule: once the show went into a town, every student had to be allowed to see the play. If there were those who could not afford the ticket price, she let them attend free.

As one might expect, she received an annual government subsidy which purchased about 20,000 tickets. It still was insufficient income to cover production and touring expenses, so she sold the show to even more schools and tried to sell more tickets herself.

Like so many producers of shows for youth, Karlojelopoulou believed firmly that children's theatre should be excellent by any standards. She aimed at the 8–9 year-old age group but felt that the show must also be of sufficient quality to entertain adults. And, although most of each show must be understandable to her target audience, she felt very strongly that there must always be elements in the play that are *not* understandable to them. Children, she said, "should know that there is always something beyond, something they do not know."[8]

Although Xenia Karlojeropoulou has emerged as the leader in the presentation of theatre for children, over the years other organizations have appeared for various lengths of time dedicated to the same audience. There is little or no evidence of their existence, but some smatterings of data tantalize the researcher. Mrs. Helen Theoshari-Perraki, inspired by the International Puppet Festival in France, founded the Athens Puppet Theatre. She created puppet plays from stories and characters indigenous to the various regions of Greece. In Athens another puppeteer, Dimos Sopkianos, presented regular shows at the Goethe Institute. The Municipal Puppet Company of Athens played almost daily and Nikos Kakosis gave puppet performances in the provinces. Various marionette theatres also played throughout Greece (e.g. those run by Frangiskos Kalaitzakis or Lakis Apostolidis). And, of course, the shadow puppet theatres, spearheaded by the internationally respected Evgenios Spatharis and Panayotis Mickopoulous, maintained a presence in every town and village.

One unique phenomenon which I did not encounter at all was the amateur Children's Companies, child actors presenting plays for child audiences. Up to at least 1973 several existed. The Mary Papastephanakis Childrens Company and the Childrens Company of Mary Soidou were only two of several which performed in Athens as well as in the provinces.[9]

I present this admittedly meager information at this point as a prelude to the next section on puppet theatre because the intentions of both forms overlap. The last theatres noted above seem to have disappeared; the Karaghiozis puppet theatre to be discussed still lives, albeit in a severely curtailed state.

Karaghiozis Theatre (see photo, page 104)

It was delightfully cool when noted Greek director Nikos Papadakis took me to a neighborhood celebration in the Filadelfia area of Athens. We joined throngs of families surging through a large park to hear folk singers, watch folk dances, listen to speeches about the then-impending Parliamentary vote on women's rights, buy home-made goodies at numerous tables lining the walkways, play in the playgrounds, eat nuts, ice cream or sun flower seeds and watch a Karaghiozis shadow puppet play.

In typical Greek fashion the place of the performance was not marked in any way, except by a kind of hearsay or generally-acquired knowledge. After asking numerous people we fought our way through a jungle of people, bushes and trees, past a small bunch of children painting Karaghiozis characters on tables set up in the woods, and finally to a small clearing which held the platform supporting the puppet stage.

This stage was a simple, free-standing, three-fold flat with a semi-opaque screen perhaps eight feet wide by four feet high on the long side facing the audience. In back of the screen and across its bottom edge was a six

A Karaghiozis Shadow Puppet Theatre performance. Karaghiozis is the bulbous-nosed character on the bottom of this fight. But rest assured he will rise again, especially when his opponent is the Turk.

inch trough on which the puppets' feet would rest during the performance. The floodlights stood on tripods a few feet in back of the screen. During a performance these flood lights shone from behind the screen and through the semi-opaque bodies of the puppets which then appeared as colored shadows when they were pressed against the screen from behind. There was one microphone for the puppet master—he spoke all the roles—and a box piled with multi-colored, two-dimensional puppets whose arms and legs were riveted loosely to the bodies so that 360 degree movement was possible for each appendage. The puppets were manipulated by flexible thin sticks attached usually to their heads or by means of strings attached to special parts of their bodies.

As the crowd waited for enough darkness to permit the shadows to be seen they jockeyed for position in their usual shoving, pushing, squeezing way. The clearing in the trees was very small for the crowd which had assembled and the low height of the stage platform made sight lines very bad. Obviously those in the first few feet would see the play easily and the rest would have to struggle. Nikos pleaded with the people shoving ahead of me to let this American professor see his first Karaghiozis play, but the needs of the children, appropriately, won the moment. I stumbled and almost fell over a large, unstable rock. I discovered that, by balancing precariously on it, I could see most of the play over the heads of the crowd. Only fathers lifting their children onto their shoulders obscured my vision.

Then the screen lights switched on. The cheers, screams of delight and applause startled me. Music, too loud for my unaccustomed ears, announced the prologue in which Karagheozis, the main character from which the theatre form gets its name, talked to the audience and danced his peculiar, limb-twirling dance. The crowd squeezed even closer, the maneuvering for position becoming deadly serious now. It was increasingly difficult to maintain balance on my rocky perch in this constantly shifting crowd.

Nikos, happily emanating Greek hospitality, tried to explain the plot as well as some interesting highlights as we went along. The character of Karaghiozis, an ugly-mug hunch-back, is derived from an ancient Turkish folk hero which had been "Hellenized" after the War of Independence. Now his antagonists are mostly Turks (even though his relatives and friends also may be on the receiving end of his many ruses and practical jokes). The plots are generally known to the audiences and the puppet master improvises on them as he wishes. The main audience-pleasing elements are, of course, the fight scenes in which completely rotating arms and legs (and in one case a huge bendable nose) spin in all directions as the puppets fly through the air, pummel each other to the foot stomps of the puppeteer, and disappear, only to reappear in another corner of the screen. Another audience pleaser is the "where is he?" scene in which a fly, bee or villain is seen by the audience but not by the puppet character looking for him or it. The kids scream wildly trying to save Karaghiozis from the impending beating. The loudly amplified voice of the puppet master, of course, "milks" the predicament for all its worth.

Curiously the relative dimensions of the puppets are logically inconsistent (e.g. the Turk is almost three times as large as Karaghiozis' son, supposedly 12 years old) but consistent in an emotional dimension. For example, the cunning rascal, Karaghiozis, himself is perhaps one of the smaller puppets and his uncle, the shepherd, one of the largest. Well, shepherds *are* more important than clever servants. His son is tiny compared to a huge, pestering bird. Somehow it made theatrical sense—the bird *was* more important than the son at that moment.

Like the audiences for all popular theatre, this one screamed and yelled at the characters, tried to help them, talked back when asked a question, milled around constantly and talked freely among themselves. yet they were attentive at crucial moments. At the end of the play, which lasted about 40 minutes, they turned and disappeared so fast that I had to blink to confirm the observation. The trees, shrubs and paths, by now all in darkness, had absorbed these 150 people in an instant. A few moments later the puppet stage was folded up and taken down and Evgenios Spatharis, the old master of Karaghiozis, was walking away with his suitcase full of multi-colored, loose-hinged puppets.[10]

Although these shadow puppets might be traceable to eleventh century China, according to Dionysius Flabouras,[11] the more immediate origin of the form is generally acknowledged to be Turkey. The Turkish form of this theatre, called Karaghioz, appeared in conjunction with the month-long Turkish holiday, Ramadan. After rigid fasting during the day the Muslims engaged in outrageous, riotous behavior at night which included feasting and attendance at a Karaghioz performance. These performances were characterized by foul language, vulgarities (e.g. scenes in a Turkish harem), and the centrality of Karaghioz's large phallus.[12]

After the fall of Ottoman Constantinople this form of popular theatre entered Greece probably in the region of Epirus where renegade Ali Pasha had established his minor kingdom. After the Sultan had that potentate killed because of his rebelliousness, the puppeteers in Epirus began mocking the dead dictator on the puppet theatre screen and the figures began dividing into Turkish and Greek characters. For example, Macedonian heroes like Alexander the Great were added to the plots, as were heroes of the Greek Revolution.[13] Too, the palace of the Pasha (the seraglio) and the poor hut of Karaghiozis were placed on opposing sides of the screen—a practice which remains standard to this day.

As more and more territories were liberated the form moved south, at first centering in Patras where there was a sizable foreign population attracted by the facilities of the harbor there. The crude entertainment met with religious and political objections of the Christian Greeks and for awhile it was rejected. By 1890, however, it was transformed into a more acceptable Greek form—the main character's phallic appendage, for example, became a very long arm with which he could pummel anyone weaker than himself; several of the particularly foul-mouthed and obscene characters disappeared in favor of Greek characters more recognizable to the public; the language became Greek. Most importantly, the stories moved away from those which took the spectator behind-the-scenes in a Turkish harem to stories and characters of the Greek Revolution and War of Independence.[14] In general, then, it had been transformed from an entertainment solely for Turkish celebrations to a form which was a mixture of Turkish and Greek influences and fully available to the common Greek. In addition it developed into a most felicitous way for the masses to express their anti–Turkish attitudes as well as to express national characteristics and themes.[15]

After the success of the War of Independence many French and German touring companies traveled throughout Greece presenting French and German classics. This was a natural result of the installation of a Bavarian king to rule the new country as well as the desires of the Great Powers to mold Greece into an acceptable European entity. Greek audiences of post-revolutionary times, however, were not terribly excited by such companies. The only almost-indigenous theatre form which was available to them was the Karaghiozis, a form which celebrated the adventures of a poor rogue who was not unlike themselves. From about 1830 to 1940, then, the shadow puppets of Karaghiozis were the best established and most generally accepted form of theatrical entertainment in Greece. By 1920 there were 15 Karaghiozis theatres in the city of Athens alone and many more traveling throughout the countryside.[16]

After World War II Karaghiozis tried to change with the times but merely changed the stories—"Karaghiozis the Astronaut," for example.

The technical aspects of the form had long been perfected and there seemed to be no direction in which it could improve. Then television and movies provided unconquerable competition for the barefooted and poor rascal. Today there is only one major Karaghiozis theatre in the Plaka district of Athens, and perhaps one other traveling the country. Some of the old masters, specifically Spatharis, have tried to teach their art to younger puppet masters, or have taken their traditions to workshops in other countries, where interest in this art form seems almost keener than in its adopted country. Recently the University of Thessaloniki created a course on the form.[17] For most Greeks, though, the Karaghiozis theatre is relegated to sporadic performances for children and to occasional neighborhood festivals, like the one in Filadelfia just described.

Amateur Theatre

Although there is an Amateur Theatre Festival each year, the amateur theatre movement still remains haphazard, occasional and non-directed. There are, for example, no strictly amateur theatres operating consistently, such as there might be in most communities in English or American cities. There are foreign groups in Athens, like the Hams which produces English-language musicals, or the Players, which produces straight plays in English. There is even an amateur group occasionally performing in English on the tourist island of Mykonos. However, to my knowledge there is no Greek amateur theatre which operates a season of plays in its own theatre.

In the schools and universities the situation is a little better. The University of Athens apparently produces a show each year; in fact Melina Halls, the daughter of the theatre scholar often referred to in these pages, Aliki Bacopoulou-Halls, was hired as the staff director for the show(s) at Athens University in 1985–1986. The students at the University of Thessaloniki produce shows, and even some small secondary schools, like the one in Veria in northern Greece, present some sort of theatrical activity. However, since there is no formalized training for theatre students in the schools or universities, educational theatre activity such as Americans are used to does not appear. It is true that the drama training schools in Athens present student productions bi-annually. It is also true that the presentations of the drama schools may be considered "amateur" because the performers are still not graduates. These productions, though, are almost completely for the purpose of evaluation and, thus, cannot be considered formal public performances. The seemingly defunct program proclaimed by former Minister Laliotis—the establishment of 300 recreation centers and amateur theatre groups—seems even more distant.

7. Some New Developments

Like everything else in Greece, the theatre scene is changing constantly and quickly. In the last few years many new projects have appeared: the municipal theatre movement, the International Puppet Festival, a summer festival in Veria. Many more have poked their heads out of the planning rooms and some have actually begun their existence. Two of them especially may be worth investigating. Both seem at the leading edge of cultural experimentalism; both are the creations of one leading Greek theatre personality, Minos Volonakis.

Festival of the Rocks

There are 38 of them, vast, craggy, forbidding places. In their awesome silences one can imagine hundreds of slaves wrestling with the rock and marble that built Athens. Their gold, rose, blue and white stone can be found on the Acropolis, in old sidewalks, on the facades of new office buildings and, ground into powder, in the most common building material of Greece, cement.

These are the quarries of Attika, a total of 138 of them which ring the city of Athens and which actually rise out of the city itself. The metropolis, seeing them as eyesores and/or possible usable spaces, proposed filling them in with the city's garbage, then paving them for parking lots or covering them with trees and shrubs to create parks and playgrounds.

One person, however, liked at least some of them in their various despoiled states. Distinguished theatre director Minos Volonakis said, "I like stone. I like hills. I like those rugged, arid, lunar landscapes. They have a certain majesty and cragginess about them."[1] Perfect, one would imagine, for ancient tragedies. He proposed to anyone who would listen that the most appropriate of these many quarries should be reclaimed as huge, outdoor amphitheatres.

No one bought the idea at first and so, in 1980, he booked into the quarry at Nikaia six concerts and 11 plays just to prove it could be done. The next summer more concerts and plays were added. In the summer of 1986 three of these quarries hosted productions, a fourth was receiving a permanent concrete amphitheatre, and it was not too difficult to believe the director's claim that the Festival of the Rocks had become a strong rival to the internationally acclaimed Athens Festival.

The idea glimmered at first in 1965. At that time Volonakis was a young director who "wanted to do something" but had no theatre in which to do it. He learned that the abandoned marble quarry on Lykabettos Hill, which still juts up as the highest point in Athens, could be used for a performance. Since he "liked that forbidding place," he encouraged the famous actress Anna Sinodinou to star in his production of Aristophanes' *Ecclesiazusae*. Almost accidentally this production became the prototype for the entire theatre-in-the-rocks project.

In 1967 the military dictatorship made working in Greece unbearable for Volonakis and, like thousands of others, he fled to England in voluntary exile. He was quite at home there, the country of his education. He worked at the Old Vic, as assistant to Sir Tyrone Guthrie, and eventually directed such stars as Sean Connery, Glenda Jackson, Suzannah York, Constance Cummings and many more.

When the dictatorship ended in 1974 the director returned to Athens and was amazed. The population explosion which had grown after World War II and the brutal Civil War which followed had now expanded to the quarries which once had been beyond the city's outskirts. In some cases housing developments had totally engulfed the gouged mountainsides.

The shock of seeing once-distant marble pits suddenly surrounded by thousands of lookalike concrete apartment buildings made him realize that the city would be faced with a series of new problems, one of which concerned the theatre. "Athens was behaving," he recalled, "like a city of 50,000, not four million." [Actually the city's population in 1974 was closer to three million.] It was ridiculous to ask those people suddenly thrust so far from the central city's theatres — those built when Athens was infinitely smaller — to travel so far in order to attend. What a shame, he thought, that there was no way to use those rugged, man-made amphitheatres which could be found in the backyards of nearly every outlying neighborhood.

So, between 1976 and 1980, and sandwiched in between his many directorial assignments, he investigated 38 of the major quarries in Athens' environs. He checked them for their proximity to population centers, for the availability of public transportation, for the likelihood of support from the municipalities adjoining the sites, for their physical configurations and for their acoustic properties.

He remembered many winter nights in 1978–1979 in which he and a few friends climbed into the silent, dark and deserted pits between 11 P.M. and 3 A.M. to test their acoustics. His device, a hand-held sound-measuring instrument, was dubbed "Kojak" because it reminded the group of the bald head of Greek-American actor Telly Savalas. Sounds of various frequencies and strengths were produced from a fixed point while the machine was carried to various other points to record the strength of the signal. Sometimes performer Giorgos Dalaras was asked to sing from assorted locations among the rocks while Volonakis made further measurements. (As a reward for this nocturnal injustice, Dalaras received the promise that, if anything ever came of this project, he would be the first performer to be featured.) After months of work Volonakis knew that his suspicions had been confirmed — the acoustics of at least eleven of these quarries rivaled the extraordinary ones at the ancient theatre at Epidavros.

It was cold and tedious work, sometimes even dangerous. The pits often were inhabited by stray dogs and at Nikaia his group actually was "attacked by wild dogs. We were in two cars and we had to roll up the windows to save ourselves."

Of the eleven quarries found suitable for reclamation as theatres the director decided that those at Nikaia and Byrona should house his first ventures. He met with a local mayor, Stelios Logothetis, who liked the idea. Unfortunately, the official could not convince his city council to support it. However, he offered the director personal encouragement and even helped with the physical labor required to clean up the nearest pit for a performance. Volonakis never forgot this show of support and, to this day, the two men remain fast friends.

Finally the dream was realized. In that summer of 1980 Volonakis presented the first formal event in the rocks, a simple concert. Featured performer, of course, was singer Giorgos Dalaras. The quarry had no access road, no water, no electricity, no audience amenities, just a rented steel scaffold theatre. Volonakis had printed 6,000 tickets, but another thousand to two thousand spectators entered free when the tickets ran out.

Parenthetically, that same shovel-wielding mayor, Logothetis, then went back to his city council and *did* convince them to support the idea. As of this writing he is shepherding the construction of the first permanent theatre project of the rocks, known as *Kokkinovrachos*, Red Rock Theatre. (See photo, page 111.) It eventually will seat 17,500 people, and its site will include athletic fields (one of which is already in place), a cultural center, tavernas, parks, parking lots, etc. It will be the first of five such theatres Volonakis hopes will be constructed.

By the summer of 1986 the rock-theatre idea had reached full acceptance. One two-night concert drew 40,000; Volonakis produced his *Oedipus* as well as a foreboding *Waiting for Godot* among the overpowering cliffs in Byrona; Peter Stein and Peter Brook both preferred the "Theatron Petros" (Stone Theatre) at Petroupoulis (see photo, page 92) to the ancient theatres for their spectacular productions of the *Oresteia* and *Mahabhrata* during the summer of 1985; two more theatres, one of which will be on the

The construction site for Red Rock Theatre, the large amphitheatre at Nikaia, Athens. Built by local and government funds, this theatre is being constructed in an abandoned marble quarry. It will eventually seat 17,500 spectators. The large circle defines the orchestra area under which will be dressing rooms, storage, rest rooms, and other support areas. Note the scale of the figure on the extreme right.

island of Salamis, were slated to open in 1987; more and more mayors, responding to demands from their constituencies, were working to construct temporary or permanent theatres in their neighborhood quarries. Most of all, the idea of theatre being important and available to all the people of Athens has come to fruition. As Volonakis boasted, the rock-theatre project was an example of "the wildest and most successful cultural planning in Athens." "It has changed the map."

The rock-theatre idea could be lauded as the latest idea in recycling. "It's simply recycling on a grand scale," Volonakis said. "You take it, a refuse dump, and you turn it into a cultural event. . . . I didn't know when I started that it would become so fashionable a notion."

Even though a fairer, demographically based distribution of theatre activity in Athens and recycling may have been the most practical reasons to engage in this vast project, the director spoke most passionately of the aesthetic reasons.

Epidavros and Dodoni are marvelous theatres. But most of the ancient theatres are not Greek at all; they're Roman, and they're vilely built.[2] They create a sort of grandeur and a romantic kind of thing because they're so old; but, otherwise, they're not really aesthetically very valuable pieces. Moreover, if Sophocles could see the Herod Atticus [the second century Roman theatre], he'd faint, because the last thing he wanted facing his audience would be a very ornate and imposing facade. He's the most imposing writer ever, but this is precisely because, I think, he doesn't impose. There's no imposition in it. . . . They [the great Greek playwrights] were all writing for a very light structure on some hillside, with the feeling of being simply away from anything that reminded them visibly of civilization. The only equivalent I could find was the rocks.[3]

Volonakis dreamed of a time when each municipality would own and operate a small winter theatre, then cooperate with several adjoining communities to operate a large, common, rock amphitheatre in the summers. Some quarries in these neighborhoods would be left in their present states — regardless of the conditions there — so that visiting troupes could plan productions specifically for those unique places — that is, a particular production idea melded to the particular stone environment. Volonakis himself looked forward to the day when he could use one of the most immense quarries (currently being fouled with illegal garbage dumping) for a production of an unnamed play of Byron. He fairly drooled over its achingly foreboding three miles of cliffs, echoing canyons, crevices and strange formations, as well as its haunting clusters of long-abandoned mining buildings — a set no amount of money could buy.

There was another quarry, tiny by comparison, sitting almost unnoticed in northern Attica. Small boys used the flat, central area as a soccer field, probably unaware of the tremendous dramatic potential of the towering cliffs surrounding them on three sides. This was "The Jewel," Volonakis' favorite quarry. It was here that he planned to produce most of his own contributions to future Rock Festival seasons. One sensed that producing in this magical space would be his own reward for his eight years of work on this project, work for which he has not received any direct payments of any kind from anybody.

Whatever the future success of this new festival may be, to date at least it has preserved and recycled truly unique landscapes. Its most significant accomplishment, however, may be the transformation of these craggy and majestic places into meeting places for community pride and the ancient Athenian spirit, a long way from those cold winter nights with "Kojak" and the wild dogs.

Bilingual Theatre

Minos Volonakis also felt strongly that the message of the ancient Greek playwrights was being muffled by the fact that the ancient plays at the summer festivals naturally were being produced in the Greek language. In the summer of 1986 he rushed ahead with his bilingual production of *Medea*, presented in the rocky ambience of the theatre at Petropoulous. Each night the language of the show alternated between Greek and English. Nearly everyone, including many of the actors involved with the project, were surprised. Few really thought that this production could have been mounted in so short a time after the idea first surfaced.[4]

In the fall of 1985 the director quietly contacted several actors whom he knew were rather fluent in English. They represented a wide range of combined nationalities: Greek with-Egyptian, -Danish, -English, -French, -Canadian, -Australian, -South African, -Libyan and -German. Without explaining fully his plans he began a series of workshops designed to explore their various levels of proficiency in the language. He began with readings of poetry, colorful prose and, eventually, drama. I was fortunate enough to be included in the instruction program, working specifically with literature from the American stage. The hidden agenda consisted of bringing the skills of as many as possible up to a performance level.

In typical Volonakis fashion he proceeded slowly and rather surreptitiously—he has always preferred to start with little fanfare and deliberate planning before "going public." For many weeks no one in the group which conglomerated in the barren upstairs apartment of Gorgos Vouros knew exactly why they were there. At the same time each knew that Volonakis just did not initiate such workshops without something specific in mind and they wanted to be involved with it whatever it was. Even at the most fundamental level, some decided to participate simply because the "great" Volonakis was involved.

When he finally announced that he intended to produce his already-famous production of *Medea* starring Jenny Karezi and Kostas Kazakos at Epidavros in Greek and then remount that same production at the Festival of the Rocks in both English and Greek, the reaction ranged from, "Fantastic," to, "He's crazy," to, "It's too early!" But the specific plan had been in the director's mind since 1977.[5]

When he was in exile in England, he became increasingly aware of his "Greekness" as well as the fact that people of various cultures really could not understand each other because of their differences in language. When he finally returned to his native land the Greek Tourist Organization asked him to produce some Greek plays in English so that the millions of English-speaking tourists could better enjoy the ancient texts. He doubted at that time that there were enough Greek actors and directors who could accomplish such a task, and so did nothing. Several years later, though, he decided to send up his trial balloon, the Acting-in-English workshop (although this seminar never had any formal title). With NYU professor and director John Chiolis, voice expert and opera singer Mikia Gematzaki, choreographer

Korais Damatis and myself, he began working with the language and the texts in earnest. These were just initial steps, however, toward his ultimate goal, "for English-speaking visitors and residents in Greece to experience for the first time the masterpieces of ancient drama in the landscape and tradition that created them, without the language barrier which has so far blunted their impact on foreigners."[6]

Medea did appear as promised, alternating Greek and English performances. The sparse information I have received regarding this production indicates that, as of this writing, the judgment on the effectiveness of the dual-language *Medea* production has not been passed. Knowledgeable and sincere adjudicators seem to have landed on both sides of its evaluation. In any case this presentation is only the first phase of a much larger project. Volonakis planned to bring foreign directors into his camp, to provide roles for bilingual Greek actors working abroad, to provide workshops in the Greek language for Greek actors living abroad who had never spoken their native tongue, to provide opportunities for great, English-speaking actors of all nations to play some of the greatest roles of all time in the particular environments that created them. His long-time friend John Chiolis already was tapped as the first foreign director to head a production in the 1987 season. Volonakis had selected three plays to be produced during a May–September season in that same year, announced his intention to tour and, in addition, to capture these performances on videotape.[7]

Greek drama was not the only focus of this new project. As the director said in an interview, Greek drama was only "our main focus to begin with. A few surprises are planned for next year and we have already commissioned something new from a well-known English writer."[8] Nor was English the only language considered.

> German is the next logical choice because we already have four German-Greek actors in the company, and at some point we will be mounting an evening of abstracts in German. Again, the point is to create a bridge of immediacy for Germans in Greece, though in general English is understood by so many people it will give us access to an *international* audience.[9]

Indeed, Volonakis is convinced that, if English is not already the world's second language, it will become so. "This is the way it will end, eventually," he stated firmly.[10]

Besides the value of the project in reaching perhaps millions more people with a more vivid impact of the ancient texts, and in bolstering the tourist economy of a country which desperately needs it, this bilingual project could become an important avenue for international understanding. The director already considered it "intrinsically and by definition a bridge between cultures."[11]

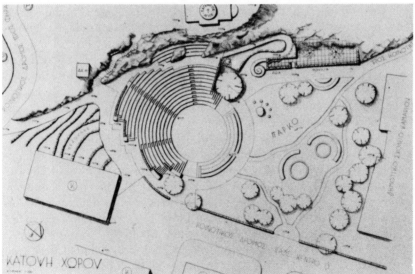

Section view and ground plan for the proposed theatre at Kalmari on Santorini.

Potential site for a new amphitheatre at Kalmari on the island of Santorini. This picture is taken from the planned stage left side of the proposed performance space. The theatron will be incorporated into that rocky hillside at the base of the chapel.

A New Theatre on Santorini?

The building bug must have reached across the Aegean to the islands too. The mayor of the small village of Kalmari on the incredible island of Santorini has served notice that he intends to construct a small outdoor amphitheatre on the grounds of the public school there. An avid arts lover-architect, Kostas Nicholaidis, from the capital town of Thira decided to donate his services to help initiate the project. Fortunately, he approached me to consult on the plans which were in the formative stages.

The theatre, to be located in a tiny park adjoining the school grounds, would only seat about 600 and would be used equally for theatre and music presentations. The latter use was necessary because the rather long-established Santorini Music Festival located in the small town of Oia has been using a wholly inadequate school building for its concerts. An outdoor facility which would adequately serve music as well as drama would enhance the reputation of this international festival as well as provide an appropriate space for theatre companies which would tour to the island.[12]

The preliminary plans for this construction are included here (see photo, page 115), as is a location shot in the school grounds. (See photo, page 116.) The architectural drawings do not include the changes suggested at informal conferences May 8–10, 1986.

III
Theatre Production and Training

8. An Overview
of Non-Production Elements

Seasons/Performances

The winter season of playgoing in Greece begins as soon after October first as production teams can mount their shows. Plays which are being carried over or remounted from the summer season, or even from the last winter season, may need relatively little preparation and so will hit the boards early in the month. Those which are starting from ground up will open later in the month or in November. By Christmas nearly all shows which are going to open have opened. Only a few which take exceptionally long rehearsal periods premiere later, for example, the productions of Lefteris Vouyiatzis which may not open until January.

The winter season continues until the first Sunday before Greek Easter which may fall as late as May 4, as it did in 1986, or as early as the second week in April. On that first Sunday immediately preceding Easter, then, all winter shows close. It may be hyperbolic, but in many ways all of Greece closes up during the Orthodox Easter week, and even in the week afterwards the country seems to run at half steam. Athens grows eerily quiet as countless thousands return to their villages, an exodus which annually strains the transportation system to its limits. I was in the tiny mountain village of Kardiani on the island of Tinos during Greek Easter week when scores of the village's Athenian relatives descended to share those holy days. Their citified clothes styles and more boisterous conversational style in that environment jarred me. But the women of Kardiani accepted the onslaught happily; after all, they had been cooking and decorating all week for just that occasion.

After the Easter celebrations a few theatres re-open their shows and continue running them until the ends of their theatre rental contracts, or until audiences diminish significantly, or until they are forced to begin preparations for a summer show, if they are to produce one. Most theatres simply close before Easter and the actors switch to rehearsals for the summer shows or simply take a vacation until next season. Major producing

organizations like the Art Theatre, National Theatre, Amphi-theatre, etc.
are expected to produce a summer show for the major festivals and,
therefore, always stop their winter productions in order to prepare their
summer ones.

The summer season, on the other hand, begins formally with the opening show at the Athens Festival or the Festival at Epidavros, around the
third week of June. This "summer season" can run three full months, or only
two to three weeks, as in the smaller festivals in Veria, Corfu, or Iraklion.
It might offer performances almost daily, as in the Athens Festival, or only
two times each week, as in the Festival at Epidavros. In general, though, the
"summer season" describes the period between June 15 and about
September 15, after which time the actors usually have a month's vacation
before preparations begin for the first show of the next winter season.

The weather determines many of these dates. Since the temperatures
in Greece can still be rather high in October (in fact I was on the island of
Hydra on Thanksgiving Day and found the temperatures perfect for eating
outdoors), asking people to attend an indoor show before the weather cools
sufficiently is foolish. Greeks are an outdoors people anyhow and naturally
prefer an activity like eating and conversing in a garden taverna to sitting
placidly in a hot theatre. Mid-October, then, has become a guidepost
around which time theatre activities might move indoors. Conversely, the
weather in spring also can be remarkably warm. Many Greeks consider late
April and May the perfect times for outdoor activities. Running a theatre
season into those months would prove almost useless since the theatres
begin to absorb the springtime heat and the preference of the Greeks is to
stay outdoors. Since almost no theatre is air conditioned, all theatre activity
after about the middle of May—with the natural exceptions of those few individualist producers who try to squeeze the turnip one more time—moves
outside.

From mid–June on nearly all productions are held in ancient outdoor
amphitheatres, theatres in parks or in other under-the-stars environments.
Usually the weather has turned bright and balmy. At times, however, as the
gods of the weather would have it, even mid–June may be too early. In the
summer of 1983, for example, June remained cold, wet and dreary—very
unusual, I was assured. The opening performance at Epidavros was the
Cyprus Theatre Company's production of *Electra* starring Irini Pappas and
directed by Michael Kakoyiannis. The show moved to Epidavros on the
Sunday before the Saturday opening but could not rehearse much in the
theatre because of the constant rain. By Friday night only a very rough
technical rehearsal for the first act had been held. Ms. Pappas had lost her
voice and tension was as thick as the fog shrouding the theatre. And still
it rained. The final rehearsal, which would also have to serve as technical
rehearsal, was cancelled, then reinstated, then cancelled again. Finally, at

about 10 P.M. the rain turned into a mist and the rehearsal was resurrected. It was a cue-to-cue rehearsal only since the use of costumes was out of the question in the rain-puddled orchestra and any request for the star to speak would have been monstrous. Besides, time was running out. So, for two excruciating hours, the actors, bundled in scarfs and heavy coats, plodded through each lighting and sound cue. Ms. Pappas whispered her lines so quietly that, even in that acoustically amazing theatre, the lighting operators in the booth 200 feet away could not hear them. Therefore, they could not initiate their cues. Kakoyiannis had to repeat each of her cue lines so that the operators could do their work. At half-past midnight I was cold and exhausted and walked back to Ligurio to a most welcome and warm bed. Rehearsal for act two had just begun.

The cast and crews stayed in that theatre until dawn when any further lighting rehearsal became impossible. The entire show still had not been rehearsed. As Dionysius would have it, though, Saturday dawned bright and warm, Pappas recovered her voice, the lighting people improvised those few cues still not rehearsed and the opening night was stunning. (See Appendix B for a first-person account of this performance.)

The weather in September still would allow outdoor shows to continue; in fact some small productions in parks do perform throughout the month. But the actors usually demand their month of vacation before rehearsals begin for the winter season shows. Therefore, the theatres close during September.

During the winter season Greek actors usually perform from Tuesday or Wednesday through Sunday with (incredibly) back-to-back performances offered on Wednesday, Saturday and Sunday. Of course this varies somewhat with each theatre, but it seems rather standard. Regular curtain times are 9:00 or 9:30 P.M. for the evening performances and 6:00 or 6:30 P.M. for the *laiki* (people's, or matinee) performances. (Rarely is there a western-style matinee at 2:00 or 2:30 P.M. That is far too close to siesta time.) Only two Greek plays which I attended started within five minutes of the announced curtain time. All the others started 10 to 45 minutes late, with the norm being around 25 minutes late. In the summer festivals there is usually only one performance which, of course, cannot begin until it becomes dark enough for the stage lighting to have effect—about 9:30 P.M. In both cases, the winter and summer seasons, spectators most often have their dinner after the show, around midnight or so. This dining time is not that different from the people's normal habits, so it all works out very nicely.

This seemingly firm schedule of performances suddenly becomes very haphazard when confronted by the usual plethora of official and unofficial Greek holidays, general strikes, sympathy strikes, transportation strikes, marches by a wide diversity of special interest groups, occasional riots, etc.

When any of these events is announced, the playgoer automatically diagnoses the march route, its proximity to the theatre to be attended, the probable disruption of the transportation system in that area of the city, the approximate degree of danger, the probability of sympathy action on the part of the actors, the cost of the ticket and the various alternatives for other entertainment that night before deciding to leave the apartment. In the case of foreigners the accuracy of this diagnosis could be even more vital. For instance, I avoided all night-time outdoor activity during Secretary of State George Schultz's visit as well as during those few days after the U.S. attacked Libya.

Facilities and Locations

Plays are produced in every conceivable space, from the best-equipped stages of the State Theatre of Northern Greece or the National Theatre to school gymnasia, from open spaces in parks or playgrounds to enormous ancient amphitheatres, from converted schoolhouses to huge, converted cinemas, from classrooms to old houses to marble quarries. Theatres and theatre spaces may be found in every major city throughout the country, but by far the vast majority are found in Athens. (See photos, pages 123 and 124.)

The largest concentration of theatres in Athens is located primarily in the very center—Kentro—of the city.[1] Athens, however, is a large and far-flung, unplanned city. Too many Athenians live too far from this central theatre district to allow easy attendance. For example, the transportation system stops at about 12:30 A.M. and the majority of the people still rely on that system for their movements about town. Many of the shows start, not at 9:00 P.M. as announced, but more like 9:30 P.M. If their announced curtain is 9:30 P.M. (not unusual) they most often actually begin nearer to 10:00 P.M. These shows, then, would not normally end until midnight or after. This is fine for those people who have cars. They simply amble to a local taverna for their dinner and loud discussions of the performance. Those without cars, however, have almost no hope of returning to their homes far from the theatre district unless they take a taxi. For many such a long taxi ride is simply too expensive.

To complicate matters further the traffic situation in central Athens is so impossible that regulations prohibit vehicles with license plates ending in an even number from entering that area on certain days of the week; those ending in an odd number naturally are permitted into the area on alternate days. Even if you did have a car, therefore, and it was not your day to be in the Kentro, you still might not attend a show for fear of being unable to get back home.

The Ancient Theatre at Philippi. Almost totally reconstructed with field stone this theatre sits in a field outside of Kavala in northern Greece. It is being set up for a performance of *Oedipus* which was canceled after 20 minutes due to a tremendous storm which can be seen on the horizon. The 500 patrons were instantly drenched by the deluge.

Ali Pasha Castle in Ioannina used as performance space. Formerly part of the barracks and stables, this space is being prepared for a performance of *Lysistrata*.

By far the largest percentage of the theatres in Athens as well as throughout the country sport the proscenium configuration. This is perhaps a logical extension of the fact that most of them are converted cinemas. I saw no full arena stage and only a few three-quarter set-ups: the Art Theatre, *I Skini* Theatre and Theatro Erevnas. The Amphi-Theatre and the Art Theatre-Plaka both have rather open stages, predominantly frontal, but allowing for a wider viewing angle than most prescenium-style theatres. All the Greek outdoor amphitheatres display, of course, that 200 degree-plus viewing area while the ancient Roman theatres hold to their usual 180 degree viewing area.

Too, almost no facility had adequate production, office or storage spaces. The State Theatre of Northern Greece and the National Theatre probably are the best endowed in these areas, but even they require substantial storage spaces scattered around their respective cities. In terms of a facility which housed all the spaces needed to prepare, mount, promote, sell and present a show, I encountered none in all my travels. Backstage space in nearly every case was woefully inadequate, as was wing space, lobby space and storage space. Even the most respected theatre in all of Greece for so many years, the Art Theatre of Karolos Koun, could claim only the bare minimal physical requirements for producing a play.

What is important and exciting, however, is that despite these sometimes overwhelming physical limitations, Greek theatre artists and their audiences continue to produce and support live theatre. Perhaps that ultimately is the attraction for me: these people love their theatre and they will do nearly anything to create it.

Agents and Finding Work

Finding acting jobs in Greece is a complicated chore. In a way each actor is his own agent, since talent agencies for these skills are rare (in fact, there were two recognized agencies in 1986). Like most endeavors in Greece, then, finding work in the theatre is almost entirely a case of whom you know and who owes you a favor. One scenario goes like this. "Suppose you are a director and you hear in a bar that Katerina is going to [cast] a role in so-and-so play. So, you have a girlfriend or the girlfriend of your son or the boyfriend of your daughter . . . so you telephone up and say, 'Hello! How are you after these ten years.' And you say 'I miss you' and things like that and you propose to me that I take person X because and because and because. And if other people propose that same person X, I say, 'Why not? I'll try it.'"[2] Another scenario goes like this: When a director has decided to produce a show, he usually sits down and makes lists of his friends whom he then calls to see if they would like to do a show. Auditions in many of these cases are not expected. Huge casting calls are relatively rare, as are auditions as the standard form of casting procedure. Many feel that too many of the open auditions which are announced are "not true" anyway— that is, casting has already taken place. It is common belief that directors cast their current lovers "many, many times . . . many, many times."

On the other side of this dilemma is an attitude among many actors that to audition means to "lose face." There "is this mentality that if they do hold auditions, actors who have already worked, they don't go. . . . They feel they shouldn't go." Therefore mostly beginning actors attend. Many actors told me flatly, "I don't audition." The possibility of public humiliation or the loss of pride is far too great. Understandably, then, auditioning as a technique to define a talent hierarchy would be abhorrent to a Greek.

Consequently, Greek actors, except for those well-known stars who in any society never need to peddle their wares, try to make the "right" contacts, to circulate among those who might be casting, to keep their ears to any available listening posts. Many maintain a kind of phone network among themselves to keep everyone "up" on the latest gossip or hearsay. Even a few of those presumably top-notch and dedicated actors with whom I worked in the bilingual theatre project confided that they were sticking close to Volonakis only because it was obvious that he would have some jobs to distribute. (In other words learning new skills was far less important than proving to the director that they were trustworthy and enthusiastic about the new project.) The typical Greek tradition of clientage-patronage was at work.

Next to pure luck and word of mouth, the next most widely used method for finding work is the frequenting of the "casting bars." Certain bars on certain nights of the week (in Exarchia the Dada Bar and in Kolonaki the Ratka Bar) are transformed into "the" places to be "seen" by producers and directors. The actors told me that it was like a huge meat market, with the clever and/or unprincipled performers (and, according to some, the talentless) sidling shamelessly up to any producer known to be looking for performers. This quality of salesmanship is often called, somewhat caustically, having "good public relations." (Others call it "prostitution.") On the other side of the equation there are also unprincipled producers who utilize their enviable positions to achieve non-theatre-related ends. Of course this kind of semi-casting-couch approach is not unknown in other countries. In Athens, however, this bar-frequenting system seems to be a major form of uniting talent with director; in fact the word *kikloma* (κικλόμα) has come to mean that circle of bar friends who help the actor find work. It is a system abhorred by a large percentage of the actors I met. On the other hand, they say, there is no other method by which actors, especially new ones, can find out what plays are being produced and by whom, if there are tryouts, where, what is required, etc. The distasteful truth is that those who play this particular game often do find work.

Because the system operates in this way, certain conveyances thought necessary in western casting circles become almost irrelevant. Resumes and photographs, while sometimes utilized, are hardly standard. Even the experienced cast of *Medea* in the spring of 1986 had to scramble for photos when the opening date for the show was announced and promotional materials had to be assembled. No one with whom I spoke, for example, had a resume or picture. Prepared and instantly available audition scenes also were rare, most auditions consisting of cold readings or, simply, interviews.

The same general system operates for playwrights. Agents are rare, if they exist at all. Playwrights, even the best ones, e.g. Kehaidis or Anagnostaki, must approach a producer and hope to convince that person to produce the script. This latter playwright has long decided that only Koun will produce her shows and so, if he refuses, she will not be produced. A new playwright, Dora Litinaki, told me that she simply took her script to Koun and asked for his help. He was impressed and offered to produce it for her.[3]

Fortunately, the Athenian theatre community is very small. Everyone soon learns the names and capabilities of everyone else. The chore of finding work, then, may not be as onerous as it may at first seem. So, even though the old-boy, the who-do-you-know? and the "casting bars" systems may be poor substitutes for an organized talent agency, they are effective enough to enable many artists their chance and many productions to reach the lights.

Most importantly, this agent-free system of matching performing talents with producers and directors seems to function with as little challenge to the Greek sense of *philotimo* as seems possible in such a competitive business. That is, one's sense of pride, of being thought incompetent in public is rather protected by a system which relies on quiet personal contact as opposed to the public rejection faced by most western actors in the audition arena. The best people may not always be hired in Greece; but by and large those who are hired have retained their own sense of worth.

Promotions

As one index of the Greek people's love for their theatre, expensive advertising in the papers and on television is not necessary to create an audience. The standard technique for reaching the theatre-going public is a barrage of huge posters, if the show is well-endowed, or, if not, a like barrage of normal-sized posters plastered on telephone poles or walls. During this recent year some expensively produced shows, like the girlie club shows at the Lido, covered entire sides of buildings with the same huge posters. The same was true on block-long construction fences. (See photo, page 128. There was an enormous amount of construction and destruction in Athens; the poster plasterers had plenty of virgin as well as already defiled territory on which to work their colorful cover-up.) Newspaper announcements in the forms of news releases, feature stories and the daily listing of the activities of each theatre were the other predominant forms of communication between theatre and audience. I never saw a prepared newspaper ad or a TV commercial for a show, nor twofers, giveaways, group

A typical method of advertising. Behind the billboards is the superstructure for the decade-long-delayed national music hall. Completion was promised by 1989.

rates, direct mail pieces, season tickets or brochures, etc. (Of course my experience may not have been universal.) But when I asked Stamatis Chondrojiannis how he advertised his plays, he said simply that he did not. The people go to plays because of the title and the star, he said. You do not have to advertise either much to get an audience.[4]

The practice, it seems, went like this: the producer sent out a phalanx of boys to put up posters a few weeks ahead of the opening. Opening nights were "papered" with friends, relatives, etc. With their good will and positive critical reviews and the appearance of a talent of star quality, the audience would build and the show "catch on." After that no advertising was necessary at all. Although it may seem like this method throws a great deal into the hands of fate, it certainly has proven to work well enough to allow scores of theatres to exist in Athens.

9. Production Elements

Difficulties in Aesthetic Judgments Across Cultural Lines

The contemporary Greek theatre attempts to utilize the whole range of theatrical devices and methods available to it through its connections with the eastern and western theatres. Therefore it maintains constant contact with devices such as the mask, oriental music forms and histrionic acting techniques. At the same time it embraces Brechtian acting methods, Stanislavskian training, the latest lighting and sound technologies, surrealistic design methods, and the like. *In toto,* then, Greek theatre today seems to behave like the theatre in any other cosmopolitan population center.

Yet the mixture of all these modern mechanisms has not jelled into a cohesive whole. The entire production schemata of the contemporary Greek theatre seems to be as fraught with contradictions as is the society from which it springs. Old and new acting styles pound the boards side by side; music sound tracks totally overwhelm the scenes which they were designed to assist; outrageous mugging and posing appear in the most realistic plays; a Brechtian *Trojan Women* premieres just a few weeks before a deeply naturalistic *Orestes,* and just after a cinematic-but-traditional *Electra.* The western observer finds himself musing, "Don't they know that they're running through laughs, that no one can see the actors under this lighting, that colors on stage should bear *some* relationship to each other?"

These observations, however, may not be valid. They may be products of a western mentality which assumes that, since Greece was the birthplace of the western tradition, then certainly it could be evaluated by the western tradition. Unfortunately, this attitude ignores the vast preponderance of Greek history which was *not* western. No part of modern Greece or any country can or should be judged on traditions established 2500 years ago.

Finding some valid and honest bases for my aesthetic judgments, then, plagued me throughout my time in Greece. In scores of plays and musicals my critical eye easily found numerous faults; however, the faults were so consistent throughout these productions that I wondered if they were products of the culture and, as such, should not have been evaluated by the standards of another culture. To complicate my confusion, many highly respected Greek theatre artists to whom I spoke agreed with my observations of their theatre's faults and furthermore refused to allow "culture" to be used as an excuse for sloppy theatre practices. "After all," they retorted, "by now there *are* international standards."[1]

That may be true, but these international standards, such as are commonly reached by the best productions of Germany, France, Great Britain, America, etc., are achieved by only a very small number of Greek productions each year. The vast majority reflect the hodge-podge of aesthetic and cultural and historical conflicts which beset the country. Moreover, the audiences who frequent these plays seem to find no difficulty in enjoying them, international standards or not. No one seems to mind the blaring sound tracks, the wild over-acting, the jerry-built sets, the thrown-together costumes, the ridiculous wigs and make-up, etc. So, who was I to find fault with the artistic accomplishments of another country's theatre when that other country was not bothered? Should I side with that minority of Greek theatre artists of international repute who find the same faults with the Greek theatre as I, or with the masses who truly are entertained by these same shows? Do I judge the whole spectrum of Greek theatre activities by those relatively few productions which achieve international standards artistically? Does this culture unconsciously judge these works according to an aesthetic of which I am not even aware? Should I believe the few who plead for guidance in advancing the state of their theatre, or the others who, once such guidance is offered, spurn it and/or manufacture countless reasons why such advice would not work in their country?

There seemed no easy way to resolve these dilemmas. With some trepidation, then, I decided to approach all aesthetic judgments from an international perspective, at the same time trying to recognize the dynamics which might color Greek performance *vis-à-vis* this standard. I chose the international standards approach for several reasons. First, the best of the Greek producers already used them. Second, educated and worldly-wise Greek practitioners and critics judged themselves by them. Third, World Market competition required that theatre which is exported to other countries achieve an international standard of performance. Fourth, Greece wished and wishes to be evaluated by contemporary western standards. This has been proven by her rushed — some would say "precipitous" — entry into the European Community and their Common Market, as well as by her wholehearted dedication to the western philosophy which posits the acquisition of material goods as the prime motivator for a full life. Fifth, television has brought western production standards into every Greek home, an influence which should eventually create a demand for higher standards on the Greek stage. Sixth, in addition to television the international festivals of music and theatre which deluge Athens in the summers cannot help but effect an increasingly demanding expectation on the part of Greek theatre-goers. Some kind of international standard already is being applied and will become increasingly difficult to ignore in the years ahead.

Interestingly, and sadly, the majority of the educated Greeks with whom I had contact outside of my direct research admitted that they loved the theatre but rarely went "because it's so bad." I was even asked to act as a kind of advance man, culling through the available productions and recommending those which might be worth seeing. It was obvious that these educated Greeks were becoming divorced from their countrymen in many ways, one of which was their higher level of sophistication as theatre-goers. This growing compartmentalization struck me as just one facet of a much larger dilemma which faces the entire culture.

Nearly every Greek parent is willing to sacrifice the entire family for the sake of one son's education in the west. When the son returns, however, (if he returns) his expectations of the Greek society may be so far removed from the actuality that conflicts seem inevitable. Far too many return to their native land only to leave again in frustration when they are unable to budge the system out of its age-old ruts. I heard of a Greek physician from Patras who traveled to America in order to study the latest techniques for the treatment of cancer. He returned to his native city to establish a clinic geared to his newly acquired expertise. After only three years he fled back to America because the local medical establishment could not accept his new concepts. This is hardly an isolated incident. A theme threading its way through many conversations was the acceptance of the fact that talented Greeks in a wide variety of fields flee Greece. Females educated in the west seem especially susceptible to a kind of reverse culture shock. Accustomed to the relatively equal treatment females receive in England or America as compared to Greece, and not accustomed to being refused work or acceptance simply because they are female, they often yearn for a return to those former days.[2]

This superior education, then, which is ardently sought by so many Greeks, colors their cultural and aesthetic expectations. To returning Greeks, other Greeks become "stupid," Athens "terrible," religion "a facade," the country "hopeless," and the theatre "not very good."[3]

This support for mediocre theatre by the peasant class and the almost total lack of support for that same theatre by the more privileged class disturbed me for some reason. Perhaps I did not expect this seemingly unfair lack of support from the more sophisticated—it seemed disloyal. I must admit, though, that even with boundless enthusiasm for my research, I, too, became so discouraged by the seemingly omnipresent problems in Greek productions that I found it extremely difficult to attend any shows after

about four months of theatre-going. I could almost determine by the promotional posters what to expect in the way of plot, acting, and setting.

Nevertheless, I would like to present my evaluations of each production element as they appeared in scores of shows which I witnessed over
11 months of playgoing. After each I would like to follow with some possible
cultural or practical explanations which might illuminate the problem or
process. I hope that any of my Greek theatre friends who might read this
section will understand that I present these judgments with the utmost love
and respect.

Elements of Production

Acting. The most obvious difference between western and Greek
contemporary theatre was the acting style. In show after show—but by no
means universally—the Greek actors seemed to "perform" rather than act.
At times shameless over-acting, strident posing, obviously dropping
character to "check out" the audience, producing passion for passion's sake,
continual and, I assume, purposeful upstaging, and total lack of ensemble
took precedence over the play and demeaned an intelligent audience. Far
too often lines were taken out of the play and "performed" directly to the
audience with a "see how clever I can be" attitude. Egotism seemed to run
rampant, especially in the leading roles. "Giving" stage seemed a concept
that the actors not only did not know but also worked very hard to reverse.
Many plays seemed artistic free-for-alls in which the loudest and most
passionate-looking won the applause. For example, the national musical
comedy star Aliki Voujiouklaki dropped character throughout the first act
of *The Merry Widow* in order to gesture angrily to the follow spot operator.
She even carried on angry conversations with other actors concerning the
problem, whatever it was, when she was not directly in the scene. Tania
Savopoulou, after delivering a moving, tearful speech of Linda Loman in
Death of a Salesman, looked for me in the first row to see if I had appreciated
that particular performance. The young actor playing Petruchio in *Taming
of the Shrew* posed and strutted to the audience so much that I thought he
was in a fashion show. The bombast and grossly exaggerated acting of some
roles in the municipal theatre of Ioannina's *The Inspector General,* or in the
role of the supervisor in the Rialto Theatre production of *The Good Soldier
Schweik,* as well as in other productions far too numerous to mention here
seemed the acting style most used, taught and appreciated by the majority
of Greek audiences and theatre artists.

There may have been several reasons for this particular approach to
acting. First, and most importantly, representational acting traditions have
not been the norm in Greece. Rather, the presentational forms, from

ancient tragedy to Karaghiozis, have better reflected the temperament of the people. The most popular form of theatre is the *epitheorisis*, the satiric musical revue, almost entirely presentational.

Second, the teachers in drama schools very often were older actors whose careers had been built upon those kinds of techniques. As I was told by their students, much of the acting training consisted of studying the old techniques of their teachers. In other words, they learned to perform a moment just as their teachers had years ago. At times I wondered if the Greek stage had unwittingly preserved the remnants of a true nineteenth century acting style.

Third, even those who might have assimilated from whatever source a basically "truthful" approach, that is, an approach that required an honest motivation for each moment and an expression of that moment in the exact terms it required, seemed forced to fight for their place on stage. The honest and truthfully motivated actor seemed out of place in a cast of ranting ones. And since Greek actors are not known for their propensity for sharing the stage, since every moment seemed a competition for the attention of the audience, these relatively quiet players were forced to play "up to" the level of their competition.

Fourth, this apparent need to attract attention seemed to lead to the lack of ensemble playing so common in Greek plays. Greek individualism, or group anarchy, whichever you choose, made tightly knit exchanges nearly impossible. The plays devolved into hundreds of individual vignettes in which each actor performed primarily for the approbation of the crowd. It often seemed like an entire cast of young "hopefuls" was frantically trying to gain audience recognition at the expense of everyone else on stage.

Fifth, repeated routines or gestures to indicate particular emotions may suggest that those activities had been taught (by direction or example) as the "proper" way to express those emotions. Frustration was often delineated like this: the so-affected character clenched his fists tightly, strode directly downstage facing the audience, then gritted his teeth while taking and exhaling a huge noseful of air. Confused anger was displayed like this: the person so afflicted paced loudly, head down, breathing very heavily, hands clasped behind his back, loudly slapping the top of one into the palm of the other.

Sixth, "checking out" the audience was almost endemic. At almost every first entrance the actor came directly downstage, and made obvious and delighted contact with the audience. This occurred in every kind of show, from musical comedy to the most naturalistic drama, and not only at the start. Dancers during *Woman of the Year* displayed great physical skill and intensity during the dances. Immediately afterward, however, they looked at the audience for approval, dropped character and even talked amongst each other about the condition of the floor that night, etc.

Many of these attitudes and devices are bred into the system. Star actors who also acted as the producers of their own star vehicles sometimes purposely surround themselves with actors of lesser talents so that they might shine the greater. Balanced casts, therefore, were extremely rare.

Cooperation, the center piece of modern theatre practice, is very difficult to create or discover in Greece. The culture posits staunch individualism and universal suspicion as two behavioral touchstones. Each major artist, then, in eons-old Greek fashion, is suspicious of each other major artist's talents and/or suggestions at the same time as he is convinced that *his* talents and suggestions are superior. And God help those supporting actors who happen to receive more favorable reviews than the star. One illustration here should suffice.

In one of the three Arthur Miller plays that opened in the 1985–1986 season the leading man, a widely respected comic, decided to prove his mettle as a tragic actor. Unfortunately, the particular mix of talents, director and setting fell short of expectations. The woman playing his wife, however, won many rave reviews. This public humiliation for the star turned him into a vindictive and impossible stage partner. In a tearful and exasperated interview the actress told me that he refused to speak with her offstage, and at times even onstage. He altered the dialogue to make her appear stupid, or to create a laugh at a most inappropriate time. Sometimes he answered her questions in such a way that there could be no further dialogue. Sometimes he refused to answer her questions at all. Once he even left the stage in the middle of a scene.[4]

This lack of cooperation, in this case particularly virulent, seems to apply equally to actors versus actors, actors versus directors and directors versus designers. In fact, is there was one emotional keynote which summarized nearly all the theatres I visited, it was a sense of universal suspicion which made cooperation at least hesitant. In close second place was the feeling of constant challenge, an eternal testing of authority in both directions. At one regional theatre the director told his underlings to do some little thing. This direction resulted in a long and heated discussion about the work to be performed and the method by which it was to be accomplished. One of the men stormed out of the office. I queried the director about this kind of behavior. He assured me that it happened all the time, that nothing was meant particularly by the worker's insubordination, that the job would be done, and that the next time they met it would seem as if nothing untoward had happened. Indeed, nothing had. He smiled, "It's the Greek way."[5]

The widely accepted "passion" of all Mediterranean people is exhibited daily in the streets of Athens or in the tavernas on Kalymnos. Every situation seems to elicit life-or-death emotional responses. To expect Greek actors to produce highly controlled and disciplined, made-for-British-television performances in a society in which control and discipline are rare occurrences would be pure nonsense.

One is tempted, therefore, to discount the productions of the contemporary Greek theatre as fault-ridden to the extreme. That would be unfair. Even though the vast majority of the shows I saw exhibited most of these faults, a healthy minority displayed truly significant accomplishments. And in so doing they compromised almost all of the supposed "explanations" of these inadequacies which I offered above. The ensemble work in Συμφορά απο το Πολύ Μυαλό by director Vouyiatzis was remarkable. It was even more remarkable in Karolos Koun's magical *Oresteia*. The control of the realistic elements of *Orestes* evoked an acting style of which Stanislavsky himself would have been proud. Russian-born Greek director Giorgos Sevastikoglou created a leading character who easily could have been written by Tennessee Williams. Volonakis' *Oedipus* was extremely disciplined; Εν Βρασμό Ψήχης actors exhibited a wonderful sharing of the stage; the two-person Κάλυ Νήχτα, Μητέρα could not have been more more realistic from an acting standpoint.

One further point warrants comment. The most natural acting sensibilities of Greek actors seem precisely in tune with their beloved ancient dramas. I saw acting students at the National Theatre portray difficult classical characters with an ease that was astounding. The acting I saw in many productions of ancient tragedy plumbed the depths of a people and its traditions. The emotional and cultural attachments of these people to their sacred literature proved at times overwhelming. Just as there is a profound connection between the English and their Shakespeare, the Irish and their Beckett, the Americans and their musical comedy, so too is there one between the Greeks and their tragedies. It may be one reason director Jules Dussin said that, what "works" in the Greek theatre of today is the ancient plays acted in those wonderful ancient theatres.[6]

Greek acting, then, can be wonderful under certain conditions: first, if it appears in an ancient play; second, if there is an extremely powerful and respected director who can texture and proportion the individual roles (directors like Kakoyiannis, Dussin, Volonakis come to mind); third, if the group has been held together by a common artistic bond over a long period of time (groups like Koun's and Vouyiadzis' come to mind). The secret in nearly all of these cases seems clearly to be the director.

Directing. If the role of the modern director is to coordinate all the myriad elements of play production toward a cohesive end, then the play director in Greece must face one of the most formidable challenges in all of theatre. In addition to the cultural obstacles he must surmount—rabid individualism, suspicion, belief in conspiracy, unwillingness to be seen as wrong or wronged in public, etc.—the director faces many practical obstacles to a full realization of his production concept, obstacles over which he seems to have little control. For example, the set design, when there is a design, does not match the style of the show; music scores overpower the scene; colors in set and costume clash horribly; scenery is so badly constructed that any hope of verisimilitude vanishes; color media in the lighting instruments draws attention away from important spaces and moments, etc. The result of these and other problems is a general lack of cohesion, of unity in the majority of Greek productions. To the general audience, however, the most obvious of the elements which prevent a sense of whole-ness is the discrepancy in acting styles.

Acting styles vary wildly. Some of the older actors, especially those who have been civil servants for many years in state-supported institutions, adhere firmly to the elocutionist-flavored styles of early in the century. Even though some of them may also teach those same styles to the younger performers, these latter do become familiar with the more realistic styles of modern theatre practice. Unfortunately, these styles are mutually exclusive; seeing them next to each other on the same stage is disconcerting. The National Theatre's wonderful and creative production of Strindberg's *Ghost Sonata*, directed by Yiannis Houvardas, was marred primarily by the juxtaposition of only two "old-timers" with a cast of talented and controlled younger performers. These two had been cast before the director was consulted, not unusual in civil service–type companies. Their poses, well-established "bits" of business, their slavering when indicating anger conflicted with the otherwise natural and honest acting all around them. The director told me that, work and harangue as he might, he could not alter their performances in a significant way. Moreover, he admitted, not only that this acting problem was a continual hassle, but also that *every* decision made during the preparation of this production "was a fight."[7]

There were other examples. In a solid production of *All My Sons* a truly beautiful monologue delivered by another of these old-timers was compromised by a truly beautiful, flowing, graceful and altogether out-of-character exit immediately afterward. Of course the exit received as much applause as the speech would have. In a generally lovely and tightly directed production of *A Flea in Her Ear,* one young actor played broadly but within the farce style, never losing the sense that he indeed was this character in this ridiculous situation. The same proved true for the young maid, a delightful young actress. Conversely, the male star, a truly wonderful comic, played to the audience as often as possible, making his "performance" of more importance than the role or the play. Even the otherwise wonderful leading lady of that theatre delivered many lines as if they were lines in a vaudeville turn, actually making visual contact with the front rows and smiling at the cleverness of her own lines. The contrast in acting styles confused me; I was not certain if this was to be a vaudeville rendition of the play — certainly a valid approach — or a normal farce rendition in which every character truly believed that she or he was a real person in a real situation.

A little later I had lunch with Greek-American director, translator and professor John Chiolis. He explained that this production was in its second year. Its first year was so successful that the producing organization, Theatro Porta, decided to remount it for a second year. The original production had been tight, controlled, unified. With time, however, the actors apparently had added more and more of the traditional routines and stylistic tendencies so that the current performance was out of key with the original intention. "There's not a Greek actor alive," he ruefully added, "who, with time, will not ruin his performance."[8] Of course such alterations of a play's performances over a long run are not unknown throughout the world. In Greece, however, if my perceptions are accurate, the potential for such alterations lies very near the surface and very near opening night.

Such stylistic conflicts are complicated by other inherently Greek situations. At the Theatro Erevnas, for example, the leading male and the director and the owner are all the same man, Dimitris Potamitis. This man sells the tickets, produces and directs the shows and stars in them. When he appeared in the American play *The War At Home*, he often was not "in" a scene but was still on stage. In those moments of "non-active involvement," he did not maintain character, but constantly looked over the audience, perhaps counting them or "checking out" their responses. Maybe it was during those times that he did not see that the woman playing the mother was operating at a decibel and activity level more appropriate to a Marx Brothers farce rather than to the primarily dramatic level of the play. In many other cases a star who still has not claimed his own theatre space may rent one and hire a director to direct him or her in a star vehicle. In most cases, I am told, these liaisons work harmoniously because the star will hire a person she or he respects and the two people probably will have a history of cooperative efforts. On the other hand one can imagine those confrontations which inevitably occur during any rehearsal process in which the actor and director disagree on some major or minor point. In this case the director has even less control over the resolution of this situation because the leading actor is paying his salary. Often a director will cast his wife or lover as a leading or *the* leading character. One can only surmise the various kinds of compromises which are made on both sides of this equation during the preparation of a show.

Many directors complained about the laziness and bad attitudes of the actors, some about the ridiculous rules of the Actor's Syndicate which made concentrated rehearsals of sufficient duration impossible. One regional theatre director whispered angrily under his breath, "They want to rehearse less and always complain about getting paid more." One well-known Cypriot director shook his head for long moments while he controlled his rage over union-mandated breaks. "By the time they look at their watches to see when the break is coming, then take their break, then report back ten minutes late, you have lost a half-hour rehearsal. Then there's the lunch break which always lasts twice as long as it should. At the end of a day you had maybe three really good hours of rehearsal." One German-Greek director fought daily battles with the union representative who required that he stop rehearsals for the required rest periods, regardless of the particular accomplishments occurring at that moment. "Impossible!" the director hoarsely shouted to me when we adjourned to the hallway. "This is impossible! I will never work here again!"[9]

Perhaps the most significant factor affecting the quality of directing in Greece is the fact that there is no formal training ground for the craft. Nearly all directors in Athens are former stage managers or actors who had worked only in Greece. (Of course it is not unusual for people in these positions to aspire to and actually achieve the position of director. With only the Greek stage as a training arena, however, many of these seem insufficiently prepared to create the cohesion, the sense of proportion and balance and focus that are the common goals of directors elsewhere.) Conversely, those few directors who had studied and worked in countries such as England, Germany, America and Russia seemed able to create a balanced and cohesive whole in spite of the problems intrinsic to the task of directing in Greece. My guess is that these few men had learned the primacy of unified productions and had acquired some expertise in achieving it. It was the one quality which clearly delineated the work of Greek directors who had had international experience from those who had none.

Once again I must state clearly that, although directing in Greece must be incredibly frustrating, the work of many directors was outstanding. Houvardas, Volonakis, Kakoyiannis, Vouyiadzis, Papjiorjiou, Koun, Michailidis, although not all in exactly the same class, all produce outstanding work. Some of these men work constantly in international arenas, some in films as well as theatre. The important point is that they comprise a very small minority of the directors available for Greek projects. The vast majority of the directors do not compare favorably at all.

Scene Design. We sat in the newly painted renovated cinema looking at her setting. It consisted of three free-hanging panels decorated with various three-dimensional attachments for texture. On the open stage and under dreadfully inadequate lights it looked at best sparse. She was introduced to me as Rena Geotoyiadi, "the best" designer in Greece, although I was certain she did not feel that way. (The superlative is nearly always attached to the playwright, each actor and every artistic contributor involved in shows about to open.) She said that there was no training for designers in Greece and most of them studied in foreign countries, predominantly

Italy. Too often when they are hired to design in Greece, the producer has no idea of the cost of settings and, so, gives them almost nothing to work with. Her present set was an example.[10] Most other theatre workers believed the same.

Actually a few courses in scene design did exist scattered in various art departments of various schools. The head of the Music School at the Odeon of Athens, Kostis Livadeas, scoffed at the idea that no training existed. The School of Fine Arts and Architecture, he said, offered a full year's worth of courses.[11] Even at that it seemed clear that truly talented and determined designers would have had to leave the country to acquire substantial training. The head of the Drama School at the National Theatre, Thassos Lignatis, admitted the dearth of design training in Greece, exemplified by the fact that the very first book on theatre design written in the Greek language had just appeared in 1986. In view of this dire need he planned to establish a full design program within the Drama School at the National Theatre.[12] What may be important here is that few theatre people knew about the availability of design courses in Greece and those who were professional designers almost all received their training outside of the country. With this kind of second-class citizenship allotted to design, one might readily understand the predominance of inadequate scenery and costume design in the midst of some vividly beautiful ones.

For every beautiful design, though, there were many which looked stitched together, or poverty stricken, or incomplete. A few reminded one of the local eighth grade class play. Colors in costume, set and lighting often clashed; costume designs did not seem to evoke the characteristics of the persons wearing them; attention to finishing detail was rare.

The best of them, however, could appear on any professional stage in the world. The *Ghost Sonata* set, the *Electra* set at Epidavros, the incredibly simple but effective set for Koun's *Oresteia,* the perfectly basic set for Volonakis' *Oedipus,* the impressive sets for the Orpheas revue, the surprisingly evocative and detailed set for *Uncle Vanya* by the Kalamata theatre and more proved that Greece has the talent and construction abilities to create stunning visual theatre. Perhaps, as someone said, there should be less theatre in Greece; that would make it better. Right now the truly talented people are spread over too many theatres vying for their contributions. A world class actor might appear in third class costumes; two extremely talented dancers may be lost in a cast of also-rans; a fine director might work with impossible talents; a fine show might be abysmally lit. Ideally, the National Theatre should have provided just such an amalgamation of the best talents in the country; unfortunately, the ideal and the reality have evolved in quite a different way.

Interestingly there was no financial aid given to any student who wished to enter the design fields. Conversely, each student who successfully passed the acting auditions for the Drama Schools at the National Theatre and at the State Theatre in Saloniki received full financial aid — that is, the entire three years were free, courtesy of the Greek government.

Lighting Design. Tom Stone sat on his patio with a scotch comfortably in his hand. He was an expatriate New Yorker living and teaching in northern Greece at Anatolia College. He had spent most of his life in the New York theatre, eventually stage managing and designing lights for various Broadway shows. He had just finished a lighting design for the Greek Lyric Opera and stated flatly, "There is no lighting design in Greece."[13]

The instruments and control equipment generally were antiquated, the methods out-dated, the personnel ill-informed. Like most of the behind-the-scenes jobs, lighting personnel probably walked in off the street looking for work of any kind. Sometimes they were placed in their positions by *koumbaroi* (κουμβάροι — godfathers) who were obligated to help their nieces and nephews find work. The production secretary for the National Theatre, Stella Zografou, admitted that there was no training for these kinds of workers in Greece. So, their ranks were filled from a wide variety of sources. All training came on-the-job.[14] She did not describe at that time a scenario which I soon learned commonly evolved from this inauspicious beginning: these new workers soon became integrated into the civil service establishments, grew in importance in their positions, then presumed to fight others who knew better, i.e. Tom Stone, when it came to designing and mounting lighting. He said that it took a few shows for him to prove to the Lyriki Skini electricians that he did, indeed, know more than they.

Given the dearth of talent in this area, it was surprising and delightful to find productions in which great care was lavished on the lighting design. Again, the National Theatre's *Ghost Sonata*, the State Theatre of Northern Greece's *Balcony*, the Kalamata theatre group's *Uncle Vanya*, Koun's *Oresteia*, and several others all exhibited exceptional lighting artistry.

Make-Up Design. To my knowledge the only make-up training afforded Greek actors takes place in a few of the actor training schools. In many cases, if interviews with the students from these schools accurately reflect the greater picture, this training consists of applying make-up as the older actors did it. There seems to have been no discussion of theory or of more advanced techniques.

This story was believable to me after sitting through scores of performances. Make-up applications were often too heavy, far too obviously "applied" to achieve some sort of effect. Wigs seemed to be over-used, achieving perhaps the right color and/or stylistic look at the expense of believability. It struck me that any of the more difficult applications, such as ancient men or haggard women, probably would have worked in huge amphitheatres or in the few large theatres found in Athens. The winter theatres in general, however, are almost all relatively small. The attempts to capture with make-up characteristics which could not be captured by the acting and costuming often did not succeed.

As in all of these production elements, some few shows revealed impeccable make-up artistry, indicating again that fully competent make-up artists can be found in the contemporary Greek theatre.

Sound Design and Music. If there was one production element which almost always achieved the level of artistry, it was the music. In production after production I was amazed at the creativity and sensitivity of the composers. In Greece nearly each show included an original score, some of which were even performed live. Composers have been creating such scores for years now and have become quite adept at it. When prerecorded sound effects and mood music were used, however, sometimes these designs were not as proficient or imaginative. To some extent that situation might have been the fault of the equipment rather than the design. In some cases Greek theatre people can legitimately cry "poor" as an excuse when the sound reproduction is inadequate. The generally under-financed independent theatres rarely can afford the high quality systems usually required to produce top-notch theatre sound.

When the production could afford quality sound equipment, and when one of the better composers was involved, and when the director found the right balance between this sound and the sound of the dialogue, the aural accompaniment to the show was often stunning. However, the overwhelming fault with nearly every sound cue was its disconcertingly loud volume. It seemed standard that each sound effect and background mood music cue as well as each microphone—if one was used—operated at incredibly high volumes. During those moments actors had to shout and still could not be heard; music, gorgeous as it might have been, became the primary theatrical stimulus.

To be fair this circumstance was so wide-spread as to be almost universal. There may have been some cultural quirk which explained this seeming imbalance which I did not perceive. My first attempts at explanations assumed a high decibel-level living environment, which anyone who has lived in Athens would not doubt affirm. It seemed possible that only an exaggerated sound cue would be perceived as dramatically contributive. But these volume levels were standard throughout the country, even in quiet little villages. Perhaps the village mentality required over-statement in order for the sound to "get across." Perhaps the composer simply argued that no one could hear his creations. Whatever the explanation(s) the westerner had better be prepared to adjust to rock-and-roll level sound tracks when she or he enters the winter theatres of Athens. As with each of the other production elements, some sound tracks were produced and played back at levels more sympathetic to western ears. Although that may have evoked a more positive response from these western spectators, it does not mean that as a consequence they were also intrinsically more effective to Greek ears.

Contemporary Greek theatre production is fraught with the same ills, confusions, contradictions, ineptitude and genius as its country. A small percentage of its productions attain international production standards while the vast majority wallow in varying degrees of mediocrity and worse. The quality of production elements even within individual shows varies wildly. Cohesiveness, ensemble, cooperation, rarely witnessed in the society also are rarely witnessed on the stage. The exceptions, which prove Greek capabilities in all of these areas, seem to center on productions of ancient plays in ancient theatres and on the work of a few directors whose strength of personality and artistic vision is sufficient to mold the disparate forces around them into beautiful wholes.

10. Theatre Training

As of 1986 serious training in scenic and costume design had just commenced, and that on a small scale. To my knowledge there existed no formal training of any substance in make-up or lighting design nor in directing. Yet there were around 40 schools of acting in Athens alone, one of which was fully subsidized by the government. In addition there were scores of private teachers whose task consisted of preparing young students to enter these drama schools.

This imbalanced state of affairs may be partly cultural. Perhaps the natural predilection of Greeks for highly visible individual performance will always favor training in acting rather than in those other, less noticeable fields. Too, actors, with the possible exception of the director, are the most independent of all a production's personnel, a circumstance no doubt preferred by the Greek psyche. All other production area heads must accept subordinate roles. The further one is from the star actor level, the further one is from independence and the ability to express one's individual personality, that *sine qua non* of the Greek character. Perhaps the fathomless desire of actors to form their own theatre companies so that they can star in their own productions is one measure of this proposition. Perhaps the desire of directors to do the same but from a directorial point of view further supports that assumption. True or not, the accomplishments of the professional theatre in Greece and the composition of the training schools there seem curiously connected.

Of the many schools in Athens which claim to train students for lives in the acting profession only two remain generally respected: the Koun school and the National Theatre school. Unfortunately, with the recent death of Koun and the disappearance of his unique leadership it seems that only the National will stand above the competition. Nearly everyone understands that the vast majority of the other schools exist more to provide incomes for their teachers than to actually prepare the students to enter the profession. Unfortunately, the continued existence of such mediocre schools deeply disturbs many theatre people in the city. By their very existence these schools encourage mediocrity and puff up their charges with unrealistic dreams about the theatre world, state their critics. Supporters of these schools, however, could point to the fact that as a group these ill-considered drama schools *do* manage to present to the diploma-granting committee several students each year, some of whom carve out careers in the professional theatre.

If a young person wishes to become an actor in Greece he must first reside in Athens. With the exception of the three programs in Saloniki (in 1983) all other acting training programs exist in the capital city. If the prospective student is truly dedicated, he probably will take private acting lessons during his high school years in order to gain experience and to prepare for the annual drama school auditions.

Until 1985 these auditions were held separately by each school. Students would trek from one to the other, probably starting at the top — the National School of Drama or the Karolos Koun Drama School — and keep auditioning for less and less competent institutions until they were accepted. Recently, however, the government mandated combined auditions — that is, all schools are now represented at one large audition. The most talented students could be offered admission at several of these and, if that occurred, could have the rare opportunity to choose.[1] (Kostis Livadeas, head of the Music School at Odeon Athenon, also told me that all high schools were newly required to teach drama, but no one else seemed to know of this rule. He may have been referring to the stillborn plans of the Youth Ministry which tried to establish recreation centers and amateur groups in schools throughout the country. If he was correct, though, it was a development which I did not pursue.)

In past years approximately 100 students auditioned for the 12 to 15 openings in the National Theatre school. In 1985 that school accepted ten Greeks and two Cypriots out of the 300 which auditioned.[2] With the recently instituted combined tryouts policy that number may soon reach a total of 500 scrambling for those 15 openings at the National, a like number at Koun's school and various numbers in all of these other organizations. Of course there are significant reasons to hustle for these top two schools. At the National, besides the training which is generally considered the best in Greece (perhaps by default), each student who graduates with an "A" average is automatically offered a contract with that theatre.[3] Koun's Art Theatre hires its own Drama School graduates almost exclusively. Those who are not hired there still may claim to possess a diploma from one of the top schools in the country, although even that is no guarantee of work in a field horribly overflowing with new graduates each year. Of the ten who graduated with such diplomas in 1982, as one example, only four have made career starts in the theatre.[4]

In 1986 the newly configured auditions consisted of three phases. In the first phase the students presented a monologue and a poem of their choice. It was relatively easy, the head of the National School of Drama told me, to select from that original group of 300 the 40 who would be allowed to continue with the audition. In the second phase each prospective student wrote an essay giving his opinion of a play in which he had acted or which he had seen. In the third phase they were tested for natural acting ability, movement and rhythm, improvisation and singing. Finally, they faced an interview. (The auditions for the less-respected schools were considerably easier.) Twelve were accepted at the National, perhaps another ten at Koun's school. The others probably scattered their talents among the 40-odd schools operating in Athens. Those fortunate enough to be selected by the National attended at no cost; some schools like the Odeon Athenon offered ten scholarships from private sources. But at most schools the students paid normal instructional fees.

An acting diploma necessitates three full years of study. Classes last eight hours each day (1 P.M. to 9 P.M. at the National and various hours at all the other schools), five days a week (although other schools may work on Saturday too) for eight to nine months, October to June. The government stipulates which academic and practical skills must be taught: acting, voice, dramaturgy, history of the theatre (which includes drama), history of Greek literature and interpretation, music, movement-dance, and stage techniques, e.g. sitting, crossing, sword fighting. Each institution, of course, addresses these topics in its own way. Lily Kokkodis, a graduate of the National School and now an actress in feature films, outlined her program there in the following way:

1. Acting: primarily scene work
2. Technical lessons:
    a. Dance: ballet, modern, historical, physical exercises
    b. Improvisation
    c. Tragedy or pantomime
    d. Swordfighting and other forms of stage violence
3. Theoretical
    a. Dramaturgy
    b. History of the Theatre
    c. Modern Greek literature
    d. Basic music theory and flute playing
4. Make-up and masks
5. Voice placement[5]

Actors from other schools admitted that they had not received instruction in some of these—in one case no dance was offered, in another only ballet and yoga, in another no stage violence other than rhythmical sword-fighting, in another no music theory. In one the vocal production class consisted of three years of singing "ma—may—mee—mo—moo" at various pitches. It seemed that adherence to the strict requirements of the government-mandated series of skills to be taught depended on the extent to which some institutions could stretch the intent of those requirements. Even acting instruction varied considerably. One actress cried that she had never received any criticism after performing her scenes except silly non sequiturs like "Don't let the audience see the bottoms of your shoes."[6] Others did receive criticism but in some cases this came in the form of demonstrations of how to perform it "better," in this case meaning exactly like the instructor. Another bitterly intoned, "It didn't matter how you did anyway. You only got jobs from the union if you belonged to the Communist Party."[7]

It was inspiring, however, to hear of the dedication of the serious students. Most of them who did not have to work at outside jobs started their day at 9 or 10 A.M., working on their scenes and studies on their own until classes formally began at 1 to 3 P.M. Many stayed after classes ended at 9 or 10 P.M. for more rehearsal. They helped each other, shared the few books they could borrow or buy and badgered the teachers to offer extra instruction. In one case the students in one class even decided among themselves to get rid of a teacher who was not teaching them anything. They were successful and concentrated on learning from the teacher who *was* exceptional in his abilities. The actress smiled when recounting this story. It was, she smiled, "a little *anarchia*."[8] Many teachers, too, deserve plaudits for extraordinary dedication.

Evdokeia Xatziioannou told me that the teachers at the Odeon of Pireaus often came to school on Saturdays and Sundays to conduct extra lessons. The instructors at the Baiaki Drama School, many of whom were paid little or nothing for any of their services (with the exception of bus or car expenses) often stayed with the students until midnight.[9] Thus, in some cases individual attention and absolute dedication to the task at hand may supplant in some degree those more expert contributions found in the major schools.

Interestingly, many of the students in the less-respected drama schools also are students at the university or are working part-time. Perhaps this parallels the well-known western phenomenon of studying one subject for the sake of one's parents, and another for one's own sake. Even in Greece parents are often thought to be "in the Middle Ages. They think that if you study in the theatre you are a prostitute."[10] Xatziioannou's parents would not allow her to attend the National Theatre school where she was accepted because it required a total time commitment. Since the family was in financial straits, she had to work. Therefore, she attended a second-rate school which allowed her free mornings so that she could hold a part-time job while attending school. Athena Pappa was within one course of finishing a pre-law degree when she decided to try acting. She told me that many students in these peripheral drama schools concurrently attended acting classes as well as classes at the university.[11] Since the Greek universities operate on the European model, that is, attendance at lectures is not mandatory, it would seem possible to accomplish this dual task.

Aside from the owners of the small private schools, most acting teachers in private or state institutions receive little or no salary. Normally these people are working performers who are expected to contribute their expertise to the theatrical education of the upcoming generation. There were 18 of them at the National in the year of my research and perhaps a few hundred throughout the system. Even the Director of the National Theatre School of Drama, the gentle and hospitable Thassos Lignatis, received a pittance for his full-time work.[12]

A former President of the National Theatre, Lignatis accepted his present position because no one else wanted it. A dramaturg and working theatre critic, he recognized many of the faults in the system and seemed to be working to improve them. He already had proposed a three-phase program to create training programs in other necessary theatre fields at the National. The first would be in design since there still was no substantive training available. Most of the current Greek designers, he said, came from the schools of graphic arts, painting or architecture. Secondly, he wished to create a program of study for theatre critics and producers, two other fields which had not been touched. Last would be a program for teachers of theatre who would eventually join the faculties of every elementary and high school in the country. Like most Greeks Lignatis had not heard of a plan to make mandatory the teaching of theatre in Greece's schools, but he supported the idea vociferously.[13]

In any case at the end of the first two years of acting training the students present the best of those scenes on which they had been working all year — perhaps three out of the nearly fifteen on which they had worked. The final year students star in one-act plays or substantial portions of full-length plays. If a particular class consists of more females than males, the males are often expected to help the females prepare their scenes. This may result in a particular male appearing in a dozen scenes. If necessary, students from the lower grade levels may be asked to help out.

It is almost a foregone conclusion that no one fails the third year exams. In the first or second year exams, though, some do fail and either drop out of school or, under special circumstances (at the National) are permitted to repeat the entire year's work. If they fail again then they are dropped. (Interestingly, the student who may be wonderful at the theoretical exams — theatre history and the like — but inadequate in acting, is likely to be dropped. The opposite is not true. Students who have little talent as actors, then, but exceptional talents as historians, simply have no other training ground available.) In addition to the acting scenes the student must prepare a scene which exhibits his progress in the technical courses, i.e. sword-fighting, dance, singing, etc. Also the assembled faculty conducts oral exams covering each of the theoretical areas, an exam that may be extremely difficult or extremely easy, depending on the school.

The Committee which sits on the final examination-performances of third year students is formed out of the office of the Ministry of Culture. This committee normally consists of working actors, directors, teachers, a representative of the union and a representative of the Ministry. This seven-member committee sits on the exams of all third year students regardless of the school involved. The students who pass are eligible to become members of the actor's union. (In past years graduation from a drama school automatically made them members of the union, once they signed the register. Currently, however, a new actor must work for about two months before being allowed to actually become a member of the union. The process is called "gathering stamps" (*ika* — ίκα) referring to the stamps which prove that one has actually worked at an acting job.) Even joining the union, though, does not guarantee them work. It does, however, make them eligible for union-initiated jobs (providing they are in the Party, according to some), and it allows them to join the 80 percent of each cast which must be union members. And it certainly allows them to begin accumulating their own *kikloma,* that circle of "casting bar" friends who will help them find work.

In Saloniki a few years ago a school director tried to make the Drama School at the State Theatre of Northern Greece a model of progressive theatre training. Theodoros Terzopoulous, a magnetic, energetic and very intense teacher who was trained by the Berliner Ensemble, tried to import for his school the latest developments in European theatre training schools. His efforts, however, seemed beset by obstacles. He found his state theatre organization stodgy and unresponsive to the realities of world theatre. He decried the conservatism of the government and, by extension, the State Theatre which, for example, withdrew a student production of a Brecht play as too *avant garde.* He bristled when describing the theatre's denial of his budget requests and for increased classroom space. Only half of his students, for example, could fit into his largest classroom at one time. He decried the one cassette recorder and 300 books stored in a dust bin which heretofore had been considered sufficient equipment for the needs of the whole school. His pleadings for decent video and exercise equipment as well as for a well-stocked theatre library went unheeded.[14] Apparently these frustrations finally overwhelmed Terzopoulous. In 1986 he was in Athens directing.

His approach while he operated in Saloniki, however, may be worth noting. It started with the auditioning process. After the usual auditions in singing, Greek tragedy and contemporary Greek drama, those who remained in the selection process were asked to perform certain tests articulated by Grotowski and Strasberg, as well as to display skills in dance, mime, music and any other performing skill which they might have had. Terzopoulous then added testing in spontaneity with images, rhythm and objects. He ended with exercises which examined the ability of each performer to work in an ensemble.

In addition to the rather small core of teachers in the major disciplines, Terzopoulous imported numerous instructors for more specialized training. For example, his program included classes in gymnastics, Bejart dance techniques, Stanislavskian techniques (with an instructor flown in from Moscow), *commedia* skills, phonetics, music theory and history, voice, and Berliner Ensemble techniques.

Terzopoulous was the only Greek who seemed sensitive to a problem that I was unwilling and somewhat embarrassed to raise among my friends, the cultural problem of young Greeks attempting to emulate western styles and traditions while ignoring the foundations of their own culture. The director called it "the bad problem of the new Greeks." These new students too often tried to copy western culture in their performing styles and approaches and thus denied the natural histrionic impulses particular to the Greek race. That was the reason, he said, that he found his best students coming from the very small towns and villages, those relatively untouched by the country's madlong rush to westernize.[15]

The majority of actors with whom I spoke would echo the opinion of one working professional actress: "Of course the schools are not good in Greece. . . ." Getting into even the best of the schools was "very, very easy . . . that has to change." Most of the training was "nothing, we were doing actually nothing . . . really nothing." Libraries were almost all inadequate and sometimes facilities were so crowded that all the students had to work on their scenes in one small room. Passing final exams often was determined as much by one's friendship with the faculty as by one's talent. In one case the Ministry's examining committee wanted to deny all but two of the graduating class their diplomas. But the elderly and respected head acting teacher "pressed them" and everyone passed.[16]

Yet, despite these trials which are probably exacerbated by the poverty of the country and, unfortunately, the greed of some of these schools' operators, performers appear who are truly wonderful. This is especially impressive when one recognizes the fact that, because theatre does not exist in the educational system, very many of the students entering drama schools probably have had no exposure, background or training in the theatre arts before that time. Many of the schools, then, must begin at the most basic levels. Some actors admitted that before they enrolled in their schools they did not even know that there were other schools in existence. They did not know the simplest things, like where to find a play to read. Consequently, many of these excellent actors know that they need further training after graduation. They almost plead for workshops and seminars in all those areas in which they feel inadequate. Such growth-producing activities, however, are extremely rare in Greece. The few master teachers who have tried to establish them in the past simply could not maintain their own activities and also provide such a service. Too, the expense of attending a workshop in Greece often is insurmountable for most impecunious actors. Most of them are convinced, nevertheless, that if a good teacher, say Minos Volonakis, were to open a school for working actors to improve their skills, he would be inundated with students. A minority of the more cynical would counter, however, that Greek actors are naturally lazy and no one would attend such a workshop. Both of these viewpoints were represented by the 20 to 30 students who attended the bilingual workshop of which I was part. The majority, I believe, sincerely wanted to improve their skills and attended whenever possible. A smaller percentage was there primarily to remain in the director's good graces in case he began hiring and, so, attended only when Volonakis himself was conducting the session.

In addition, there is almost no instruction in acting for film or television, two of the major sources of income for actors. Many new graduates find their first work in such activities and admit to absolute ignorance of the techniques involved. This may explain some of the dreadful performances which appear daily on Greek-produced television.

IV
Epilogue

11. Spotlights and Darkspots

Playwriting

My language skills in Greek are hardly up to the poetic subtleties required for a full comprehension of Greek dramatic literature, nor was that the intention of this work. Such a literary study will have to be undertaken by someone much more versed in the language and in literary analysis. Several observations about the experience of being a playwright, however, can be made at this time.

Members of the theatre community in general recognize the fundamental importance of new writers. If they were to name one element which would significantly improve the Greek theatre overall, nearly every person would name playwriting. I would venture to say that nearly every Greek theatre company is looking constantly for a bright new playwright whose work would illuminate the Greek situation to the Greeks. The problem for these companies, of course, is that, even if they find a decent new play to produce, they must make a profit on it. The independent companies especially are often financially strapped and must feel strongly about a new piece in order to present it to a public which is not known for its acceptance of non-traditional art forms and ideas. Even though many of these companies do produce new works, it is more likely that well-established companies like the Art Theatre or the Theatre Stoa or the Amphi-Theatre would attempt them. In fact the Amphi-Theatre produces a newly found sixteenth–nineteenth century Greek play nearly each year. The National Theatre produced three one act plays by Almenis, Papadojeorjou and Xaritaki in 1985, and the Art Theatre produced a new play by fledgling playwright Dora Litinaki in that same year.

This last example may provide an interesting viewpoint. Since Greeks in general abhor hierarchical social or political structures and, conversely, truly believe in absolute egalitarianism, many Greeks feel that they may approach any official at any level as equals. Producers, therefore, are probably more approachable in Greece than in most western countries. Litinaki, who was educated in England as an actress but has not performed in Greece, wrote her first play, and took it right to the "top," to the great master,

Karolos Koun. He thought it was brilliant and offered a full production on the spot.

Dialegmenos still distrusts theatre interests in general and prefers to produce his own plays. He refuses to have his plays translated into English because, as he said, such translations will never capture the essence of the language, and language is the essence of his plays.[1]

Anagnostaki, widely respected as perhaps the best playwright in Greece, refuses to have any other theatre than Koun's produce her plays. He is the only one she can trust, she said. And although Koun mounted all of her earlier plays meticulously, and although they all looked about the same on opening night, at least, she continued, she knew that her work had been respected and she had been consulted on any changes which might have arisen. (One wonders whom she will trust now that Koun has passed away.) In addition, she still refuses to allow just anyone to translate her work. Her only translator, she said, will be Aliki Bacopoulou-Halls, an extremely busy teacher, President of the International Theatre Institute and government representative on granting committees.[2]

Playwright and prize-winning short story writer Kostoula Mitropoulou, conversely, has had great difficulty receiving productions in Greece, even though she has been widely produced in France and Germany. She even has agents in Paris and in London. Her plays, very modern in the Ionesco sense, seem far too *avant garde* for the regular Greek audience, she said. And when she was produced in Greece, she was produced badly "because they [producers] don't know the language of the modern theatre." Too often when they asked for a play and she gave them one, they more often than not returned it with, "Don't you have something with a beginning, middle and end?" Productions, she continued frustratedly, "productions are *not* what the writer wrote . . . . Only Anagnostaki and Kehaidis have a *chance* . . ." to have very good productions.[3]

All playwrights who were interviewed expressed their almost universal suspicion of the producers who were to mount their shows. (Koun and Volonakis seemed to be exceptions.) No doubt this paranoia accompanies most playwrights' treks to the boards, regardless of the country. In Greece, however, a nation conditioned by history to embrace this psychological stance, it seems endemic. Dialegmenos produced his own shows to avoid the trauma of fighting the producer; Skourtis generally produced his own shows; Anagnostaki only allowed Koun to have her shows; Mitrolouous would allow only Volonakis to do hers.

Of course many would disagree that these writers above represent the best Greece has to offer. Unfortunately, my attempts to ascertain such a superior group met with failure — no one could agree who were the "best." (I must admit that Loula Anagnostaki's and Lefteris Kehaidis' names appeared repeatedly.) Therefore, I would like to offer here a list of the "best contemporary Greek playwrights" according to just one of my respondents, Thassos Lignatis, past president of the National Theatre Board, Director of the National Theatre Drama School, as well as a dramaturg and practicing critic.[4]

The list is by no means exhaustive and may well have changed had I given the critic more time to weigh his responses. It may provide, however, a starting point for researchers who might become interested in the literature of the contemporary Greek theatre. Many of these plays are one-acts, a form which seems to be favored by many writers.

Kehaidis	Dafne and Cloe,
	Festival
Maniotis	Saint Sunday
	The Match
	Common Sense
	The Pair
Pondikas	So Be It
	Spectator
Anagnostaki	Victory
	Cassette
Ziogas	Comedy of the Fly
Dialegmenos	Ma . . . Mama . . . Mom
Matisis	Civic Right
Moursalas	The Friends
Korres	Old Age Homes
Limberakis	Ring of Geese
Chrisoulis	The Name
	The Adolescent
Efdimiadis	The Killer
Doxaras	Exorcist
	Strip Tease
Christophilakis (in Poland)	Provinces

The Actor's Syndicate

Blonde and beautiful actress Emilia Ipsilandi was the head of the actor's union in Greece in 1986. A dedicated and gracious lady, as well as a persuasive Communist, she seemed to have only the health of the art and the availability of theatre to all the people of Greece as her operative goals.[5] Unfortunately, she also told *Ta Nea*, the largest circulation paper in Athens that, if the Party told her to shut down the theatres, she would.[6]

Greek "Equity" was established in 1917 but has become a real force for the proper treatment of actors only recently. Not unlike performers in other parts of the world, Greek actors often faced various kinds of instability and maltreatment. They often were not paid for performances or rehearsals.

They were worked for long hours without rest. They were sometimes employed for a day instead of months and then fired when the production collapsed. Perhaps they lost other work by accepting that fruitless job.

Consequently, through the efforts of the union a law was passed requiring each producer and actor to enter into a firm agreement with each other. The actor was to be paid for a minimum of three months regardless of the financial conditions of the producer; he was to work only eight hours a day with appropriate breaks every hour; he was to be paid for rehearsals. We have seen in our interviews with working Greek actors that, unfortunately, this system still does not work completely. Producers often will ignore the terms of the contracts. (Actors also are not blameless, often challenging the limits of producers' patience in attempts to carve out more free time for themselves.)

Ipsilandi and her associates wished to stop this malpractice by requiring that the producers deposit with the union sufficient funds to cover actors' salaries for the primary three months. Then, regardless of the show's financial future, at least the salaries could be distributed in case of the show's failure. The union and the government, however, have not been able to resolve ideological differences of opinion in this regard. Even many actors feared that placing that much of their money in a government agency would not be wise. It seems that the spectre of the *junta* and its misuse of such available funds hovers uncomfortably close. Consequently, actors' salaries still cannot be guaranteed. Ipsilandi admitted that the union did not have enough money to initiate litigation in every one of these breach of contract cases but, in those court cases which were engaged, the union inevitably won.

The union also acted as a clearinghouse in an attempt to connect out-of-work actors with producers. Apparently those actors who were also members of the Communist Party were heavily favored in the distribution of these jobs, if the testimony of the actors I interviewed was a fair indicator.

This very active and focused union also tried to apply pressure to various parts of the production and educational systems in order to effect improvements in the overall availability and quality of the Greek theatre. For example it required 40 days of rehearsal for each show at the National Theatre (although it preferred 45 days). It helped sponsor the Municipal Theatre Conference in 1979–1980, a meeting to explore the various models upon which their then-incipient municipal theatre project could be based. It established the Organization for Cooperative Theatre Companies both to provide production funds outside those of the government or the box office and also to allow theatre-producing groups to rise out of native soil anywhere in the country. (Naturally the charge against this facet of the union was that it only helped Communist-affiliated organizations.) It managed to organize a system by which the Ministry of Labor gave away up to 500,000 show tickets to students and factory workers — and they were working to increase that number. They tried to change the graduating requirements for the drama schools in the country because they recognized that these schools simply were not providing sufficient training. (In a curious paradox the union believes that whatever takes more theatre to more people is good, even if the quality of the efforts has to suffer for a time. When the theatre is well established and the audience better educated, so the theory goes, then both the audience and the theatre productions will increase in quality.)

For years, in order to become "professional actors," graduates of these drama schools would complete their studies, pass the final examination and simply sign their name on the union's register. New Syndicate rules, though, now require a drama school diploma *as well as* 50 working days as a paid professional. (The Catch-22 here is recognized more by the new actors than the union. How can they get these required 50 days of work experience if they need to be a member of the union to get the work experience?) Too, just a few years ago only drama school graduates could claim work as professional actors. With the increasing use of TV and rock stars on stage for commercial purposes, though (many of whom had no such education), union regulations changed so that only 80 percent of any cast had to belong to the union. The rule allowed some star performers to work in plays; unfortunately it also allowed nearly anyone the producer could convince to appear on stage. The results are sometimes embarrassing.

Ipsilandi almost glowed when she spoke of her dreams for the union and for Greek theatre. Foremost she wished for greater employment among the actor population. She wanted to make Greek TV really Greek. (Its programming was almost 80 percent foreign at that time.) She was working for some infallible method by which the actors would be paid regardless of the producer's circumstances. She hoped that some way could be found to improve all theatre training, by state-imposed methods if necessary. She felt passionately that theatre should be incorporated into all schools, not only as a spectator activity, but also as a hands-on one. She looked for the establishment of even more municipal theatres and some way to "fix" the state of the state theatres. And she wanted to create the infrastructure and "nests" from which new theatre groups could spring anywhere.[7]

Opinion concerning the viability and usefulness of the union ran the gamut from total support to total derision. We have already seen that some directors decried the union's mandated breaks, not because actors did not deserve breaks, but because they were forced to take them at specific times and they inevitably took twice or three times as much time as was mandated. Or they did not return to work exactly as scheduled, after lunch, for example; still they expected their breaks. Some respected directors felt that all those union rules simply placed obstacles in the way of significant artistic achievement. Non-Communists detested the alleged favoritism displayed by the union in providing work. On the other hand the 32-year-old head of the Communist Youth section of the union felt that it was absolutely necessary to protect the workers' rights because without such protection the producers would ride roughshod over everyone.[8]

Perhaps the reader may recognize the fact that nearly all of the above is true and, moreover, adheres to typical Greek behaviors and patterns. Producers often *do* ride roughshod over actors, even *with* union contracts. Union contracts *are* considered simply pieces of paper. Verbal agreements, infinitely malleable, have long been the norm in Greece. Formal agreements are considered valid only as long as they are profitable. Communist actors *do* receive preferential treatment, but that is typical of any Greek affiliated with any organization—familial, village or political. Many Greeks, if left alone, probably would take breaks every ten minutes and would take even more time at their lunches. But time does not make the same impressions on the Greek soul as on the soul of a westerner. Conversation, political discussion, second jobs or paving the way for some future "deal" are infinitely more important than being obedient to some nebulous and artificial time schedule in the sky. It simply goes against traditional village behaviors to worry terribly about time.

Both sides of these battles, it seems, are at fault. The basic problem is that most Greeks, if they recognize rules at all, recognize them grudgingly. For evidence just observe the traffic violations on any thoroughfare in Athens (which will include, if you are not very careful, your own demise when a hurried Athenian taxi driver decides to park on the sidewalk where you are standing).

At the same time a growing proportion of the population is slowly beginning to realize that rules will be necessary to progress—the one thing they dearly wish for—in this twentieth century. With 20,000 taxi cabs plus countless thousands of other cars and buses in Athens alone, some kind of accommodation between personal freedom and the good of all others in those mad traffic crushes must take place. Adherence to rules, personal and social discipline, increased productivity, subordination of self to a larger organization—all these necessities of twentieth century industrialization fight constantly with the traditional Greek ways of going about their daily affairs. It is this continuous, heart-wrenching necessity to impose rules and at the same time stretch or ignore them that colors all of modern Greek history, including such relatively insignificant parts of it like the relationship of the actor's union with its old and new members.

The International Theatre Institute

The Hellenic Center of the International Theatre Institute is located at 25 Voucourestiou in downtown Athens. When I first climbed the stairs to their offices in 1983 I found only two pleasant women who admitted that they had almost nothing to offer my research. For years, they said, the Institute published an important annual, *Thespis*, but funds for the publication ceased and the complete series is difficult to find. Recently the Institute acquired a new President, Aliki Bacopoulou-Halls. Mrs. Bacopoulou-Halls seems to have created a new excitement there. During the 1985–1986 season the Institute hosted at least an international conference on Theatre-in-Education in Saloniki and another international conference on Drama for Minorities held in Athens. Although the second was attended by very few people, its very existence may have indicated a new energy and purposefulness in this organization.

The Theatre Museum

Housed in the basement of the Greek Cultural Center, 50 Akadimias Street, the Theatre Museum is the primary source of research materials in the Greek theatre. Built in 1840 as a state hospital, the neo-classic building began accumulating theatrical memorabilia in 1938 under the inspiration of Theodoros Sinandinos. Today, primarily because of the work of its intense advocate, George Sideris, it houses many photographs of ancient and modern productions, one entire room of famous stars' dressing room artifacts, wonderful posters, costumes, masks and a small library of books and newspaper clippings primarily in Greek, but with a few in other languages.[9]

Playwright and President of the Greek Playwright's Society, Manolis Korres, is the administrator of this collection. He has tried to maintain and increase the library's holdings, but it has been difficult with only private donations covering all expenses. Only in the last few years has the government offered some financial support, but not enough to cover the operational costs. This is unfortunate, since the collection could become a center for the international study of the Greek theatre. As of this moment, however, the library is not much; but it is the only game in town. Whatever deficiencies the library may have had as a research tool, the cooperation and hospitality of the director and his staff were not among them. I wish I had been able to address their desperate pleas for more volumes of any sort on any theatre in the world.

12. Summary

The world today, especially the theatre world, still tends to think of Greece as if it were a glorious democracy at the peak of its power in the Mediterranean. It has been the purpose of this book to introduce to the modern reader a more realistic view of present Greece and its theatre as well as to excite other researchers with the possibilities of contemporary Greece as a focus for their studies.

Almost no work has been done, for example, on the religious plays and festivals of Byzantium during the 400–1400 A.D. period. No translations exist of those plays of Greece's "renaissance" period of 1600 to 1800 when they were under the influence of the Italian Renaissance. I found no evidence indicating the existence of those Greek plays which may have been composed outside of the Ottoman Empire and smuggled into key Greek cities within those boundaries during the pre-revolutionary period. I wonder if those plays exist and what they might tell us about Greeks living under Ottoman dominion. Indeed, translations of Greek plays composed after the fourth century B.C. are remarkably rare. Yet some of these post-golden age plays may offer unique insights into the condition of being Greek in the twentieth century. Moreover, these translations, if they existed, might afford westerners a more perceptive look into the hearts and values of this nation which eternally sits astride critical cultural, geo-political, strategic and ideological routes. The contemporary Greek satiric revue is an immediate touchstone to the feelings of that people yet no study of it has been done. The work of Karolos Koun, the first and most important individual to strive for connections between the ancient texts and the modern Greek seems particularly important as a subject for investigation as it may describe methods of discovering like connections between the pasts and presents of many of the newly emerging nations.

Whatever work might follow this present one, it must deal with the fact that the Golden Age of the fifth century B.C. represents just a fraction of the total life and output of Greece. It must recognize that Greece's history has formulated the present theatre and that the vast percentage of that history had little to do with that one glorious century 500 years before Christ. Thus contemporary Greek theatre cannot be judged either on those ancient standards nor on western biases without considering fully the numerous historical threads which weave the present Greek theatrical tapestry.

We must remember that Greece had profound ties with the peoples and cultures of the Middle East, places like present-day Turkey, Iraq, Syria, Egypt, Libya. The first colonies to the Greek mainland and to the various islands came from those regions. The "cities" thus established grew into important bartering centers for civilizations around the Mediterranean. Natural bartering and negotiation skills developed probably along with concomitant characteristics—cunning, deception, cheating, paranoia, secrecy, argumentativeness. It is not too difficult to accept the evolution of these latter characteristics if one accepts the critical importance of "success" in those negotiations with occasional traders.

By 450 B.C. one city-state, Athens, emerged as a cultural and military leader in the region. By that year it had defeated the Persians and, in a way, created the first in what was to be a centuries-long conflict with its prehistorical forefathers from Asia Minor. From the earliest years, then, Greece and Turkey have been involved in a blood-feud of sorts with first one and then the other subjugating each other in turns. After that miraculous victory Athens spread its colonies to the African coast, to Turkey and Italy, even to the Black Sea. The "Golden Age" which followed altered somewhat the characteristics which had been accumulating about the race for centuries. By then one might find argumentativeness balanced with a striving for reasonableness, cunning fighting with a pursuit of excellence for its own sake, an acute sense of proportion confronted by total unreasonableness—Athenian Apollo engaged in constant battle with oriental Dionysius. Like the gods in ancient Greek literature whose erratic and outrageous behavior confused even themselves, the Greek people manifested like behavior probably because that seemed inevitable.

Macedonian Alexander the Great spread the Greek "word" an incredible distance, all the way to the Indus River in present-day India. In doing so he reunited the "new" Greeks with their Asia Minor roots while at the same time coloring the newly evolving culture with Persian and even Indian influences. This was especially true in Persia with the enforced intermarrying of local princesses with his military officers. In probably less direct ways the cultures of those regions in present-day Egypt, Afghanistan, Iran, Syria all probably contributed in some way to the development of Greece's culture in the fourth century before Christ.

By 146 B.C. the Greeks were totally controlled by the Romans. For the first time they experienced as a nation the helplessness of "subjects." No doubt the "hubris"—overweening pride—of their Golden Age took a beating. One might imagine that what remained might have looked a lot like their present-day *philotimo*—pride with a degree of arrogance. Certainly their ability to bargain and their general shiftiness were noted in Roman times and may have contributed to their continued survival. At the same time they took advantage of the demands on the part of the Romans for copies of Greek arts, literature, philosophy and theatre. Bastardized and boring Greek tragedies appeared from time to time in the Roman salons and circuses, but of course could not provide the blood and excitement required by Roman audiences.

When Emperor Constantine moved his capital to Constantinople partly to renew the purity of the Christian faith, he created yet another wrinkle in the Greek psyche. Greek language and thought mingled with Roman administration and discipline within a quasi-oriental region to create what has become known as the Byzantine era. Their glorious pagan beginning became fused with a glorious Orthodox present. The spendor of religious rite, the conservatism and intransigence of religious thought, the convoluted machinations of "Byzantine" administrative processes, the tendency toward oriental-like metaphysics all combined to produce a society still reflected in much of Greek governmental and religious custom. Greek Byzantium lasted 1000 years.

The Ottoman Turks captured Constantinople in the fifteenth century and imposed a sometimes iron-fisted, sometimes *laissez-faire* structure on this Byzantine one. In a way the Turks might have been repaying the Greeks for the conquests of Alexander centuries before. (One might consider this episode a continuation of the blood brother-to-brother feud which seems to have been continued even to this present day.) The consequent exodus of Greeks to Crete and to the Western Empire helped incite a renaissance of Greek playwriting on Crete and the Renaissance in Italy. Those Greeks who lived outside the Ottoman Empire smuggled nationalistic plays to their brothers still living within the confines of that mega-state, thus preserving the idea of a free Greece.

At the same time these 400 years of Turkish rule influenced the development of Greek society in numerous ways, e.g. in their foods, language, use of metaphysical/emotional rather than logical thought processes, etc. Mostly, however, these 400 years created in the Greeks an overwhelming determination to be a free country once again, preferably with some external manifestation of the splendor that once was attached to Byzantine Constantinople or even to old Athens.

The Greek War of Independence began in 1821. By 1934 England, France and Russia guaranteed their newly won freedom. England, especially, caught up in the romanticism of the Greek fight for freedom, spawned a view of this "new" Greece which had little to do with the most recent 2000 years of its history. Rather, it skipped blithely to 500 years before then and with its European friends determined to mold Greece into an image of the ancient world as well as a viable entity in the modern world. England's support of a monarchy in a country which never had one, its support of a new language, when the language of the people served perfectly well, its idealistic superimposition of ancient ideals on a society which had long adapted them comfortably to the various exigencies it had faced over millenia all probably sowed the seeds of a schizophrenia which the Greeks are still trying to control. Indeed, it may not be too radical a hypothesis that the imposition of these kinds of romantic notions by too many Philhellenes in the nineteenth century has ultimately proved a grave disservice to Greece in the twentieth century and may be largely to blame for its present confusion.

Nevertheless, the contradictions inherent in such a violent transitional period abounded. Greeks were told that their forefathers had created the first true democracy, but they found themselves ruled by a succession of despots, *coup* leaders, *juntas,* monarchs and corrupt democracies. They had fought for and won independence, but their reliance on outside guidance and support belied that feeling of independence. They were told that they should attend the Boulevard plays from France but they really preferred their beloved rough-hewn Karaghiozis puppet plays, which they had by then transformed from the Turkish. They were told that they really ought to like their own classics but these were presented in the ancient Greek language, a tongue few spoke; so they leaned toward their crude satiric revues.

By the end of World War I all of the false hopes and false starts toward this new and glorious Greece led inexorably to the disaster known as the Megali Idea, the plan to re-establish a Byzantine-like Empire predominantly out of Turkish territories. Even though rational Greek voices cried out in horror, the Greek armies did attack Turkish provinces outside of Smyrna, a Greek colony with roots back to 450 B.C. Unfortunately the Turks counter-attacked to preserve their own newly emerging determination to be an independent state and routed the Greeks in a few weeks. Dreams lost, from 1923 to World War II the Greeks flailed out at every government which attempted to restore some semblence of order and unity in the country. Governments of every conceivable stamp entered and exited in incredibly rapid fashion. Then Mussolini helped unite Greece, possibly for the first time since the Persian attack 2400 years before.

When Il Duce demanded that the Greeks allow him free entry into their country, it must have seemed to those northern Greeks that not only had their dream of empire been crushed, but now their very freedom was being threatened again. Still not to be free! Still to live under a foreign power! Then, for one brilliant moment the factious Greeks stood strong and united to repulse Mussolini's invasion from Albania. For a few heady weeks they succeeded. Then Hitler's Panzer divisions attacked and rumbled cruelly all the way to the Aegean.

The Führer's occupation of Greece was not a gentle one. Yet once again the eternal Greek dream of freedom from foreign intervention after millenia of servitude captured men's hearts. The Resistance movement bloomed on Crete. *Any* freedom fighter was a hero and for years Greeks could not be bothered by these fighters' particular political leanings. Unfortunately, the freedom fighters did bother about their particular political leanings and fought among themselves with as much ferocity as they fought the Germans. After the retreat of the Nazi forces and the end of the war they continued to fight among themselves along the same political lines. The Americans and British supported the forces which eventually won this civil war, but by then the country was hopelessly divided—free but divided. American guarantee of Greece's freedom as well as its enormous infusion of dollars and technology and technocrats firmly established Greece in the western sphere. The subsequent Hellenic attachment to Europe and the Common Market, while it may have been an economic necessity, certainly did not accurately reflect its ten-fold experience as a mid-*eastern* culture. Once again Greece found itself caught between its oriental roots and its classical past; but now this dilemma was further complicated by its foreign-imposed, romantically created pseudo-classical present and the survivalistic functionalism of its economic policies.

In theatre this post-war period was marked by a burst of experimentalism. Suddenly the existentialists were accepted. American playwrights were celebrated. Amateur theatre erupted, and several puppet theatres blossomed. The most significant movement, however, might have been Karolos Koun's attempts to find connections between the plays of ancient Greece and the Greek people of the post-war period. In its own way Koun's work may have been an attempt to find the threads which would allow this people to trace their *entire* history and, thus, to embrace the fullness of their culture.

Yet, in 1967 the people's freedoms were once again denied. Colonel Papadopoulous led a successful *coup* under the guise of preserving Greek freedoms. To the people it became obvious (eventually) that his actions had proven that the Right (Rigidly Conservative Dictators) was just as obnoxious as the Left (Communists). For yet one more time the people were asked to define "democracy," "freedom," "independence," "radical," "conservative," "progress" from diametrically opposed viewpoints. To many, definitions had by now become far too ephemeral. Identification with a particular past seemed impossible, given the kinds of "pasts" available. Defining political systems accurately, too, seemed an impenetrable task. Deciding who the good guys and the bad guys were frankly seemed impossible, especially since both sides changed roles for no perceivable reason and at no pre-determinable times. Just like the ancient gods of the *Iliad* and *Odyssey* who changed sides at a whim, and whose words could be believed for only as long as the god was being served, so the leaders in Greek society could not be believed very far or very long.

It is no surprise that the average Greek today suspects all political leaders and believes passionately only in his own personal politics and his particular view of life. It is also no surprise that these beliefs are second to the efficacy and singular importance of his family and of his village. This rallying around these two social units recalls the survival tactics of ancient Greek villages as well as modern villages in developing parts of the world. When faced with an uncertain future and able to control only a few of life's forces, a person is most likely to form a strict protective shield around the basic building block of any society, the family, and that collection of families, the village. When a modern Athenian returns to his village for Orthodox Easter, he is responding not only to the traditions of life in Greece in the twentieth century, but also to the eternal threads of life by which humans have survived for thousands of years.

So in 1986 these highly suspicious Greeks, steeped in millenia of foreign domination and local ineptness, glorying in their participation in empires as well as surviving a remarkable string of racial and national indignities, these clever Greeks have elected a new kind of government—at least new to them—a Socialistic Democracy. It may prove the perfect answer to the demands of their latest re-configuration of the "Greek culture."

In 1986, though, life in Athens seemed to be moving too quickly to allow any consideration of this longer view. In the last 40 years many Athenians have gone from living in small but comfortable houses in which there was no electricity, water or indoor plumbing, to huge, impersonal, concrete apartment houses with VCRs in the living rooms and Mercedes-Benzes parked on the sidewalks outside. In the space of 40 years they have gone from neighborhood gossip as the major form of communication to instant world-wide telecommunications via TV sets in virtually every living room in the country. In that same four decades many have passed from a meager or even minimal existence to individual entrepreneurship.

The theatre of course reflects this cultural turmoil. It attempts anything. Ancient tragedies are presented presumably in exactly the same manner as they were 2500 years ago or with the latest technology and couched in terms of the latest avant-garde-ism. Plays are presented as over-miked harangues or as examples of the most quiet Stanislavskian kind of realism. Greeks copy American musicals and Italian operas. They create children's plays out of their ancient myths as well as out of life in Athens. At the same time as they love their covertly anti–Turkish Karaghiozis puppet plays, they invite a Turkish puppet theatre to their mime festival and reveal a surprisingly widespread understanding of the Turkish language. Their revues satirize whatever government happens to be in power, whether left, right, radical, conservative or dictatorial. Their acting styles vary on the same stage between elocutionistically inspired presentationalism to the most realistic form of representationalism. Production standards in their professional theatres vary from the most obvious amateurism to the most polished professionalism. Lighting equipment varies from a few display floodlights to lasers and computers. Eighty percent of their television programming comes from England and America, the latter of which they claim to abhor for having too much influence on their affairs.

This constant play of contradictions has existed in Greek affairs almost from the beginning. We cannot expect them to settle into a focused and integrated approach to life and its theatre as might have been possible in that small city-state of so long ago. The stability that was essential to the development of tragedy certainly is rare not only in Greece but anywhere in the world in the latter half of the twentieth century. In fact, until the country can forge or discover a means to integrate its diverse and opposing historical forces with the unique and often terrifying demands of the last quarter of the twentieth century, we probably should not expect to witness a Greek theatre renaissance of any sort. What we can do, however, is to revel in the incredible range and quality of its theatre, seeing in each group of performances the mind and soul of this unique Greek people.

Appendix A. *Helen* (A Review)

Produced by the State Theatre of Northern Greece at the Athens Festival, July 10, 1983.

It was obvious from the audience's first entrance into the theatre that this *Helen* was going to be different. The enormous, narrow stage of the ancient Herod Atticus Theatre was filled with "Stonehenge"-type obelisks of various heights, each embedded with a gold mask near the top. These forms surrounded a huge tent just left of stage center. Several more of these vaguely phallic erections marched off the stage and into the old Roman orchestra where they became part of that semi-circular form by means of a low stone edging which, in turn, surrounded a grey and sand space where the old orchestra lay. A small, water-filled pool near the stage held a prone, half-submerged statue. Horizontal netting draped from sticks completed the encircling of the orchestra. Most impressive was the fact that it all somehow seemed to emerge out of that enormous old facade and thereby retained its own focus. This was not going to be a production upstaged by impressive ancient structures. It also was not going to be a production unbefitting a queen of the Trojan War. At the same time, however, there was something a bit quirky about the whole effect.

Like so many productions in Greece this one started fifteen minutes late. As usual those who had come early to claim the best of the reserved rows applauded several times to urge an earlier start. Finally the gong sounded for the third time; the house lights clicked off and the entry music blared from loudspeakers disguised as old stones.

The entry procession confirmed the suspicion that this was going to be a *Helen* of a different stripe. The oriental and Turkish flavor of the fantastical twelfth century B.C. costumes, the strange make-up, the bare-breasted servant girls, the *Ubu-Roi*-like breasted Theonoe, the myriad costume bells, jingles and cymbals spoke of a production with only one, half-open eye on the script and the other dazzle-bright on the director's fancy.

This strange play, which solves the Helen-Menelaus relationship by assuming that Paris stole only a god-designed copy of her, concentrates on getting husband and wife back together and away from Egyptian king Theoklymenus, who hotly pursued Helen throughout the play. You see, when Menelaus was returning from Troy with the copy of Helen, he was shipwrecked on the shores of Egypt. Remarkably, Zeus had taken the real Helen to that very same place for safekeeping at the start of the war and . . . well, one need not bother with the plot—the director surely didn't.

Director Andreas Voustinas changed it all into an expensive sex comedy anyhow. All soliloquies were played presentationally along with all the mugging. All sexual references were over-played, as were the sudden, inexplicable crying scenes by Menelaus. Music smacked of antiqued contemporaneousness. Farce routines like the Neanderthal Menelaus frightening the orange and yellow-organdied chorus, and they frightening him in return, pleased the audience but seemed better placed in a TV sitcom. The "fuck you" gesture by the Messenger (wonderfully played by Stelio Kappatos) screamed twentieth century, as did the sudden skyrockets and spouting fountains when Menelaus and Helen recognized each other and ran into an embrace. This last effect, admittedly incredibly well-timed, frightened me right out of the theatre. Imagine being involved in a romantic scene; then, at the crucial moment, the sky behind the Herodeon explodes with fireworks and various incendiary devices, the lighting changes drastically and suddenly to romantic blues and pinks, the small pond erupts in a dozen geysers of water and the sound track swells into a 1940s cinematic climax. Perhaps you, too, would have found yourself totally out of the play in such circumstances. Admittedly, the audience loved it. To me it seemed at first that a director fresh out of drama school had been given an unlimited budget and felt that he had to use it all. Then, on second thought, I stopped and smiled. Why look for Euripides and serious comment? This silly, romantic, gimmicky interpretation was well-done and consistent. Antiquity be damned! On with the show! On with the vaudeville routines, the pratfalls, the mugging, the hilarious asides, fireworks, chases, screaming, naked women and the horrible overacting!

Even though I found it sometimes hard to swallow some of these too-obvious directorial gimmicks, I must admit that, within the framework established, they were almost all consistent. Here was the admission that all stops would be pulled to give the audience a good time. No one could have possibly expected a subtle, deeply psychological or even symbolic rendering—the very first chorus girl giggle dispelled that preconception. And if one thought that Euripides was going to deliver an angry tirade at the culpability of man and the deviousness of women and the strangeness of the gods, that thought was promptly dispelled by the Neanderthal costume and grunts of Menelaus and the pouty foolishness of Helen. Quite clearly, after one thought about it a moment, this was intended to be a *Helen*-ized *Midsummer Night's Dream*-ish romantic comedy.

One-third of the international crowd of 4500 gave this show a standing ovation. The other two-thirds applauded solidly.

A few days later in a discussion of the show with various other Athenian directors, I was told that Voutsinas, the director of *Helen*, was a personal friend of Mel Brooks. That was consistent too.

Appendix B. *Electra* (A Review)

Produced by the Cyprus Theatre Company at the Theatre Festival at Epidavros.

Over the last several years the opening of the theatre festival at the ancient theatre of Epidavros has acquired the status almost of a national holiday. Last summer the announcement that the high-flying Cyprus Theatre Company would produce Sophocles' *Electra;* that noted film director Michael Kakoyiannis would direct; and that national star Irini Pappas would play the title role heightened the normal excitement to fever pitch. The best seats were sold out as soon as the box office opened and by the day before the first performance over 12,000 people had tickets for this grand event.

I arranged with a friend of director Kakoyiannis to attend the dress rehearsal in order to interview him. This rehearsal, called the "general rehearsal," is peopled by friends of the company and residents of the nearby village of Ligurio. Tradition has it that ancestors of the village's inhabitants helped discover the ruins of the theatre and also helped in its excavation. Therefore, all their descendents are invited to attend the final rehearsal as long as the festival exists. Even though there was a brief but heavy rain storm at 7 P.M. that night, and even though it continued to drizzle, a few hundred of us trudged toward the theatre for the scheduled 9 P.M. "general rehearsal."

As I searched for the director in the actors' cabana area behind the theatre, it became clear that everyone's nerves were taut—the director shouted; actors bowed their heads; assistants scurried. The all-night lighting rehearsal the night before had covered only half of the play and the rain was threatening to force cancellation of tonight's very important rehearsal. To complicate matters Ms. Pappas' throat was sore and she was coughing badly. With that kind of tension I decided not to bother the director.

The rain vacillated between heavy and light. The rehearsal was called off, then on, then back and forth a few more times. Finally the director decided that they needed at least to complete the lighting cues regardless of the circumstances. After all, tomorrow the world would be watching. The depressed company trudged the 100 yards through the soppy woods to the theatre.

The rehearsal went slowly, lighting cue to lighting cue. The director shouted lighting instructions from the sixth row, counting on the theatre's unbelievable acoustics to carry his voice to the operators at the top of the theatre. Unfortunately, it also carried very loudly to the actors who were obviously bothered by his shouted instructions during their attempts to act. Ms. Pappas barely whispered her lines, making it impossible for the control operator to hear his cues. The director resorted to relaying her lines to the operator in a hoarse shout. It was all very painful. I left

169

at midnight for one of the few rental rooms left in Ligurio while the cast and crews, bundled in sweaters and scarfs against the unseasonably cold and wet evening, continued to plod through the ordeal in the best theatrical tradition.

Opening day dawned clear and bright. The town, normally laid-back and sleepy during the rest of the year, paused expectantly. Everyone knew that this was the day of the festival's opening. By 7:30 P.M. a steady stream of cars, broken and elongated by dozens of tour buses, droned and roared and beeped through the single street in town, a long snake headed for the theatre site one mile distant. Datsuns, Fords, Mercedes-Benzes, Citroens and Asconas fought for positions between the occasional tractors being driven home by late-working farmers.

Nearer the entrance to the theatre thousands of theatre pilgrims funneled up the few roads to the sacred precinct. I had heard actors at the National Theatre of Greece repeatedly call Epidavros "magical" in their attempt to describe their feeling toward it. And no matter how many times they performed there the magic never waned. As I joined the crowd jostling toward the theatre I started to understand that feeling.

The "magic" of about 12,000 people of all nationalities, social spheres and ages (there were many children), bound together for a short moment in time by a common interest, gathered in what had become once again for similar reasons a "holy" place, seated on stones that connected them to human beings of all time as darkness crept over their new world has to be one of the most awe-producing spectacles possible, at least to theatre people.

Dignitaries arrive and receive applause, the acoustical properties of the theatre obvious in the reverberations of the greetings. The house flood lights click off. A hush as ancient as time settles on us. A group of black shadows magically appears from the darkened grove of trees behind the old skene. A cymbal roll segues into eerie electronic music and the black forms slowly cross to the stage area. The tension is riveting. A deafening cymbal crash, the roll of kettle drums. The stage lights burst on. Three men rush onto the metal-plated orchestra carrying torches. It is impossible not to applaud this re-birth — and we all did.

Call it passion, the eternal rocks in the history of these people, the sun, the geography, the open appraisal of death, whatever it is called, it creates a theatre form that seems perfectly suited to this physical theatre, the tragedy, the people. The depth of passion that American actors can read into but not achieve in these tragedies is second nature to these people. The Greeks, obviously, are more Dionysian than Apollonian.

Upstage seven or eight enormous, two-dimensional, vertical, steel-plated towers, curving toward the orchestra at their bottoms dwarf the actors. Two three-foot steel balls stage left are balanced stage right by half a dozen curious, vertical steel sculptures. The earthen orchestra is covered with more steel plate. Costumes are primarily black with deeply colored underskirts for the Chorus, red for Clytemnestra. Only Cassandra wears all white.

The music, composed by Michalis Christodoulides, was magnificent, even if over-used. Lighting shifted imperceptibly, a remarkable performance given the trauma of the last two nights. Acting was uniformly good, helped by highly trained and controlled voices which were, in turn, helped by the theatre's acoustics. Ms. Pappas' voice, although a little hoarse, showed few signs of the coughing and sniffling of the night before.

This *Electra* was a talky play and Mr. Kakoyiannis tried to keep the Chorus, costumes and lights moving in order to help its visual austerity. Perhaps he went too far. The constant movement of the Chorus, for example, often attracted attention rather than serving as background for the main action in front of it. Conversely, he played all the important speeches in the center of the orchestra where the acoustics are best. I had hoped for more balance on both sides of this movement spectrum.

He did, however, stage several scenes exceedingly well. I was not the only one crying when Electra received the false news that Orestes was dead, or when she was given the urn supposedly containing his ashes, or when she was finally re-united with him. And I was not the only one with goose bumps when the usurping king, Aegisthus, was presented with the body of his dead lover, Clytemnestra, who was clad in a blood-red cloth streaming out in a train 20 feet behind her. Her dead form was stood up vertically and the sheath stripped away, revealing her body in an identically colored gown. She stood there for a terrifying moment, then fell into Electra's arms. As Electra lowered her to the floor, her train was divided by the Chorus into two huge pieces. They maneuvered these large sections into a barrier through which Aegisthus could not escape. As Orestes closed in for the kill the blood-red cloth closed into a tighter and tighter circle. After one slash of the avenging sword the undulating material entangled Aegisthus like a net and he fell. The theatre erupted with applause.

A few moments later the play was over. Ms. Pappas received ten curtain calls. People broke through the police lines surrounding the orchestra to kiss her or to give her flowers then hurry back to their places.

The invocation, preserved after so many centuries, had been resurrected.

Then, like a group of happy spectators whose team had just won the championship, we cattled our way down the hill to the noise, dirt, fumes and shoving of Greek civilization in the twentieth century.

Notes

1. A Brief History

1. A.R. Burn, *A Traveller's History of Greece* (New York: Funk and Wagnalls, 1965), pp. 1–9.

2. The term "Romios" referred to a Greek living away from Rome who displayed those behavioral and belief characteristics of a "true" Orthodox Greek. The term is still used today.

3. We must always remember that Greece had no Renaissance and has been always caught in its intellectual and artistic lives between the pagan glory of ancient Greece and the glorious Oriental excesses of Orthodox Byzantium. It had no National Gallery until just a few years ago. Its architecture has been either Byzantine religious or ancient pagan, for example the three major buildings of the present University of Athens. It was only after the 1950s that any sculptor dared *not* to do classical imitations.

4. S. Victor Papacosma, "The Historical Context," in *Greece in the 1980s*, Richard Clogg (ed.) (New York: St. Martin's, 1983), p. 32.

5. Clogg (ed.), p. 40.

6. David Holden, *Greece Without Columns* (New York: Lippincott, 1972), p. 136.

7. Quoted in Holden, p. 157.

8. Holden, p. 160.

9. In the summer of 1986 a statue of Truman, erected in the 1950s as a symbol of the Greek nation's appreciation of his efforts in Greece's hour of need, was blown off its pedestal by a small bomb. After weeks of demonstrations and scores of editorials and public debate for and against its replacement, the Parliament decided not to reinstall it.

10. Holden, pp. 303–308.

11. Much of this material is taken from *Greece, Background Notes,* published by the United States Department of State, Bureau of Public Affairs, April, 1985.

2. The Greek Character

1. Nikos Kazantzakis, as quoted in Holden, p. 30.

2. Holden, p. 21. Some readers may reject the repeated use of Holden as a reference in this chapter. After living in Greek society, however, it is my opinion that his perceptions most accurately reflect my personal experience.

3. Holden, p. 23.

4. William McNeill, *The Metamorphosis of Greece Since World War II* (Chicago: University of Chicago Press, 1976), p. 8.

5. Holden, pp. 288–289.

6. Holden, p. 24.

7. Quoted in Holden, pp. 94–98. It is interesting that, as of this writing, the Greek government has embarked on a 10-year program to save that same Parthenon by totally reconstructing it stone by stone.

8. Holden, p. 173.

9. John Koumoulides, *Greece in Transition* (London: Zeno, 1977), p. 285.

10. Holden, p. 276.

11. Name withheld, in an interview, June 11, 1983.

12. William Ammerman, "A Home of One's Own: A Cautionary Tale," *The Athenian*, April, 1986, p. 39.

13. McNeill, pp. 226, 228.

14. Holden, p. 280.

15. McNeill, pp. 11–12.

16. Quoted in Holden, p. 20.

17. As quoted in Holden, p. 88.

18. Name withheld, in an interview, May 8, 1986.

19. Katerina Bakopoulou, in an interview, March 10, 1986.

20. Holden, p. 25.

21. Holden, p. 36.

3. *Theatre Between Worlds*

1. Holden, p. 324.

2. Quoted in Aliki Bacopoulou-Halls, *Modern Greek Theatre: Roots and Blossoms* (Athens: Diogenis, 1978), p. 13.

3. Bacopoulou-Halls, p. 12.

4. Bacopoulou-Halls, pp. 16–17.

5. *Ibid.;* and John Sideris, *The Modern Greek Theatre*, translated by Lucille Vassardaki (Athens: Hellenic Centre of the International Theatre Institute, 1957), p. xiv.

6. Sideris, p. 15. This period of Venetian rule (1204 to 1669) generally is considered to end in Greece's own "renaissance," an explosion of artistic expression in general and some remarkable playwriting in particular. One noted director, Spyros Evangelatos, has made it a personal quest (and quite a career, one might add) to discover, resurrect and produce these old texts. Others, however, feel that these plays are highly derivative of Italian Renaissance plays, which are hardly models of exceptional playwriting. What seems important is that they were written at all given the circumstances.

7. Bacopoulou-Halls, p. 29.

8. Alexis Solomos, in a preface to Geiorgos Hortzadis' *Erofili*, third ed. (Athens: Galaxias, 1969), p. 9.

9. Sideris, p. 2.

10. Sideris, p. 8.

11. Sideris, p. 11.

12. Sideris, pp. 15–20.

13. Interestingly, the satiric musical revue as we know it in America was probably created in Paris also in 1894. It was the *Follies Marigny* by C.T. and J.H. Cogniard.

14. Name withheld, in an interview, October 18, 1985.

15. Minos Volonakis, in an interview, February 18, 1986. More cynical Greeks maintain, however, that Greeks go to the theatre just to go out at night, a tradition much more rooted in social rather than theatrical culture.

16. Jules Dussin, in a telephone interview, December 12, 1985.

17. Estimates based on *Statistical Abstract of the U.S.*, 1985, and various theatre Managing Directors' statements on Greek government contributions.

18. One indication of this fact may be the audience support of touring companies from other countries. In nearly every case these shows are sold out before their arrival in Athens.

19. "Traditional Values and Continuities in Greek Society," J.K. Campbell, in Clogg (ed.), pp. 184, 192.

20. *They Have Blown Our Umbala*, June 10, 1983.

21. At a performance of *Captain Michalis*, July 24, 1983.

22. One may be horrified at the types of programs they import from the U.S.; in fact, one might conduct a most revealing study of Greek attitudes toward America based solely on the TV fare America sends them. Nevertheless, there is no doubt that production standards for features, serials and slick, Madison Avenue–produced or –inspired commercials, are generally far better than in those Greek programs produced in cooperation with ERT-1 or ERT-2, the two government-controlled television channels.

23. Yiannis Houvardas, in an interview, April 7, 1986.

24. Holden, p. 24.

25. Nikos Bakolas, in an interview, July 7, 1983. I was with Minos Volonakis when he visited the State Theatre about this same time. One of the elderly women who was being terminated approached him in the lobby, crying that she didn't know what she was going to do. She had been with the theatre most of her professional life. And, like any Greek she went to someone who seemed to her a "fixer," someone who could pull the right strings and save her job.

26. Miranda Voglis, November 15, 1985.

27. In discussions with Minos Volonakis from April through June, 1986; interview with Yiannis Houvardas, April 4, 1986.

28. McNeill, pp. 224–226.

29. F. Eletheriou, "Long Days of Dormancy," *Athenian*, February, 1987, p. 13.

30. Name withheld, in several discussions, June, 1983.

31. Bakolas interview.

4. Difficulties in Research

1. Playwright Dora Litinaki, in discussions, October 27, November 13, 1985.

2. Varos Paselidis, in an interview, April 21, 1986.

3. Minos Volonakis, in an interview, June 21, 1983.

4. Paselidis interview.

5. Holden, p. 32.

6. J.K. Campbell, in Clogg (ed.), p. 191.

7. Kostas Laliotis, in an interview with Haris Livas, January 17, 1985.

8. Holden, p. 31.

9. On a television news show in December, 1986. Even though subsequent events have proven the validity of that paper's claims, at the time of Regan's statement no one challenged him.

10. Name withheld, in a discussion, December 16, 1986.

11. In my daily log, October 21, 1985.
12. Konstantinos Papalexis, in a discussion, December 15, 1986.
13. Campbell, pp. 189–190.
14. Nikos Bakolas, in an interview, July 7, 1983.

5. Government-Supported Theatres

1. Names withheld, in discussions, June, 1983.
2. Various actors in the cast of *Trojan Women*, at Epidavros, June, 1983.
3. Tasso Kavidia, in an interview, June 3, 1983.
4. Name withheld, in a discussion, June 2, 1983.
5. Christos Tzangas, in an interview, June 21, 1983. See pp. 69–72.
6. Karolos Koun, in an interview, July 16, 1983.
7. In the summer of 1983 one of these operas was scheduled to open the Festival. The confusions of a new government, the lack of strong artistic leadership at the Opera and the demands of a militant musician union led to a fiasco. The production was in such terrible shape that a new director, Minos Volonakis, was called in two weeks before opening. In an orgy of activity he recalled the designer who had flown back to London in disgust; redesigned the entire show; hired a phalanx of seamstresses to re-costume the production; re-rehearsed and was prepared for opening. I saw these frantic last hours of the rehearsal two days before the first performance. Unfortunately, the musicians' union called a strike the day before the opening. The strike lasted the entire summer. All productions were reduced to using recorded music or hiring student musicians. Obviously, the opera never was presented.
8. Interviews with Costas Paskalis, June, 1983 and Spyros Evangelatos, March 17, 1986.
9. Spyros Evangelatos, in an interview, March 13, 1986.
10. Name withheld, in a discussion at a U.N. celebration, October 24, 1985.
11. Evangelatos, March 17 interview.
12. Most Greeks still consider Cyprus part of Greece. There remains an emotional tie, therefore, with anything Cypriot. When the State Theatre of Cyprus produced a gripping *Electra* at Epidavros starring Irini Pappas and directed by Michael Kakoyiannis, there was more than an appreciation. There was an emotion-ridden communication between the mostly Athenian audience and their "lost" brothers. See Appendix B for a first-person description of that event.
13. Stella Zografou, in an interview, June 2, 1983.
14. Christos Tzakopoulos in a discussion, July 7, 1983.
15. One careful Salonikian taxi driver, while threading his way through the mad crush of rush-hour vehicles, told me proudly that Greeks finally have their freedom; then, after a heart-stopping swerve to avoid a careening, lane-weaving truck he added, "Maybe too much freedom."
16. Nikos Bakolas, in an interview, July 7, 1983.
17. One example may be the National Theatre's production of *Taming of the Shrew* at the Piraeus theatre. It was truly awful. When I asked where they found the obviously incompetent director, I was told that everyone in Athens knew that he was incompetent but that he always had "the right friends" in the National Theatre.
18. Thomas Gressler, "The Oresteia," *Theatre Journal*, March, 1984, pp. 119–120.

19. Koun interview.

20. Koun interview.

21. Iakonas Kabanelis, quoted in a promotional release in the files of the Art Theatre.

22. Even though everyone calls these theatres "new," they are not newly constructed. I saw almost no such theatre construction at all in Greece, with the one exception being an enormous outdoor amphitheatre being constructed with the Greek equivalent of urban renewal funds in the neighborhood of Nikia in Athens. All other "new" theatres are refurbished warehouses or, most likely, renovated cinemas. Construction of a new, national symphonic hall has been temporarily suspended for the last ten years. Minister Mercouri promised in 1986 that it would be completed by 1989.

23. Evangelatos, March 17 interview.

24. Nearly everyone caught up in this money-for-everyone whirlpool admits that there are many theatres not worthy to receive this kind of support. If the government could grant monies based on excellence only, they say, the Athenian theatre standard would be much higher. As has been shown, however, organizational decisions based on excellence simply are not the way the Greek people manage their affairs. Besides, one can barely imagine the chaos which would descend on the Minister of Culture's office if she suddenly revoked the assistance privileges for a large group of theatres.

25. Giorgos Dialegmenos, in an interview, June 5, 1983, Sofie Dialegmenos translator.

26. For a fuller discussion of these two project ideas, see Chapter 7, New Developments.

27. Yiannis Houvardas, in an interview, June 23, 1983.

28. From Thomas Gressler, "Athens Report," *Performing Arts* Magazine, November, 1984, pp. 76–78.

29. Dimitris Kostis, in an interview, July 4, 1983.

30. I had planned to visit Komotini in April of 1986 since I was already up in Veria. However, there was no plane ticket available, all the buses were full, and there was no hotel room to be found in that city. I discovered that every weekend is the same: Komotini is the R and R center for all the Greek soldiers guarding the frontier with Turkey only a few miles away.

31. Nikos Charalambus, in an interview, December 7, 1985.

32. Mayor Vangelis Pavlides and Deputy Mayor Litsa Papathanassi-Fraraki, in interviews, November 5, 1986.

33. It is unclear as of this writing if the city has offered them a more appropriate space in which to house the theatre, now that it has government sanction.

34. Stratis Papamanoussakis, in an interview, July 27, 1983, translation by his son.

35. Nikos Papadakis, General Manager, in an interview, January 9, 1986. He was able to supplement this salary by directing one or two shows each year.

36. Nikos Siafkalis, in an interview, December 28, 1985.

37. Siafkalis interview.

38. Although the staffs of all the municipal theatres varied somewhat, depending on local requirements, this break-down reflects a general personnel distribution common to all of them.

39. Elpidophoros Gotsis, in an interview, April 18, 1986. It was in Serres that I experienced vivid examples of the Greek character in action. All those characteristics which seem to work against a smooth and efficient and excellent artistic

endeavor were displayed openly—the individualism, the pride; the refusal to take orders, to be subordinate, to be wrong; the necessity to save face, to have the "right" answer. Gotsis barked orders to subordinates who obviously had to fight with their emotions before complying. Both sides were in particularly vulnerable situations because a foreigner was in the same room. How could each side save face, demonstrate its superiority and still get the job done? Again, one side barked directions; the other side argued for better ways to do it, then acquiesced glumly, even antagonistically. One side complained about the ineptitude of the actors and the other side complained about the ineptitude of the director. The overall sensation was that of two opponents constantly at odds over the slightest decisions.

40. Jules Dussin interview, December 12, 1985.

41. From Thomas Gressler, "The Magic of Epidaurus," *Dramatics*, January, 1984, pp. 7–13.

6. Commercial, Children's, Puppet and Amateur Theatres

1. Sideris, p. 20.

2. In the revue *Praskina Damaskena kai Psiles Elies*.

3. Name withheld, in an interview, January 13, 1986.

4. Sideris, p. 20.

5. Dora Litinaki, in a discussion, June 12, 1983.

6. Lucy D. Spathari, "Children's Theatre," *Thespis*, December, 1983, p. 128.

7. Xenia Karlojelopoulou, in an interview, July 10, 1983.

8. Karlojelopoulou interview.

9. Spathari, pp. 128–129.

10. At a Karaghiozis performance in Filadelfia, July 13, 1983.

11. Dionysius Flabouras, "World Shadow Theatre and the Greek Karagheozis," *Zygos*, May–June 1976, pp. 39–60.

12. Bacopoulou-Halls, pp. 63–64 and Linda S. Myrsiades, "The Karaghiozis Performance in Nineteenth Century Greece," *Byzantine and Modern Greek Studies*, Vol. 2, 1976, pp. 83, 86.

13. Myrsiades, p. 95.

14. Bacopoulou-Halls, p. 65.

15. Myrsiades, p. 96.

16. Bacopoulou-Halls, pp. 66–67.

17. *Ibid.*

7. Some New Developments

1. Minos Volonakis, in an interview, May 28, 1986. The material for the rest of this section comes from this interview and from discussions with the director conducted intermittently from July, 1983, to June, 1986.

2. Nearly all ancient Greek theatres were constructed after the Golden Age in the fifth century B.C., then later were destroyed or over-built by the Romans according to the needs of their own theatre forms. The rare fourth century B.C. Hellenistic theatres which have survived, therefore (like the glorious one at Epidavros), have become irreplaceable treasures.

3. Volonakis interview.

4. Intermittent discussions with members of the company, January through June, 1986. Much of the information in this piece also was taken from an undated publicity release handed to me by the director in April of 1986.

5. Volonakis had already directed an English version of the play for the Circle in the Square on Broadway in 1973 starring Irene Pappas and a Greek version of the play in Athens in 1976 starring Melina Mercouri.

6. Quoted in Nigel Lowry, "Unmuffling Greek Tragedy," *Athenian*, August, 1986, p. 26.

7. *Ibid.*

8. Nigel, p. 27.

9. *Ibid.*

10. Volonakis interview, May 28, 1986.

11. *Ibid.* (*Author's note:* By February of 1988 this project had ceased to exist, much to the dismay of many who had worked to make it a reality. After Volonakis had accepted the post of Artistic Director for the State Theatre of Northern Greece he seems to have totally forgotten his wonderful plans of just a few months before.)

12. Kostas Nicholaidis, in an interview, May 9, 1986.

8. An Overview of Non-Production Elements

1. This concentration is one of the reasons director Volonakis has worked so hard to erect or have constructed theatres in the more distant neighborhoods. His quarry project is one example of taking theatre physically to the people. He also is delighted that the quarry project has apparently convinced some governmental officials that theatre edifices closer to more people will increase availability and attendance. Several cinemas have been designated as future live theatres and full architectural drawings for their conversion have been completed by the government. Interviews with Minos Volonakis and Stelio Logothetis, June 19, 1986.

2. This quote and the many others which appear in this short section came from interviews I held with various members of the *Medea* cast on March 6, 11, 12, 18, 1986. None of their names are given because of the possibility of professional repercussions.

3. Dora Litinaki, in an interview, October 27, 1985.

4. Stamatis Chondroyiannis, in an interview, December 13, 1985.

9. Production Elements

1. In conversations with various members of the *Medea* cast, January–February, 1986.

2. Discussions with several female teachers, among whom were Christina Angeloussi, Ariane Kotsis, Katarina Isroilidou, Mary Koutsoudaki.

3. The clearly-felt need to educate their sons (and peripherally, their daughters) to be successful in the twentieth century world, as defined, unfortunately, by TV series such as *Dallas* and *Falcon Crest*, certainly is altering the country's standard of aesthetic judgment, and may be altering some basic cultural traditions.

4. I saw the show on opening night and, so, was not a witness to these events. Too, some leeway must be allowed for normal human hyperbole. Nevertheless, I find it quite easy to accept her descriptions, given my knowledge of her and my admittedly incomplete knowledge of the star.

5. Nikos Siafkalis, during an interview, December 28, 1985.

6. Jules Dussin, in a phone interview, December 12, 1985.

7. Yiannis Houvardas, in an interview, April 7, 1986. Interestingly one of the more believable actors in this production was the same young man who had strutted and over-acted so horribly in *The Taming of the Shrew* a few months before. Obviously, his director in that show had allowed him freedoms the director of *Ghost Sonata* had not.

8. John Chiolis, in an interview, November 9, 1985.

9. Names withheld, in discussions and interviews, June and July, 1983, December, 1985.

10. Rena Geotojiadi, in an interview, March 5, 1986.

11. Kostis Livadeos, in an interview, October 11, 1985.

12. Thassos Lignatis, in an interview, April 4, 1986.

13. Tom Stone, in an interview, February 21, 1986.

14. Stella Zografou, in an interview, June 2, 1983.

10. Theatre Training

1. Kostis Livadeas, in an interview, April 4, 1986.

2. Thassos Lignatis, in an interview, April 4, 1986.

3. Stella Zografou, in an interview, June 2, 1983.

4. Vaso Sakellari, in an interview, March 11, 1986.

5. Lilly Kokkodis, in an interview, July 16, 1983.

6. Name withheld, in an interview, March 10, 1986.

7. Name withheld, in an interview, March 28, 1986.

8. Name withheld, in an interview, March 18, 1986.

9. Evdokeia Xatziiaonnou and Athena Pappa, in interviews, March 12, 1986, and March 18, 1986, respectively.

10. Athena Pappa.

11. Pappa interview.

12. Lignatis interview.

13. *Ibid.*

14. Theodoros Terzopoulous, in an interview, July 8, 1983.

15. *Ibid.*

16. Names and dates withheld. (*Author's note:* This difficulty with a lack of teachers, textbooks, facilities, etc. pertains to nearly all public education in Greece. In 1988, for example, the university students staged yet another in a long series of strikes to demand a redressing of the school's problems — staff shortages, unavailable student housing, too few lecture halls, etc. After three months of continuous strife they occupied the office of the Minister of Education, Antonis Tritsis, and held him captive for eight hours. These kinds of activities, of course, lend credence to Greece's educational critics who charge that Greece tolerates the shortest school years in all of Europe.)

11. Spotlights and Darkspots

1. Giorgos Dialegmenos, in an interview, January 1, 1986.

2. Loula Anagnostaki, in an interview, October 18, 1985.

3. Kostoula Mitropoulous, in an interview, April 2, 1986.

4. Thassos Lignatis, in an interview, April 4, 1986.
5. Emilia Ipsilandi, in an interview, April 3, 1986.
6. Yiannis Houvardas, in an interview, April 7, 1986.
7. Ipsilandi.
8. Aristotelos Sofianos, in discussions, April 9, 1986.
9. Jeanne Valentine, "Hellenic Thespians," *Athenian*, October 21, 1985, p. 30.

Bibliography

Books

Bacopoulou-Halls, Aliki. *Modern Greek Theatre: Roots and Blossoms.* Athens: Diogenis, 1978.

Burn, A.R. *A Traveller's History of Greece.* New York: Funk and Wagnalls, 1965.

Clogg, Richard, ed. *Greece in the 1980s.* New York: St. Martin's, 1983.

Diehl, Charles. *Byzantium: Greatness and Decline.* New Brunswick, N.J.: Rutgers University Press, 1957.

Gage, Nicholas. *Eleni.* New York: Ballantine, 1983.

Greece, Background Notes. Washington, D.C.: United States Department of State, Bureau of Public Affairs, April, 1985.

Holden, David. *Greece Without Columns.* New York: Lippincott, 1972.

Hussy, J.M. *The Byzantine World.* Westport, Ct.: Greenwood, 1961).

Jenkins, Romilly. *The Dilessi Murders.* London: Longman's, 1961.

Koumoulides, John. *Greece in Transition.* London: Zeno, 1977.

Kresta, Rena, comp. *The Modern Greek Theatre.* Athens: Greek Playwright Society, 1983.

McNeill, William. *The Metamorphosis of Greece Since World War II.* Chicago: University of Chicago Press, 1976.

Sideris, John. *The Modern Greek Theatre.* Trans. Lucille Vassardaki. Athens: Hellenic Centre of the International Theatre Institute, 1957.

Articles

Ammerman, William. "A Home of One's Own: A Cautionary Tale." *The Athenian,* April, 1986, p. 39.

Colebourne, Jimmy. "The Lyriki—Sad Conditions." *The Athenian,* February, 1988, p. 38.

Constantinidis, Stratos E. "Existential Protest in Greek Drama During the Junta." *Journal of Modern Greek Studies,* October, 1985.

"Continuous Confusion." *The Athenian,* February, 1988, p. 12.

Cowell, Alan. "Linguist Pleads for Glory That Was Greek." *New York Times,* April 19, 1987.

_____. "Ye Gods! Hoots Are Heard on Socialist Olympus." *New York Times,* March 14, 1987.

_____. "Fearing AIDS, Idyllic Greek Island Seeks New Image." *International Herald Tribune,* May 26, 1987.

"Dangerous Driving." *The Athenian,* April, 1987.

Eleftheriou, F. "Long Days of Dormancy." *The Athenian,* February, 1987.

Flabouras, Dionysius. "World Shadow Theatre and the Greek Karagheozis." *Zygos,* May–June, 1976, pp. 39–60.

Gressler, Thomas. "Athens Report." *Performing Arts* Magazine, November, 1984, pp. 76–78.

_____. "The Magic of Epidaurus." *Dramatics,* January, 1984, pp. 7–13.

_____. "The Oresteia." *Theatre Journal,* March, 1984, pp. 119–120.

"Gunfight Injures Three." *Athens News,* February 24, 1988, p. 2.

"Heaviest Smokers." *The Athenian,* April, 1988, p. 11.

Jorgensen, Brigette. "The West's Highest Abortion Rate." *The Athenian,* January, 1987.

Katsoudas, Dimitrios. "World Premier." *The Athenian,* February, 1988, p. 41.

_____. "Paschalis' Triumphant Return." *The Athenian,* April, 1988, p. 42.

_____. "A Triple Celebration for Opera." *The Athenian,* March, 1988, p. 45.

"Larissa Protests Block Highway." *Athens News,* March 18, 1988, n.p.

Lowry, Nigel. "Unmuffling Greek Tragedy." *The Athenian,* August, 1986, p. 26.

Minotis, Alexis. "The Theatre in Athens." *The Charioteer,* Summer, 1960.

Myrsiades, Linda S. "The Karaghiozis Performance in Nineteenth Century Greece." *Byzantine and Modern Greek Studies,* Vol. 2, 1976, pp. 83, 86.

"ND Leader's Remarks on Ex-King Draws Gov't Fire." *Athens News,* February 5, 1988, n.p.

"National Opera's auto-da-fe." *The Athenian,* January, 1988, p. 44.

Psellas, Jimmy. "The One True Church Looks Forward." *The Athenian,* February, 1988, pp. 16–17.

Reed, Carol; Elliot, Sloane; and Lazarus, David. "A Festival of Discontent." *The Athenian,* February, 1987, p. 9.

Smith, Helena. "Greek Education: the 'year of living dangerously'" [sic]. *The Athenian,* March, 1988, pp. 16–17.

Spathari, Lucy D. "Children's Theatre." *Thespis,* December, 1983, p. 128.

"Trouble in the Air." *The Athenian,* February, 1988, p. 11.

"Turkish-Greek Relations Appear Improved." *The Sunday Oregonian,* February 14, 1988, p. A10.

Valentine, Jeanne. "Hellenic Thespians." *The Athenian,* October 21, 1985, p. 30.

Williamson, Raichel. "Housing Problems for Music." *The Athenian,* January, 1988, p. 28.

Interviews

(This list includes those people with whom I spoke just once as well as those with whom I spoke several times, sometimes at length, during the 1983–1988 period.)

Loula Anagnostaki
Antonin Andipas
Kristina Angeloussi
Aliki Bacopoulou-Halls
Nikos Bakolas
Katerina Bakopoulou
Nikos Charalambous
John Chiolis
Stamatis Chondroyiannis

Giorgos Dialegmenos
Stavros Doufixis
Jules Dussin
Spyros Evangelatos
Rena Geotojiadi
Nikos Germanacos
Elpidophoros Gotsis
Melina Halls
Yiannis Houvardas

Index

DATE			